HOW TO BE A REFUGEE

Simon May was born in London, the son of a violinist and a brush manufacturer. Visiting professor of philosophy at King's College London, his books include *Love: A New Understanding of an Ancient Emotion*; *Love: A History*; *Nietzsche's Ethics and his War on 'Morality'*; *The Power of Cute* and *Thinking Aloud*, a collection of his own aphorisms. His work has been translated into ten languages and regularly features in major newspapers worldwide.

'A poignant tale of three sisters who buried their Jewish roots to survive in a hostile world.'
Neil Fisher, *The Times*

'May embarks on a quest to uncover his family's true history: a story of steadfast denial of their Jewish heritage through extraordinary means in order to escape the fate of Jewish people living in Hitler's Germany.'
Hannah Beckerman, *Observer*

'More than just a family story, it is an essay on belonging, denying, pretending, self-deception and, at least for the main characters, survival.'
Julia Neuberger, *Literary Review*

'May's large cast of characters shows with dizzying variety the human ability to live in a state of constant flight from horror, long after the shooting stops. His broad and intriguing book suggests that these survivors were exiled not just from time and place, but also from themselves.'   John Phipps, *Irish Times*

'The paradoxes of identity so brilliantly explored in this memoir are intriguing and absurd, as well as tragic.'
Oldie

'May is at his best when he writes about his own experience of loss and displacement . . . a beautifully told story of a second-generation refugee coming to terms with his family's German past.'
David Herman, *Association of Jewish Refugees Journal*

'A deeply moving and perceptive memoir of a family caught in the jaws of a terrible history, May shows how individual lives and relationships reflect the larger tragedies, the losses, hopes and loves, of oppressive and destructive times. It is a powerful story beautifully told, and at the same time a significant document in the record of the twentieth century.'
A. C. Grayling, author of *The Frontiers of Knowledge* and *The History of Philosophy*

Also by Simon May

Love: A New Understanding of an Ancient Emotion

Love: A History

Nietzsche's Ethics and his War on 'Morality'

The Power of Cute

Thinking Aloud: A Handbook of Aphorisms

Nietzsche's 'On the Genealogy of Morality': A Critical Guide (ed.)

Nietzsche on Freedom and Autonomy (co-ed.)

SIMON MAY

HOW TO BE A REFUGEE

The gripping true story of how one
family hid their Jewish origins
to survive the Nazis

PICADOR

First published 2021 by Picador

This paperback edition first published 2022 by Picador
an imprint of Pan Macmillan
The Smithson, 6 Briset Street, London EC1M 5NR
EU representative: Macmillan Publishers Ireland Ltd, 1st Floor,
The Liffey Trust Centre, 117–126 Sheriff Street Upper,
Dublin 1, D01 YC43
Associated companies throughout the world
www.panmacmillan.com

ISBN 978-1-5290-4286-3

1 3 5 7 9 8 6 4 2

A CIP catalogue record for this book is available from the British Library.

Typeset by Palimpsest Book Production Ltd, Falkirk, Stirlingshire
Printed and bound by CPI Group (UK) Ltd, Croydon, CR0 4YY

Visit **www.picador.com** to read more about all our books
and to buy them. You will also find features, author interviews and
news of any author events, and you can sign up for e-newsletters
so that you're always first to hear about our new releases.

With inexpressible gratitude to Marianne, Ursel,
and Ilse — my mother and my two aunts; to my grandfather
Ernst and great-uncle Theo, who died long before I was born,
but whose lives have inspired and challenged me since childhood;
and to my beloved father Walter and my grandmother Emmy,
both of whom I knew only briefly.

CONTENTS

PRINCIPAL CHARACTERS

Relationship to the author is shown in brackets

ERNST LIEDTKE, 1875–1933 (maternal grandfather): born Christburg, then in West Prussia. Lawyer; husband of Emmy; father of Ilse, Ursel, and Marianne. Converted from Judaism to Protestantism. Died in Berlin after being expelled from his profession in April 1933 under the Nazi ban on non-Aryan lawyers.

EMMY LIEDTKE, 1890–1965 (maternal grandmother): born Emmy Fahsel; wife of Ernst and mother of Ilse, Ursel, and Marianne. Lived in Germany all her life. Converted to Catholicism.

THEODOR LIEDTKE, 1885–1943 (maternal great-uncle): brother of Ernst Liedtke; uncle of Ilse, Ursel, and Marianne; salesman at Tietz department store in Berlin; deported to Sachsenhausen concentration camp in 1942, and from there to Auschwitz.

HELMUT FAHSEL, 1891–1983 (maternal great-uncle): Catholic priest and philosopher. Left Germany in 1934 for Switzerland on a tip-off from Franz von Papen, Hitler's deputy chancellor. Apart from a brief spell in Germany after the war, spent the rest of his life in Switzerland.

ILSE LIEDTKE, 1910–1986 (older maternal aunt): photographer who spent the war in Berlin. Lover of Harald Böhmelt, composer and Nazi Party member. Except for a few years in Kiel from 1948, she lived in Berlin all her life. Converted to Catholicism.

URSULA (URSEL), COUNTESS VON PLETTENBERG, 1912–1995 (younger maternal aunt): born Ursula Liedtke. Actor who became a

Catholic; secured 'Aryan' status in 1941 with the help of Hans Hinkel, a senior official in Hitler's regime; married Franziskus, Count von Plettenberg in 1943; fled to the Netherlands in 1944; returned to Germany soon after the war and lived there for the rest of her life.

MARIANNE MAY, 1914–2013 (mother): born Marianne Liedtke. Violinist, stage name Maria Lidka; emigrated to London in 1934; married Walter May in 1955. Converted to Catholicism.

FRANZISKUS, COUNT VON PLETTENBERG, 1914–1968 (maternal uncle by marriage): married Ursel in 1943; deserted the German army in the Netherlands in 1944 and went into hiding with Ursel.

WALTER MAY, 1905–1963 (father): born in Cologne. A banker and then a brush manufacturer; emigrated to London in 1937. His first wife Hilde May was also a cousin; his second wife was Marianne Liedtke.

EDWARD MAY, 1903–1968 (paternal uncle): born in Cologne. Doctor, amateur cellist, and master chef; emigrated to London in 1934.

KLAUS MELTZER, 1943–2017 (putative cousin): claimed to be a grandson of my great-uncle Theodor Liedtke. Son of Ellen Liedtke and Nazi *Staffelkapitän* Walter Meltzer. Lived in Cologne. Photographer; painter; educationalist; founded a community centre for Turkish women.

ELLEN LIEDTKE, 1919–1971: putative daughter of Theodor Liedtke, whom Ernst, Emmy, Marianne, Ursel, and Ilse all believed to be a childless bachelor.

LIST OF ILLUSTRATIONS

1. My maternal grandparents and their three daughters on holiday in the Swiss Alps in the mid-1920s. (Marianne Liedtke-May's *Nachlass*.)
2. A room in my grandparents' Berlin apartment at Blumeshof 12. (Ibid.)
3. Ernst's certificate of his exit from Judaism in 1910. (Ibid.)
4. Ernst's certificate of baptism, 1910. (Ibid.)
5. Ernst and his brother Theo sailing from Bremen to New York on board the *Kaiser Wilhelm II* in 1909. (Ibid.)
6. Marianne, Ursel, Ilse. Berlin, 1917. (Ibid.)
7. Ernst and Emmy on the North Sea island of Helgoland in 1926. (Ibid.)
8. The Liedtkes' boat on the Wannsee. Ernst in the peaked cap, Emmy next to him and Ilse to the left of the gangplank. (Ibid.)
9. The final page of Marianne's concert and theatre notebook, in April 1933, with performances by Wilhelm Furtwängler and the quartet of her violin teacher, Max Rostal. (Ibid.)
10. Ilse. (Ibid.)
11. Ursel. (Ibid.)
12. Marianne. (Marianne Liedtke-May's *Nachlass*. Photo: Ilse Liedtke.)
13. The three sisters as teenagers. (Marianne Liedtke-May's *Nachlass*.)
14. Marianne and Ursel playing violin and accordion with canine audience. (Marianne Liedtke-May's *Nachlass*. Photo: Ilse Liedtke.)
15. Ursel and probably Katta Sterna in a Berlin cabaret. (Marianne Liedtke-May's *Nachlass*.)
16. Ursel, Emmy, Ernst and Marianne having tea on their boat. (Ibid.)
17. Ilse and her boyfriend, Harald Böhmelt, at the Trichter dance hall on Hamburg's Reeperbahn, late 1930s. (Werner Finck, *Witz als Schicksal – Schicksal als Witz*. Marion von Schröder Verlag, Hamburg, 1966, p. 60.)

18. Ellen Liedtke, putative daughter of Theo Liedtke, and her fiancé, Walter Meltzer, in 1939. (Archive of Simon May. Gifted by the late Klaus Meltzer.)

19. Walter Meltzer with comrades in Nuremberg during the 1933 Nazi Party rally. (Ibid.)

20. Ursel with Maria 'Baby' von Alvensleben, probably Lexi von Alvensleben, and their mother, Countess Alexandra von Alvensleben, at the yacht club Klub am Rupenhorn, Berlin, 1931. (ullstein bild Dtl. / Contributor)

21. My mother, Marianne, with violin. (Marianne Liedtke-May's *Nachlass*. Photo: Ilse Liedtke.)

22. Marianne playing in a wartime concert at the National Gallery in London. On the reverse of the photo she writes: 'The concert was moved to the basement as a bomb had just fallen upstairs.' (Marianne Liedtke-May's *Nachlass*. Photo: Erich Auerbach)

23. A Czech Trio programme from 1941. The Trio was sponsored by the Czech government-in-exile in the UK and provided my mother's first legitimate earnings as a refugee. (Marianne Liedtke-May's *Nachlass*.)

24. Ursel's letter of thanks, dated 17 July 1941, to SS officer Hans Hinkel, who was key to her achieving Aryan status. (Bundesarchiv Berlin. BArch, R9361V/56771.)

25. The resident's cards on Ursel in Bremen City Hall, 1931–43. (Staatsarchiv Bremen. StaB 4,82/1 – 0909, Bild 231 und StaB 4,82/1 – 1185, Bild 278. Einwohnermeldekarten der Stadt Bremen für Ursula Liedtke.)

26. A letter of 17 September 1943 from Count Franziskus von Plettenberg's military commander permitting him to marry Ursel and enclosing his medical certificates and proof of Aryan origin. (Bundesarchiv – Abteilung Militärarchiv, Freiburg im Breisgau; BArch, PERS6/158762, 'Heiratsgenehmigung für Hptm. (Tr.O.) Graf von Plettenberg (Franz)' erteilt vom 'Höheren Kommandeur der Flakausbildungs-und Flakersatzregimenter', 17 September 1943.)

27. The bombed idyll of Blumeshof 12 in 1945. (Marianne Liedtke-May's *Nachlass*. Photo: Ilse Liedtke.)

28. The ruins of Ilse's studio at Budapesterstrasse 43, Berlin, in 1945. (Ibid.)

29. Ilse's temporary studio in 1945, with her portraits of US soldiers. (Ibid.)

30. The temporary graves of Geri and Eva, Ilse's neighbours, shot in their home by Soviet forces and buried by her, Berlin, 1945. (Ibid.)

31. My father, Walter May, in London in 1958. (Marianne Liedtke-May's *Nachlass*.)

32. My mother, Marianne, my brother, Marius, and me in 1959/1960. (Marianne Liedtke-May's *Nachlass*. Photo: Marianne Samson.)

[E]verything must be earned, not only the present and future, but the past as well . . . and this probably entails the hardest work of all.

Franz Kafka, Letters to Milena[1]

'That was your father you found. You've been carrying your father's bones – all this time.'

Toni Morrison, Song of Solomon[2]

FOREWORD

The most familiar fate of Jews living in Hitler's Germany is either emigration or deportation to concentration camps. But there was another, rarer, and today much less well known side to Jewish life at that time: denial of your origin to the point where you manage to erase almost all consciousness of it. You refuse to believe that you are Jewish. In reaction to a long history of racial and religious persecution, and out of intense love for German culture, you repudiate your birthright.

This feat of repudiation, epitomized by my mother, her sisters, and her parents, did not originate with Hitler's rise to power. The ground for it was prepared long before, in the late eighteenth and early nineteenth centuries, when some Jews, such as Rahel Varnhagen – the great woman of letters, whose extraordinary intellect and sensibility were admired by Goethe, Schiller, and Wilhelm von Humboldt, among other luminaries of her time – came to regard their heritage as a curse that poisoned their whole existence and debarred them from full belonging in the world of German culture, to which they were so fervently devoted.

But in my mother's family such repudiation of origins was pushed to an extreme, becoming an ethnic purging of the inner world – a profound alchemy of the soul. Nor did it cease with Hitler's defeat. Though my mother had fled to London from Nazi Germany and I was born well after the war into a vastly more tolerant era, I was forbidden to think of myself not only as Jewish but now also as German or British.

I have attempted to tell the story of the extraordinary German-Jewish world from which my family came – as well as of my own quest to carve a path to both its heritages – principally through the remarkable lives of three sisters: my mother and my two aunts. Their very different ways of grappling with what they experienced as a lethal origin included conversion to Catholicism, marriage into the German aristocracy, securing 'Aryan' – non-Jewish – status with high-ranking help from inside Hitler's regime, and engagement to a card-carrying Nazi under whose protection survival in wartime Berlin was possible. But we also meet other figures with a similar heritage, such as my maternal great-uncle, who became a Catholic priest and translator of St Thomas Aquinas; and the love child of a Jewish woman and a passionate Nazi, who, so far unknown to us, claimed me and my family as his sole surviving relatives.

To recount these contortions of ethnic and cultural concealment is – categorically – not to criticize them. Who are we who have never experienced racial hatred in its vehement forms, let alone in the form of state-sanctioned persecution, to criticize anyone's strategy to survive and flourish in such conditions? Who are we who have lived free lives where our particular heritages have been accepted and sometimes even admired, to cast judgement on ancestors who were forced to find ever more ingenious ways of appearing harmless to the majority – and to themselves? Their choices are only my business because to be born into this strange tributary of the Jewish experience was to be commanded to construct an identity out of everything that I was not. Following the early death of my father, also a German-Jewish refugee, I was raised a Catholic and mandated, on pain of betraying my mother and her parents, to live as a refugee in the country of my birth. In effect, I was instructed never to arrive anywhere: to be a hereditary refugee.

The urgent questions that this raised for me – questions of identity and belonging that seem to be everywhere around us today – are these: Are we not all in some way exiles in an era that is shedding its past at unprecedented speed? Can the worlds we have lost be restituted, even if minimally, along with their rich networks of meaning, without fruitless, and possibly self-destructive, efforts to set the clock back? Or is all restitution a pipe dream: are lost worlds necessarily the unattainable territory of ghosts who powerfully inspire our lives from a great distance, but with whom we can never live or speak again? Either way, how many generations can it take for a refugee family to feel at ease in their adopted country, no longer pining for a place from which they were once uprooted? And at a time when identity is becoming a choice rather than just a given, will it get easier – or harder – to be a refugee?

INTRODUCTION

Death at the German Embassy

i.

It was only after my mother departed for England that I discovered the circumstances of my father's death.

I was eleven years old and finishing dinner with my mother's two sisters, Ursel and Ilse, both of whom had come from Germany, where they lived, to spend the summer holiday with us in the Swiss Alps. We were sitting in the kitchen of our rented chalet in the hamlet of Gsteig, nestled in a corner where one valley makes a sharp, ninety-degree turn into another. Ilse had whisked the plates from the table and was already scrubbing them before I'd finished eating. Wherever Ilse was, German orderliness reigned. Outside, the sun was sinking behind the glaciers, turning them a brilliant pink, and I could hear the owners of our chalet pottering about in their vegetable garden and the occasional shot from a nearby rifle club, when Ursel said to me, apropos of nothing, 'Simon, do you know how your father *really* died?'

Shock at Ursel's abrupt summoning of a loss that I had no idea how to grasp struggled, almost at once, with guilty euphoria at hearing his name. What a wonderful question to ask me! 'Do you know how your father *really* died?' My father had collapsed, out of the blue, when I was six, and had been buried in silence. He'd been present at breakfast; then left the house and never returned.

I wasn't taken to the funeral on the grounds, I later learned, that this would be traumatic for a child. But I prayed for him at least once a week, hoping that he would be happier as a result, and that speaking to God would also be a way of speaking to him, even if he couldn't answer me back; but doubting that it could be that simple.

The silence was echoed by his almost total absence from our home. Nothing personal of his remained: no tie, or pair of shorts, or book that he'd marked up, or love letter, or the silver cigarette case that my mother told me she had given him for the birthday on which he had finally decided to quit smoking. I had rummaged through cupboards and drawers many times looking for a relic of his life. But everything had been cleared out.

Everything except for the magnificent drawings and lithographs on the walls of our living room. These emblems of his life should have been my link to him. Instead they were mocking reminders of his absence; ghostlike markers of a presence that was no more – their own life frozen when they lost the person who chose them and of whose striving they spoke. Since childhood I have found the idea of inheritance peculiarly burdensome – tolerable only if we, the living, have justified it through an understanding of this person's relation to what they have bequeathed us, and gratitude for the effort they invested in acquiring and caring for it.

I also had no memories of my father, or of family life with him, except for four fragmentary scenes. One was of him showing me how to hold my penis when going to the toilet, so as not to splash the seat, and, as an afterthought, telling me to stop holding it while walking in the street. Another was when it began pouring with rain into his open-topped convertible, a hulk of a car with red leather seats that had a whiff of well-hung meat, and we had to stop and haul the roof closed, faking breathlessness as we struggled with the heavy tarpaulin. The third was when we landed at London's Heathrow airport and I realized that I had left my beloved one-eyed teddy bear in the departure lounge at Frankfurt and he resolved to fly back at once to look for it, in the teeth of opposition from my mother, who said that children had to learn to accept losses. And the last was when, as was the custom on Sunday mornings, my brother Marius and I were allowed into our parents' bed and we all had a boiled egg, and after I had wolfed down mine he spotted me looking covetously at the remainder of his and handed it to me with the warmest wordless smile, and it tasted even better than mine, as the food of those you love so often does.

Aside from those memories and the pictures, he'd left few traces. I couldn't remember his voice, though I remembered the voices of many others at that time, for example of his doctor, Ernst Lucas, who would visit my parents every Saturday morning with his strangely silent wife, Lilly Reifenberg, who died not long after my father without me ever hearing her speak. I remembered Lucas's gravelly intonation and the chocolate cigarettes, thin as Gauloises, that he gave me and my brother with a warm, knowing chuckle that only German refugees seemed to have, before the two men disappeared into our severe living room to play chess, still addressing each other, after decades, with the formal 'Sie'.

Occasionally he would visit me in dreams, almost always in the back garden of the house to which we had moved after he died. We exchanged few words and no kisses or hugs or presents or smiles or tears; but the pure current of life flowed between us, the only current that ultimately matters, the one that enlivens and affirms your existence and speaks of that too easily used word, 'love'. The questions I'd wanted to ask him – where he was now, how he felt there, how much of my life he could see, whether he missed us – usually died on my lips. No answer would ever tell me what I wanted to know.

It was always over in a few minutes, as if he'd been granted only brief terrestrial visiting rights. Our leave-taking was as silent and unsentimental as our meeting had been. He disappeared and I crept back to my bedroom, taking care not to scare my mother or brother. I accepted that he had to keep to his allotted time, and once back in bed I'd usually wake up.

It had happened so long ago: that day five years before – I was about six and a half – which marked for me the end of the semi-pretence that there is a separate realm of experience called 'childhood'. The eighteen-year-old girl who looked after me and my brother while our parents were out had taken us to a nearby park, just a few minutes' walk from our house, to break the news.

We were approaching my favourite path, flanked by a riot of brightly coloured flowers, when she stopped and said there was something she needed to tell us.

'Your father has gone to heaven,' she announced nervously.

Sally then half put her arm round us. Sally Marshall was her name.

It was like being hit by a car at speed, followed by a reflex struggle to master the impact. I knew at once that this was the shock of the real. It didn't provoke the disbelief that floods the freshly bereaved adult: the sense of being swept up in a bad dream and the expectation that the loved one will surely return; that he will need to eat, fetch a fresh shirt, and find his credit cards. A child's life doesn't have the momentum that years of habit give an adult's expectations; it's freer of the illusion that what was once normal cannot possibly have vanished, freer of the sense of unreality when the anchors of existence are destroyed in a moment.

Unlike many adults, I didn't ask 'why me?' I didn't seek a justification or feel self-pity, not because I was being stoical but because self-pity isn't really in a young child's repertoire. Grief is, though. At once the world felt very dark and the future blank and void. The thought floated through my mind that I'd got to know him as well as I ever would, and that he would never hear anything more about my life. He'd never teach me anything again. We'd never do anything else together. This poured-out world was the new order.

And I remember my brother standing next to me. I was sure he hadn't grasped the cataclysm. He didn't react. He seemed helpless and innocent, in a way that I'd never noticed before. I wanted to protect him forever.

Unsure what to say next, Sally muttered, 'You *will* see him again, in heaven.'

Those words made me angry. Yes, I'd already realized that he wasn't about to stumble back into the house and confess to having departed in error. As for seeing him in heaven, that wasn't something she was in a position to promise, and her reassurance felt mockingly empty.

Then I thought of my mother. Where was she? How was she? I could protect her too, I was certain of that.

The three of us stood there in silence, huddled but not touching. Dread and a strange exhilaration took hold of me, egging each other on. This was overwhelming fate at work; not malevolent, just heedless; knowing nothing of its impact on little mortals. It had brought the curtain down on the old world, with its breakfasts and quarrels and laughs and playtimes and silences, and catapulted me into a new universe of horror and of freedom – the horror of destruction and the freedom that I would have to explore, to make a life for myself. And I would rise to the challenge. An enormous whoosh of energy welled up within me, coming to my rescue and taking command of my bewilderment. I would be fine, not because others were to hand with consolation or promises of heaven, but because that energy would prevail, no matter what.

We remained a little longer at that spot, still marked today with a sacredness visible only to me. Nothing more was said. I looked at my brother again, unable to fathom what he was feeling. As we turned to walk home, the world felt as if it was vastly expanding, shedding its predictability and becoming flooded by emptiness and doom, but also, inseparably, by reality and light.

ii.

After that day in the park, my father died a more leisurely death. The few vestiges of him began to fade. Talk of him dwindled, like the volume on a music player being gradually turned down. It dawned on me, as it hadn't while he lived, that there were no relatives. Didn't he have siblings, like my mother did, or perhaps parents or cousins, nephews or nieces?

My mother told me that his parents had died long before I was born. Eventually it emerged that there was a brother, Edward May, who was a doctor and a brilliant amateur cellist, and lived near us. Eddy had a wife and two sons, but nothing was said of them. I met him only once, a couple of years after my father died, when we dropped in to his house near London's Marble Arch and he took me for a spin in his Jaguar, racing from one end of Park Lane to the other and then back up again, at a clip that today would set off a frantic relay of speed cameras. He was clearly a class rascal, big-spirited and humorous. Like all Mays, he loved the holy trinity of food, wine, and music. As for other relatives, Mother didn't know who or where they were. Either my father hadn't liked them much, she said, or they had emigrated from Germany to Palestine or America. Their names were unknown so they couldn't be traced.

Occasionally I would try to keep the subject of my father alive by asking schoolfriends how many fathers *they* had, a question the absurdity of which would provoke the retort, 'One of course; how many do you have?' And then I could tell them that I had none.

There was a single clue to a hinterland of family, but I didn't join the dots. The Christmas after my father died, the postman delivered two large boxes containing presents for me and my brother. The presents were a suitcase for each of us, and the sender, our mother said, was father's eldest son from his first marriage, which had been to his second cousin, a Hilde May. My half-brother was called Tommy, and he was about twenty years older than me and lived somewhere in the English countryside. Every year, at the same time before Christmas, the presents would arrive. I was exhilarated that Tommy's hands must have touched the paper that I was unwrapping; and that I now had my own suitcase – which meant that I too could emigrate, though to where I had as yet no idea.

A few weeks after my father died, I awoke to torrential rain of a viciousness that I have never experienced since, not even in monsoon season in Japan. My mother and brother were already downstairs and peering excitely out of the kitchen window. It was about ten in the morning, but the sky was dark and the shape of everything outside was distorted by the rain sluicing down the windowpanes. Mother had turned all the lights on, which made the safety of being indoors all the more delicious. But the clouds were getting denser and blacker and closer, until it was hard to imagine that they would ever allow the sun through again. Soon the pouring rain became a tempest, pummelling the house and soaking the land. A shaft of lightning shot to earth, turning the sky into a kaleidoscope of colour, followed by a huge thunderclap. Streams of water began to flow down the sloping yard in front of our house, and one more crash

from the heavens sent all the lights out. Had we been directly hit?
Excitement quickly turned to fear. Then we saw water seeping under
the front door. My brother and I started crying. Worst of all, Mother
started crying. It seemed to get even darker outside. The carpet by
the door was becoming soaked and water began invading our living
room. Within an hour it had risen several inches and was threatening
to destroy the Pembroke table and the Persian carpet and leather-
bound volumes of German classics that my father had rescued from
Nazi Germany, and the pictures on the wall that he had left us – all
the remaining traces of his life.

As the water accumulated, we panicked. What should we do?
Run upstairs? The flood surely wouldn't reach that high. We were
all paralyzed, until we realized that we were going to have to scoop
up the water as quickly as it was flowing in. And for an hour at
least, we tipped it into the kitchen sink and into the toilets, until
only the carpets and the legs of the furniture in the living room
were submerged and most of father's possessions had, for the time
being, been spared.

For years afterwards I thought of 'The Flood', as we called it.
That furious sky and its deluge of terror echoed – confirmed – the
violence, the suddenness, of father's disappearance. It wasn't
punishing humans for their misdemeanours, like the biblical flood;
it was hitting us indiscriminately, regardless of right and wrong. It
was saying to me: 'Yes, this is how the world works. Your blameless
father isn't the only one who is vulnerable to disaster: everybody
is, at any time.' The flood was an omen after the event – a sign that
something very extraordinary and very catastrophic must have
happened to bring about my father's demise.

iii.

'He fell like this,' said Ursel, standing up and then tumbling backwards into a wicker chair in the corner of the kitchen, her head
thrust back, her neck stretched out, and her mouth gaping. 'He
gestured to say something, but he collapsed before he could say it.'

'How can you say that?' Ilse chimed in indignantly. 'He's a child.
I find that tasteless, Ursel. Outrageous.'

'You were there?' I asked, irritated by Ilse's protests, which I feared would inhibit the flow of revelation. 'You saw him die?'

Ursel then explained that my father was helping her and her husband at a meeting that needed to be conducted in German. He was someone they both trusted. They had asked him to join them. She was in the room when it happened.

'Who was your husband? Which room? Why did my father die?'

'He had a broken heart.'

'How can someone's heart break?' I asked.

'It's like a plate,' she said. 'Under great pressure, it breaks.'

'But a heart is flesh, and flesh can't break.'

She looked flustered. Why did she have to bend the truth for a child?

'It just fell apart,' she explained lamely.

She then repeated her enactment of his fall, but in slow motion, with more emphasis on his shocked face, his open mouth, his still-ness – and the finality.

Ursel was a mimic of genius and her evocation of the scene was so vivid that it was bringing my father back to flickering life, for the first time since he disappeared.

'Where was that room?' I asked.

'At the German Embassy in London.'

'Why the *German* Embassy?'

The reason, she explained, was that she and her husband needed to consult a lawyer qualified in a specialized branch of German law. In those days it was hard to find one in London.

'Your father was a Jew,' she added – strangely, as if I didn't know. 'How bizarre, what an astonishing coincidence, to die on German territory – on the territory of the country he fled in the 1930s.'

Images of my father's expression in that last, horrific moment flashed inchoately through my mind. I couldn't settle on one. Shock. Fear. Incomprehension. Nothing at all. Did he realize this was the end? Was his face pale? Was it flushed?

'My father was a German too,' I protested, indignant at him not being identified as a German as well as a Jew, which seemed to evict him from his homeland for a second time, depriving him – and therefore me – of our heritage as Germans.

'No, he was no longer a German,' Ursel snapped, with a defiance that unnerved and confused me. 'He became an Englishman, but he remained a Jew after the emigration.'

My tussle with Ursel over my father's identity humiliated me. But I was also elated that she had evoked him and his last moments at all: in making his death so vivid, she seemed to restitute to me at least a shadow of his reality, perhaps the greatest gift anyone has ever made me.

This was all I'd been told about my father at the age of eleven: that he was a Jewish German, born in Cologne in 1905, who'd fled to England just before the Second World War; that with a small loan he'd bought a bankrupt brush factory in Wales, and by the early 1950s had made it into a gleaming, efficient place, churning out the highest quality brushes; and that with the money he made he'd bought paintings and sculptures, our house, and his car. Art, I was told, was his passion. If he hadn't come to England without a penny to his name and left school at fifteen with no further education, becoming a bank clerk to earn money for his parents and to pay for his older brother to go to medical school, he'd have become a museum curator or an art historian.

But Ilse had become really angry, and demanded that Ursel stop at once. Horrified though I was by the thought of his final moment and by his eviction from Germany, I was also euphoric at the determination this called up in me: the determination to square up to truth, like wrestlers squaring up to each other in the ring; to stare back at his disappearance as hard as it stared at me; but also to allow myself to feel its real presence, however painful, so that it might reveal itself more fully.

From that day on, Ursel was my favourite aunt – my favourite relative – no doubt about it. A lifeline to the past. To my father. And so to his homeland.

iv.

'My father was a German too.'

This wasn't said out of mere nostalgia – that deadly and vital force, at once seductive trap and source of the most powerful energies (and we can seldom be quite sure which it is). It was the life-giving truth that must be preserved at all costs. Without it I would be lost in a dimensionless world, unable to sleep. Heritage as powerful as this can't be excised. Nor can its universe of memory and meaning, no matter how painfully or patchily preserved, be ignored. By my eleventh year, or perhaps long before, I felt as much of an exile as my parents – or rather I felt *more* of an exile than they did, because at least they had lived in their homeland before their displacement, whereas I had been born displaced, a German who had never lived in Germany and was barely able to speak a word of the language. My two aunts, I decided, couldn't understand this. They thought Germany was behind me, a non-issue, just because I had been born in London.

As I lay in bed, picturing my father collapsing, I was overwhelmingly grateful to Ursel for conjuring his presence back into my life. But I continued to refuse her denial of his homeland, and so of a whole world of experience and feeling that it had bequeathed, raw and unshapen, to me. Though my parents were both German Jews who had fled their country of birth, my mother in 1934 and my father in 1937, they hadn't fled their identity as Germans. They hadn't fled the German language – the only language that they spoke to each other and to nearly all of their friends. They hadn't fled German music – which never stopped being at the centre of their lives. They hadn't fled German recipes or cleanliness. They hadn't fled their accents, which after decades in England remained stubbornly stronger than those of young Germans I would later meet at university who had only been in the country for a matter of months.

Nor had they entirely fled their home towns. The names of Berlin places and streets in which I had never set foot, repeated by my mother like incantations, came to have a magical resonance for me: the Bendlerstrasse, the Landwehrkanal, Motzstrasse, Maassenstrasse, Nollendorfplatz, Pallasstrasse – places that only a local would know – meant more to me than any equivalent in London. I could feel myself walking over the Bendler bridge a few steps from my grandparents' home, holding on to its wrought iron balustrade and peering down at the Landwehr canal, with its lazily flowing water. I could picture the *Flugverbandhaus*, at the corner of Blumeshof and Schöneberger Ufer, where my mother saw the veteran airmen from the First World War as well as Russian émigrés gather for their reunions throughout the 1920s. I can see her as a twelve-year-old, still living in a world that could be taken for granted, meeting her friend Luise Borchardt, who later became my godmother, and the way they used to ask each other every morning as they walked to school together, '*Gehen wir Motz oder Maassen?*' – 'Shall we go down Motz or Maassen Street?' Above all, my mind's eye clings to the neighbouring Tiergarten – the huge park in the centre of Berlin where my mother and her sisters would play, where her family would go for long walks, and where I sense that moments of deep contentment were enjoyed. In winter the children would skate on the frozen lake around the Rousseau island, which as a little girl she thought was spelled 'Russo', named after an anonymous Russian, rather than after the Swiss-French philosopher (an error that amused her until her death); and afterwards the family would go to a nearby cafe, nestled among the trees, which sold foot-long frankfurter sausages and lentil soup and cakes topped with whipped cream. Though Berlin has become my second home, or maybe my first, to see the word 'Tiergarten' on a road sign or at the S-Bahn train station is still to be accosted by an entire world. Our world. This was the world that my parents brought with them to a street in central London and that lived immortally, it seemed, in our English home with its leaky windows and erratic plumbing.

Indeed, far from not being German, my parents and their fellow refugees in London seemed to me, as a child, to be the only genuine Germans. Each time I visited Germany – which we did every year while my father was alive and then three times a year after he died – the Germans there never seemed really German. They somehow missed a third dimension: the rich, quietly intense warmth, pervaded by deep, unselfconscious integrity, which I had been taught to associate with the real Germany, non-Jewish and Jewish. Indeed, no nation was capable of greater nobility and integrity of spirit, my mother drummed into me, as exemplified by non-Jewish musicians such as the violinist Adolf Busch or the conductor Erich Kleiber – just as no nation had demonstrated greater venality.

Though the intricacies of memory, denial, and guilt had made life in Germany seem so psychologically rigid back then, in the late 1960s and early '70s, and though the overt love for German culture that I felt even among our friends in London who had survived the death camps was so complicatedly impossible there, or at least unspeakable, I fantasized about going 'back' to Germany and living in a homely town, where people quarrelled and laughed and insisted and in particular complained in ways every nuance of which I recognized, and had a soul with which I was intimately familiar and that seemed to offer a refuge from being a refugee.

And every time I arrived in Germany my spirit lifted. I loved the autobahns, with their impossibly smooth surfaces and their comforting blue signs, which gave way to gleaming yellow the moment you drove off them. I relished stopping at the oddly intimate *Raststätten*: highway restaurants where I would choose *zwei Spiegeleier mit Erbsen* (two fried eggs with peas), brought to the table by immaculately dressed servers, their cash tinkling in black pouches concealed under white lace pinafores. I felt consoled by the cozy expressions of elderly people meeting their friends for *Kaffeeklatsch* over cakes of unreal dimensions. I was overcome by the beauty of German landscape, the silence and scents and melancholy and secrets of which spoke directly to my soul. I was endlessly fascinated by German rigidity, some forms of which seem to provide a brilliant structure to life that makes possible the highest achievements of the human spirit; while others are mere prison houses for the mind that demand sterile conformity and are guarded by peculiarly mean-minded hostility towards all dissenters and outsiders. Despite its provincialism and often its pettiness, Germany felt richer in spirit than any other country I knew. For all its narrowness it was broader, more complicated, more generous.

I resolved that when I grew up I would return to whatever Germany the future would bring. I would honour my father by planting myself back in his land and, unlike him, I would cease to be a refugee. Then I would be where he had come from and where I belonged. And Adolf Hitler, who had wanted to empty Germany of us, would not have won completely.

*   *   *

To do this, however, would be a rebellion of the first order. Against my mother. The Germany she loved was no more. Hitler had destroyed it by throwing out the Jews and neutering the remaining Germans. The country, according to her, had been reduced to a vast factory churning out high-quality goods so that, by distraction through wealth, it could keep itself numb. Which it did superbly. The real Germany had ended with the war, so I would be returning to what she saw as an illegitimate, materialistic orphan of a country that in betraying its Jews had irredeemably betrayed itself.

I was permitted only fleeting access to this half-Germany, and forbidden to enjoy or to say anything good about it. No German goods of any kind were allowed in our home. Above all, the language was off-limits to us, the next generation. Though German was *the* language of belonging, of our souls and our histories, it was more strictly out of bounds than even the new Germany itself. Though, within the walls of our London home, it was the language in which she and my father exclusively conversed; though almost all her friends were from Germany, Austria, and other German-speaking regions and spoke to each other only in their native tongue; though when the telephone rang I nearly always heard my mother answer in German, for us it was the prohibited language: *die verbotene Sprache*. Complete editions of Goethe, Schiller, Hölderlin, and other classics lined our shelves – in some cases in two copies, one inherited from my father's family and the other from my mother's – all of them carted over to England with the few possessions they took; yet to me and my brother she resolutely spoke her broken and heavily accented English, and found it ridiculous when, from my mid-teens onwards, I tried to reply in my broken and heavily accented German.

But a Jewish identity was even more out of the question. For I wasn't really a Jew either, she often said, and so I had no right to identify myself as such. Or at least I wasn't more than partially Jewish. That her father had been was never in question, but her mother, she usually maintained, was 'Aryan'; and so Jewish law, which states that you are Jewish only if your mother's line is, or if you convert, would pronounce her – and therefore me – to be an outsider. (Of course, Nazi law, she added, would have stipulated precisely the opposite, deeming me, even with three Jewish grand-parents, a full Jew, with all that would have entailed.)

Yet there were times when my mother spoke of her mother's Jewish grandmother and other maternal Jewish ancestors, who would briefly come into focus before disappearing again. Which would mean that she herself was Jewish after all, and that I was.

Which of these identities she attributed to her mother depended on states of mind whose laws I struggled to decipher. Her ethnic position was clear only in the company of most Jews, when she was categorically non-Jewish, and in the company of most non-Jewish Germans, when she was categorically Jewish.

To add to her palette of identities, my mother had become a Catholic just after Hitler came to power and not long before she emigrated to England in 1934. She hadn't, though, converted from Judaism, but rather from the Protestantism in which she had been raised and to which her father had belatedly converted.

The result of these ethnic-religious contortions was always the same: I was not allowed to identify myself as Jewish, just as I wasn't allowed to be a contemporary German. But nor was it permissible to consider myself English or British. Indeed, this was the greatest taboo of all, because the English spirit was deemed alien in a way that neither the Jewish nor even the post-war German spirit was. Though not a word of criticism was ever to be uttered against the country that had given my parents refuge, to feel English would be a betrayal of everything that I really was, whatever that might be. Worse, it would be to admit – or rather to pretend – that we had abandoned the pre-war culture of our origin, even though that culture no longer existed.

Above all, it would be to betray the sacred duty of a refugee: never allow yourself to arrive. Contribute everything in your power to your host country, in order to say thank you and to be accepted; be unflinchingly patriotic; support its institutions, and even be pillars of those institutions; but do not succumb to its inner life. Be fully in your new home, but never of it.

So who was I? The answer became strangely clear: I was an émigré (though I had never left anywhere), who belonged to the culture of a Germany which was now extinct (though I had never lived there), with a Jewish origin (sometimes admissible, sometimes not), and permanent temporary residency in the country of my birth. My only legitimate identity, according to my mother, was to somehow recreate a bygone German world that was the only world worth living for. Her mandate, in short, was to live a life rooted in a culture that had disappeared before I was born, and whose language I was not permitted to speak, but that was nonetheless my golden inheritance – and make it shine in an alien country and era. Oh, and I was to do all that as a practising Catholic, which, being a universal faith, did not confine me to any particular country or era – or indeed ethnic group.

As I was growing up, this lost culture and country were represented above all by one idol – German music, as performed by always dead, usually German, and often Jewish musicians. Though that culture had vanished, it was the only dimension of life not to feel provisional. Everything else existed in limbo, as the émigré's world so often does.

For me, this inheritance came to be embodied within our family in one man. Not my own father, whose death, as spellbindingly recounted by Ursel, had triggered my search for this world of the assimilated German Jew, but whose own life had been too decisively extinguished to provide any road map for that search. Rather, this loved heritage became personified by my mother's father, Ernst Liedtke, whom she held up as the paragon of an assimilated German Jew: cultured, educated, deeply moral, law-abiding, and patriotic. Born in 1875 into a poor family of grain traders in West Prussia, he was a contemporary of that extraordinary generation of German-speaking Jews who had so richly reimagined German and indeed world culture: Albert Einstein had transformed our understanding of the universe; Arnold Schoenberg had produced an entirely new music; Franz Kafka had invented a unique literature; Sigmund Freud had fathered a revolutionary conception of the mind; and so on, in nearly every field of endeavour.

These largely non-religious Jews seemed to Ernst to vindicate his highly assimilated life, and even to guarantee its safety. More than that, they confirmed that though Jewish tradition might have been a ladder to the heights of German culture, and though its values and sensibility might have enabled some Jews to become more creatively German than the Germans, it was now a ladder that could and should be discarded.

By the age of eleven, five years after my father began to disappear, I was sure that I couldn't hope to make sense of this inheritance and to solve the enigma of identity that it had handed to me unless I could first find a way into the life that Ernst and my grandmother Emmy had created in the Berlin of the early twentieth century – a life that my mother had spoken of for as long as I could remember. I would need to understand the very different fates of Ernst's and Emmy's respective brothers: one of them, Theo, a shy salesman in a Berlin department store who was deported and murdered; the other, Helmut, a convert to Catholicism who, it has been said, was the most famous Catholic orator in Germany of the late 1920s and early 1930s. Above all, I would need to trace the very different lives – before, during, and after the Nazi tyranny – of Ernst and Emmy's three daughters, and to understand what they had each made of this common inheritance, of which they were the direct bearers and witnesses.

My quest to regain some vital connection to my dead father, and to the German-Jewish world from which he came, supplied the motive; but the thread that led me into that labyrinth was the life of Ernst, who lived on through my remaining parent and two aunts with a vivid presence that my own father was denied. And I was determined from that evening in the Swiss chalet to go after him, his family, and his legacy.

PART I

A Berlin Idyll
1910–1933

I have always loved assimilated Jews, because that was where the Jewish character, and also, perhaps, Jewish fate, was concentrated with greatest force.

Aharon Appelfeld[3]

1

Blumeshof 12

Christmas Day, 1932. In retrospect his world might look fragile and delusory, a house of cards waiting to collapse. The menace of anti-Semitism is nothing new: it has been there for as long as he can bear to recall it. Nonetheless, it is a reality against which, grandfather Ernst is sure, the solidity of his life insulates him.

He has it all: A respected position in one of Berlin's leading law courts, the Kammergericht on the Elssholzstrasse – which still exists, indeed is Germany's oldest surviving court. Three talented daughters – Ilse, Ursel (Ursula), and Marianne, my mother – unusually, for those days, all embarking on professions. A large apartment in prosperous 'Berlin West' – Berlin W. – the magic 'W', pronounced 'vey' and spoken with awe by my mother and her sisters, for it denotes a protected zone of high bourgeois *Kultur*, with its impregnable ethic of seriousness and learning and its veneration of music and philosophy, art and theatre. No more Jewishness – that he sees as behind him now, banished to the past, conquered, extirpated, anachronistic, inauthentic; a problem finally solved, not just to the outside world but even, somehow, in his innermost soul, where the sensibility and instincts of millennia no longer hold conscious sway. A cultured, beautiful, and officially non-Jewish wife – who is aware that she is halachically Jewish and yet, decades after her death in 1965 and right into the twenty-first century, my mother continues to speak of her sometimes as Jewish but usually as 'Aryan', and in either case with equal conviction. Above all, there is his beloved Germany: a nation of deep thinkers, dazzling musicians, epoch-making scientists, discipline, order, and integrity. Germany: a culture of incomparable richness, from which the human spirit has grown to transcendental heights. In which innocence and knowingness, divine naivety and self-consciousness, all flourish in fertile tension. In which the austere and the overwrought restlessly coexist. Germany: for him and his kind, the greatest culture in the contemporary West, and probably in the world. Athens on the River Spree. Without slaves.

My grandfather fills his days with law and his evenings with cultured conversations around the dinner table with his wife Emmy and their daughters – though, according to my mother, from about fourteen Ursel, the middle daughter, begins to absent herself. Her home and especially her father make her uncomfortable. It all seems frighteningly, oppressively, serious. And, I imagine, perhaps the seriousness conceals something else: the perilous unreality of her parents' belief in the safety and solidity of their lives; and their terror before the fragility of civilization.

After dinner, Ernst and Emmy usually read German classics aloud to each other: poems of Schiller or extracts from Goethe's *Italian Journey*, in the footsteps of which Ernst had followed as a young man and which still inspire the annual trips he makes to Italy each summer, accompanied by either Ilse or Marianne (Ursel refuses to go). Sometimes he reads Novalis and Tieck, or he gets his mind around Kant, Hegel, or another of those dense German philosophers. And Emmy occasionally interjects with a poem or two of the hundreds that she learned by heart in her childhood and at the finishing school in Montreux where her rich Jewish uncle and adoptive father, Artur Rosenthal, sent her in her late teens.

Or Emmy goes to the piano and accompanies herself singing *Lieder*. Though her voice is small, she is highly musical – more so than Ernst, who lacks her innate understanding of phrasing and tonality. She is naive, though also intensely aware, given to wild exaggeration, and easily infatuated with the latest fashions in healthy eating, such as Graham bread, herbal teas, and anything that comes from England. Even in her seventies, when I knew her – she died when I was nine – she had an evergreen youthfulness, walked briskly on spindle-thin legs, found most things either unbelievably wonderful or unbelievably terrible, craved the protection of others yet was formidably self-reliant, and had an unnerving stare betraying, I was sure, intelligence and stubbornness of a high order.

Most Saturday afternoons she makes English tea and combs Berlin for bread that is textureless enough for truly English sandwiches. She has her furniture upholstered in English material by the down-stairs neighbour, a Baroness Schlippenbach, who imports fabrics, and swoons over its delights, saying, 'Ach, children, isn't it beautiful? It's so tasteful! It's so *English*!'

The domestic idyll is occasionally interrupted by friends who drop in after dinner. The benign lawyer, Wilhelm Krämer, my mother's god-father, who was in the same student fraternity as Ernst and is soon to be promoted to the *Reichsgericht*, Germany's Supreme Court, in Leipzig, where he will stay right up to 1945, regularly breaks into their quiet time after dinner for a drink. So does another lawyer, Herr Hans-Harald von Hackwitz, a tall, reedy, and handsome loner who deputizes for Ernst while he is on holiday. Hackwitz's gait and speech are as stiff as his name and he is unaware of being followed around the large living room – my mother always chuckles as she tells me this story – by Ursel, who mimics his mannerisms behind his back and pretends that she can't wait to get her hands on him. 'I don't understand that child; I just don't understand her,' Ernst says disapprovingly as Ursel turns the gestures, tics, and eccentricities of her parents' friends into festivals of clowning. The mutual incomprehension, even mistrust, between Ernst and Ursel is already there; subtly she is repudiating him, her millstone of earnestness. 'But,' Ernst continues, 'why such a charming young man refuses to get married, I don't know.'

Occasionally, my mother tells me, Gregor Piatigorsky, a great Russian cellist who would emigrate to America in 1940 on the last passenger ship to leave France before the German occupation, knocks on the door unannounced – less to visit Emmy and Ernst than to feast his eyes on 'the three graces', as he calls the teenage daughters of the house. 'You are lovely graces!' he exclaims in his elegantly Russified German with its rolling 'r's. 'But, I am sorry, none of you –' and he pauses teasingly – 'is a patch on your charming mother!'

Piatigorsky's excuse for dropping in is that he needs a room to change into his white tie for the concerts at my grandparents' downstairs neighbours, Baron and Baroness Schlippenbach, who have converted their twelve-room apartment, minus the kitchen, bathroom, and four bedrooms, into a concert hall, complete with a platform and curtains that two domestic staff draw back to reveal the artists for the evening. Baron Schlippenbach is a dandy who dabbles in poetry, likes to dress in eighteenth-century court costume, claims to have written a novel longer than *War and Peace* which is tucked away in a drawer waiting for its time to come, and has befriended many of Berlin's leading musicians. He persuades virtuosos like Fritz Kreisler, Carl Flesch, reigning professor of violin in Berlin, and Piatigorsky to rehearse their programmes at his soirées; and few of these men are indifferent to the beautiful women whose animated conversation lights up the shadows of the reading room at the back of the apartment.

The concert hall is big enough for Schlippenbach to stage operas in full dress, performed by such singers as the then-legendary soprano Irene Eisinger, a decent-sized choir, and a chamber orchestra drawn from the *Staatsoper*, one of the city's three opera houses, under its leader Josef Wolfsthal. The writer Walter Benjamin – whose own grandmother, Hedwig Schönflies, lived, until her death, in the apartment directly above my grandparents – gives a sense of the spaciousness of the apartments in Blumeshof 12:

> The rooms in this apartment on the Blumeshof were not only numerous but also in some cases very large. To reach my grandmother at her window I had to cross the huge dining room and attain the farthest end of the living room. Only feast days, and above all Christmas Day, could give an idea of the capaciousness of these rooms.[4]

*　*　*

'Above all, Christmas Day'! Preparations for this most deeply contented day of the year begin at least a week beforehand in Ernst and Emmy's household, as in those of millions of Germans. The windows on the Advent calendar are nearly all open; the tree is carried in and decorated with candles and baubles; cookies of ginger, almond, and other *Weihnachtsgebäck* are laid out on brightly coloured plates beneath the tree; and finally, the presents, concealed until the previous evening in a locked cupboard, are distributed on three tables, then covered with cloths embroidered with a big woven 'L', a wedding present from Emmy's adoptive father, Artur Rosenthal.

The girls have not been allowed into the room with the tree and the gifts all day, until, at precisely 7 p.m. on Christmas Eve, Ernst, chuckling with delight at his daughters' excited anticipation, rings a bell. They rush out of Ilse's room, where they have been confined out of sight of the last-minute preparations, and each of them sweeps the cloth off 'her' table. The tree is addressed with the traditional German Christmas song, '*O Tannenbaum, O Tannenbaum*', followed by '*Stille Nacht, heilige Nacht*', before a large goose, steaming in its basted golden-brown skin, is wheeled in by the proud cook, who is followed by the other staff, all dressed in their best and giggling conspiratorially.

As my mother lies dying in a London hospital ward some ninety years later, just three weeks before Christmas, she sings '*Stille Nacht, heilige Nacht*' over and over again to the nurses; to a magnificent cockney called Dorothy in the next bed, who seems perplexed enough by the stream of foreign words to briefly cease complaining about the scandalous lateness of meals and the 'madhouse' that she deems the hospital to be on account of its inability to produce cheese sandwiches with unbuttered, crust-free, chewable bread; and to a Muslim woman in the bed opposite, her female relations sitting round her in veiled silence, her charming son 'inspired', he tells me, by the vivid happiness of my mother's memories as she recalls the deep contentedness of the Christmas room, and the symphony of church bells in the distance, and the creaking of the staircase in her building as neighbours, non-Jewish and Jewish, return from church. The tenderness of Mother's voice overwhelms me as she pauses, her eyes large with the wonder of childlike happiness, and repeats:

Holder Knabe im lockigen Haar,
Schlaf in himmlischer Ruh!

(Lovely boy with curly hair,
Sleep in heavenly peace!)

The idyll of Blumeshof is potent. Its moral order seems in-destructible. Even when their lives are beset by anxiety, Ernst and Emmy's marriage is free of it. It is a marriage of dovetailing desires and dislikes, rhythms and sympathies, unburdened by drama, boredom, jealousy, suspicion, or unfilled expectations. Their love is undisturbed by those torments where one person seems achingly elusive or, on the contrary, to press in on and crowd out the other's inner world; unoppressed by the emptiness that couples can feel when they possess each other too securely. Their needs for each other never go beyond what they can give (with perhaps one excep-tion). There are no rows, only loving disagreements. Her penchant for wild exaggeration is perfectly cushioned by his natural under-statement, his self-control balanced by her spontaneity. They offer each other that deep security and well-being that is happiness.

At least, this is how all three daughters spoke to me of the marriage. As if in a dream reporting a dream, they would recall its perfections with identical superlatives and in the same self-evident tone. Over decades I heard paeans – entirely convincing – to its harmony and order, spoken by each in unvarying sentences that seemed as wholehearted as they were automatic. Even Ursel concurred that it was a remarkable match, though absolutely not to her dramatic taste.

The apartment itself embodied this contented union. The three sisters, their parents, the staff, and the relatives and friends who came to stay all had their own quarters where they slept, ate, relaxed, conversed, and worked; and when they crossed into other parts of the apartment they were like visitors on foreign turf. Each room had its distinctive atmosphere and furnishings, as if it were designed to support one particular life form. There was a room where my grandfather and grandmother had breakfast together, another where he worked or read, a third where she could be private, the library where they spent their evenings, the salon with the piano, an office in which his secretary banged away on a typewriter every morning from eight until noon, and another where he received colleagues. And there were the rooms at the back where the girls were confined while they still played with dolls, though Ilse stopped doing that at ten and found Ursel and my mother rather stupidly obsessed with the puppet theatre that they had built together and the private language that they had developed: their so-called 'Maminasprache', a playful perversion of German, replete with dramatically lurching cadences, based on the West Prussian dialect spoken by Ernst and his parents.

It was an upholstered universe of impeccable structure. Its laws felt palpably self-sustaining. The rougher sides of Berlin – poverty, anarchy, bigotry, and later the brownshirts – were literally out of sight and out of mind.

As Walter Benjamin said of his grandmother's apartment upstairs, poverty, and even death itself, 'could have no place in these rooms.' To which he added mysteriously, but also illuminatingly: 'Blumeshof has become for me an Elysium, an indefinite realm of the shades of deceased but immortal grandmothers.'

And, of course, grandfathers.

2.

'Musician must always look beautiful'

'Musician must always look beautiful,' my mother remembered Piatigorsky saying in a stern tone that revealed a steelier side to the jocular Russian charmer than he normally presented – 'Not just play beautiful, but appear beautiful! Even in a heatwave, he will still wear white tie and correct shoes – and always comb hair! No excuse!'

Apart from that advice, he encouraged my mother, then aged twelve or thirteen, to take up the violin professionally. The conversation on one of his visits was succinct:

'She looks perfect; she must play perfect!' the handsome cellist commanded. 'She is a natural, but she needs a top teacher. Enough with children's teachers!'

'Who is the right person?' Ernst asked, in his relentlessly focused way. 'The very best.'

(Whatever really mattered in our family always had to be 'the very best'.)

'There are only two in Berlin who would be right for her,' Piatigorsky replied. 'Josef Wolfsthal and Carl Flesch.'

Wolfsthal was Carl Flesch's former student and among his most distinguished disciples. The master had written the definitive book on the subject, *The Art of Violin Playing*, and his student, who had been appointed professor at Berlin's renowned Hochschule für Musik at twenty-six, followed its teachings to the letter.

The question was which teacher it would be. Flesch was the more famous and had the more illustrious students, but he liked to teach each of his students in front of his whole class. This was an efficient use of his time and trained the young men and women to perform before a demanding audience. Technique, musicianship, performance – you learned them all at once. Wolfsthal, by contrast, was willing to teach one-on-one.

'So, do you want to do it?' Ernst demanded, turning to my mother.

'Of course I want to do it.'

'And with whom?'

'With Wolfsthal.' The class thing was intimidating, especially as you were up against some of the greatest talents of the day, such as Henryk Szeryng.

'It will be arranged,' her father answered, 'but you will need to cease your school studies immediately, and devote everything to the violin. Are you prepared for that?'

'I am.'

A few weeks later, at Piatigorsky's introduction, my mother began her studies with Josef Wolfsthal.

3.

Where Germans and Jews
secretly met

Once a week at least, and usually on a Thursday evening, Ernst
would walk straight from the law court in the Elssholzstrasse to
meet Emmy at the Philharmonie, Berlin's greatest concert hall.
There they heard the Berlin Philharmonic Orchestra conducted by
Wilhelm Furtwängler, Bruno Walter, or Erich Kleiber – and musicians like the pianist Artur Schnabel or the 'cold but dazzling' violinist
Jascha Heifetz, who had all the prodigious talent that, they held,
Eastern Europe and Russia could nourish in their Jewish natives,
though they failed to foster the supreme cultivation that only the
German-speaking lands could instil. Or Ernst and Emmy would go
to one of the three opera houses that flourished in the city: the
Staatsoper, where my mother's teacher was concertmaster and where
they heard Erich Kleiber's famous performance of *Wozzeck* and
Furtwängler conduct *Tristan und Isolde*; or the more experimental
Kroll Oper, where Otto Klemperer reigned with his uncrompom-
ising ways; or the Städtische Oper, presided over by Bruno Walter.

They had a long-standing disagreement over who was the greatest
symphonic conductor of this extraordinary collection. Ernst
preferred the more controlled, yet sensuously rich, Walter – a Jewish
conductor who had replaced his real surname, Schlesinger, with his

middle name. He loved Walter's classical vitality, his scrupulous emotional hygiene, and the refined joyousness of his phrasing; while most concert-goers' favourite was the more mystical Furtwängler, whose incredible intensity of feeling evoked a religious sense of redemption. According to my mother, it was often said in Berlin at the time that Walter tended to be the Jews' favourite and Furtwängler the non-Jewish Germans', reflecting, she maintained, the reality that Jews have a quite distinct sensibility, no matter how German they felt, or how successfully they could articulate Germanic culture. It seemed from some of her accounts that there were parts of a Jewish sensibility that assimilation, however ardently and even violently pursued, never managed to touch.

At the same time, Ernst was not immune to the yearning of many German Romantics to find the divine immanent in the world, and to discover the absolute through music, art, and thought. Perhaps their unquenchable passion for spiritual purification rooted in the rigours of learning was where Germans and Jews of his times secretly met. In any event, such yearnings deeply appealed to those German Jews, like him, who wished to rise beyond their origins into what they saw as the grander, richer world of the German soul, a world that, unlike their ancestors' effete traditions, was overflowing with new life. Not surprisingly, perhaps, Ernst loved Wagner's *Parsifal*, that orgy of redemption set to the profoundest music, in which an angelically androgynous youth who doesn't know even his name redeems a woman, Kundry, whom he transforms from a mocking denier of the Cross into a kind of spiritual bride. He also revered German philosophers in the tradition of Hegel who, though they might have criticized Judaism, were devoted to a vision of absolute reality in which history is destined to culminate – a vision that bore striking parallels to the ancient Jewish promise of a redeemed reality beyond history, in which unity will be brought to a fractured world.

Above all, for Ernst as for Hegel, such a culmination of history could only be German. From his earliest years, my grandfather was determined to make Germany – the spirit of Germany, the texture of Germany – his own, and to turn his back once and for all on his Jewish ancestry, with, as he saw it, its myriad of embarrassing customs and no longer spiritually relevant laws. For him, Jewish culture was the airless, parochial past; German *Kultur* the free, fertile future.

He longed to serve Germany in any way he could. In the First World War he had lobbied to join the cavalry and fight on the front line, but after falling off his horse within days of joining the service, he was quickly transferred to Intelligence and a desk in Berlin. Applying his formidable willpower to this new assignment, he was awarded a medal by the Kaiser for unscrambling enemy code. He was deeply proud of the medal, though kept it locked up in a secret place and was reluctant to talk about it outside the family. It didn't just recognize his unwavering loyalty to Germany; it was also, he was sure, official proof of his acceptance by Germany and of the power of an enlightened state to override or somehow to render harmless the anti-Semitism that refused to sleep.

As a child I liked everything about this story – that my grandfather was a German patriot; that he was too steeped in the dreamy heights of German culture to ride a horse; that he was able to see through a sophisticated enemy aided by no more than a smattering of rumours and quarter-truths. His pristine demeanour, perfectly groomed hair, and trimmed moustache exuded a sense of duty, efficiency, order, and discipline – those quintessentially German virtues, so deliciously reassuring and life-giving when devoted to noble ends. His lips pouted with precision. His rimless glasses rested on a straight no-nonsense nose and framed his melancholically determined eyes. But I kept all this Teutonic bliss under wraps during my high school years in 1970s England, a time when anti-German sentiment and memories of both world wars were still very much alive, when classmates would jack their right arms up in mock Nazi salutes on hearing my mother's accent, and when having two German parents marked me out as inescapably alien.

Or at least I hoped it marked me out as alien, because, like both my parents, I refused to accept that Germany had been lost. And that they had really emigrated.

4

Ernst's conversion

Ernst was raised in Christburg, a town of fewer than 3,300 inhabitants, then in West Prussia (now Dzierzgoń in northern Poland). Born in 1875, it seems extraordinary that my grandfather – only a long generation removed from me – could have been alive when Otto von Bismarck, his political hero, was chancellor of Germany, Benjamin Disraeli prime minister of Great Britain, and Ulysses S. Grant president of the United States; and that he had grown up well within the lifetimes of such figures as Tolstoy, Victor Hugo, Emily Dickinson, Wagner, and Nietzsche.

His father, a trader of grains, had died young, and his mother – warm, quiet, and intense – doted on him and his less energetic brother Theodor. After attending high school in nearby Graudenz, today's Polish city of Grudziadz, he became the first member of his family to go on to higher education, studying law at the University of Königsberg – the open, free-trading capital of East Prussia, founded by the Teutonic knights in the thirteenth century, that had been home to the philosopher Kant as well as to the world's best marzipan.

But Königsberg – later renamed Kaliningrad by Stalin, who turned it into one of the Soviet Union's 'closed' cities where the Kremlin built its top-secret military bases – felt too confining to Ernst, despite the freedom it enjoyed as one of the great seaport cities of the ancient Hanseatic League. On graduating in 1898, he left for Berlin to seek his fortune as a lawyer, first working for an import-export business, then joining a firm of commercial lawyers, and eventually gaining admission to the family law division of the Kammergericht in 1906. He married Emmy Fahsel-Rosenthal, seventeen years his junior, in 1909, and became an exemplary member of that uniquely German social class: the *Bildungsbürgertum*, literally translated as the 'cultivated citizenry'.

Ernst had risen into this burgeoning class by dint of willpower and education, and he was fervent in his loyalty to it on account of its cultured ideals: its devotion to music, literature, philosophy, and, to a lesser degree, science as the way for the individual to tap his or her humanity at its deepest sources – indeed, as sacred activities. The *Bildungsbürgertum* had emerged as recently as the mid-eighteenth century, just a few decades before the beginnings of Jewish emancipation. Inspired by the egalitarian ideals of the Enlightenment, it looked to a future in which the nation would be glorified by learning and liberty. For Ernst, it came to seem like a sanctuary that politics couldn't touch, a realm of freedom and equality and belonging and respect for the dignity of the individual, which would be left in peace by rulers who, mercifully, had little interest in its cultural ideals. It was, to him, the most elevated and *authentic* source of German patriotism; it was where the German soul, in all its richness, found its purest expression.

If the *Bildungsbürgertum* was conscious of any danger, so my mother would say, that danger came not from the bearers of power above but from the petit bourgeois below: from the world, again uniquely German, of *Spiessertum*.

Long after the war, *Spiessertum* continued to be seen by my mother and her sisters as the real enemy – the barbarian spirit permanently at the gate. If they wanted to damn a person, an idea, or even an article of clothing they called it *Spiessig*, by which they meant riddled with pretence, small-mindedness, a cringe-making desire to impress, and above all no feeling for *Kultur*.

Everything the *Spiesser* did was insistently petty, affected, trivial.

He was obsessed with securing comfort and predictability for himself. He spoke with just-so hand movements, pleased at mastering his narrow universe, and quick to resent outsiders who he perceived as threatening it. All this perversity was deemed to have a single origin: his inferiority complex, or *Minderwertigkeitskomplex*. I remember this as the one universally applicable accusation that would be levelled at whatever anyone did of which my mother or her sisters disapproved. (Nor was I exempt from this all-purpose diagnosis of *Spiess* rooted in a *Minderwertigkeitskomplex* when my ideals departed from theirs, or were deemed too 'modern'.)

But my grandparents' hostility to the *Spiesser* wasn't directed just at their alleged small-mindedness or lack of cultivation. In addition, they feared something else entirely, against which they might be defenceless: the festering resentment that was stoked, as they saw it, precisely by the inferiority complex of the *Spiesser* and that was truly menacing because it was insatiable. In the Germany of the early twentieth century, it made such people extremely dangerous, especially to semi-outsiders like Jews. Many in the ruling classes might also be crass and uncultured, but they were 'secure' in themselves, and therefore unlikely to become hostage to violent hatred. They might be nationalistic and anti-Semitic, but never with the bitterness of the *Spiesser*. In the phrase so often used by my mother, 'they didn't *need* to be angry'.

And then, beyond the borders of the ruling classes as well as of *Spiessertum*, lay a class the very existence of which was as painful to my grandparents as it was barely spoken of by them: the true poor. 'We knew little of the terrible poverty in Berlin,' my mother so often said to me. She recalled encountering these people at close range only when accompanying Emmy to choose domestic staff. There, in scenes that would haunt her for life, row upon row of emaciated faces stared out of rags at this passing woman in her fine dress, their sallow eyes beseeching her for the chance to scrub a pantry. To what dwellings they would return if not offered the salvation of domestic work was unclear. How they would feed themselves – and perhaps children kept well hidden lest they deter an offer of employment – was a question that suggested a vista of horror best not seen.

Not seen but nonetheless not entirely suppressed: thus did their own bourgeois 'solidity' appear all the more impregnable to my grandparents. A glimmering awareness of this Hades of penury made it all the harder for them to imagine poverty invading the Elysium of Blumeshof. And the numbness of those crumpled faces, their sole focus on the practicalities of surviving another day, seemed to insulate the poor from the anti-Semitism and nationalism that made the *Spiessertum* feel so sinister.

Of course, the *Bildungsbürgertum* could also be infested by nativist impulses that saw Jews as interlopers who threatened to corrupt the primordial Germanic spirit, which it was the goal of *Bildung* to cultivate. But, Ernst and Emmy were sure, such impulses would always be subordinate to the egalitarian ideals that defined its calling. It was, after all, a class indebted to heroes like Beethoven and Schiller and Lessing, whose visions of tolerance and universal brotherhood it saw as emblematic of the humanistic ethos in which it so passionately believed. These geniuses demonstrated, my grandparents were convinced, that German culture could take both a national form – for they supremely expressed the German soul – and yet be devoted to the broadest humanistic ideals. More than that: they demonstrated that German culture, and above all music that was loved all over the world, was *uniquely able* to respond to an egalitarian and universal calling.

And so, within the protective embrace, real and imagined, of this class – a class into which he had risen only a few years beforehand – a momentous further step away from his Jewish inheritance eventually seemed to Ernst not merely natural but essential.

On 28 November 1910, just over a year after his marriage to the Protestant Emmy and shortly after the birth of their first child, Ilse, he took just that step and formally renounced the faith of his ancestors. He filed an official form, which was stamped by Department 9 of the Royal Prussian District Court of the Schöneberg district of Berlin and authorized by a law passed on 14 May 1873, with a single signature bringing thousands of years of belonging to an end. It was an odd business: how could a covenant made between a people and its god and recorded in holy scripture be undone by a document stamped by a German bureaucrat? What role could the German state conceivably have in confirming that a relationship between a human being and the creator of the world did or didn't exist?

In fact, Ernst's abandonment of Judaism must have been something of an afterthought, as he had already had himself baptized two months earlier, on 22 September 1910. Some official might have reminded him that in order to be a Christian one had to cease being a Jew, and so he had hurriedly gone along to Department 9 to get his exit visa. In practice, he continued to live something of a double life in which he and Emmy lit the Shabbat candles with his mother on Friday evenings, though, it seems, as strangers in their own home, and were occasionally seen in the pews of their local Protestant church on Sundays. But he irrevocably spurned those Jews who identified openly with their religion or who were less 'German' than he. It was they, he felt, who attracted anti-Semitism with their alienness. He came to see himself, to his marrow, as a Prussian, a Protestant, and a patriot, and remained unshakably convinced that Germany – *his* Germany – was the most profound, vibrant, and creative culture in the world.

As to the rise of Hitler, he found that a sick joke. 'You will see!' he announced to his family after Hitler had wangled his way to power in January 1933. 'That man won't last more than six months.' When he saw my grandmother silently weep as Hitler's furiously rolling 'r's fanned out from the radio into the cultivated restraint of their apartment, he would gently admonish her premature fears. 'Don't cry,' he would say tenderly, 'please don't let this distress you so.' And he would turn anxiously to his daughters: 'This whole thing is absurd: the Germans will wake up soon and repudiate it!'

5.

'Get out of here immediately, you East-Asian monkey'

A few weeks later, his life collapsed. On 17 April 1933, a Monday, he walked, as usual, from Blumeshof to the law court near the corner of Elssholzstrasse and Pallasstrasse, arriving, as he always did, punctually at 8.30 a.m., to an unexpected greeting from his normally courteous clerk, which my mother would repeat in disbelieving horror until the day she died:

'*Hau hier sofort ab, Du ostasiatischer Affe!*' – 'Get out of here immediately, you East Asian monkey!' – the young man yelled, contemptuously using the familiar '*Du*' that would otherwise have been an inconceivable way of addressing any colleague, let alone a superior. He then slammed the door in Ernst's face.

Of course, Ernst knew that Jewish lawyers were supposed to be thrown out of work in their thousands. With the exception – for now – of First World War veterans who had served at the front, which he hadn't, as well as of some of his older colleagues. But he didn't believe it happened like this, without a word of explanation, an embarrassed excuse about orders from high up, or a written notice of dismissal with long reference numbers and the customary sign-off '*Im Auftrag*' in the official German style. How could his clerk just lose it in this unstructured, chaotic way?

No, he must go in and discuss it properly. But first he must have a talk with a senior colleague.

He warily opened the door to the offices. His clerk was standing with his back to it, chatting to someone else. The young man swivelled around, stared furiously at this interloper, grabbed him by both shoulders and heaved him to the edge of the landing. He then hurled him down the stairs.

'*Hau hier ab, Du dreck Jude!*' – 'Get out of here, you filthy Jew!' – he yelled, incensed by the Jew's nerve in trying to enter. 'East Asian monkey!' he repeated as his former boss tumbled down the stone steps.

From halfway down the flight of stairs, the older man looked up to see the clerk staring victoriously down at him. Without mockery. The young man's hate was too vast for the subtleties of mockery. The door slammed shut again.

Alone, stunned, and enveloped, I imagine, by terror that all his bearings in the world might be illusory, Ernst enquired silently of the closed door above him what he was to do now.

Normally his clerk was waiting attentively for his arrival. Ernst would often glimpse him as he entered the Kammergericht, bending over his boss's desk with dutiful concentration, preparing the files that were needed that day. He liked his clerk, and though they maintained the strict distance between a senior and his junior that was customary in the Germany of those times, there had been undeniable respect and even affection between them.

For the next few weeks, Ernst spent most of his time sitting in inconsolable gloom in his study at home. As my mother recounted it, he didn't agonize out loud about how he could so suddenly be expelled from his profession for a Jewish origin that he thought he had repudiated more decisively than any Aryan could on his behalf. Though he was by then well aware that Hitler was evicting Jews from all public employment, he was sure he sensed pragmatism behind the bluster. The poetry of hatred so beloved of the ranting Austrian would be replaced by the prose of economic interest; and the sacking of the Jews would be temporary. Sometimes he thought of asking Herr von Hackwitz, who deputized for him when he was on holiday, to take over his whole practice for the time being, but then he abandoned the idea as too hasty.

He would perk up after dinner when friends dropped in, as some continued to do. Rechtsanwalt Krämer now came almost every evening and offered his holiday home in Berchtesgaden, near Hitler's own house, as a retreat. Baron Schlippenbach and his fabric-obsessed wife from downstairs continued inviting Ernst and Emmy to their musical soirées. Their upstairs neighbour, an elderly Jewish woman who had inherited the apartment from Walter Benjamin's grandmother, Hedwig Schoenflies, seemed to think that Germans loved their Jews too much to support the government's racial obsessions, and was remarkably relaxed about everything. Most touching of all was Werner von Alvensleben, the father of Ursel's best friend, Lexi Alvensleben. He would come over unannounced. 'I am so sorry, Herr Liedtke,' my mother reported him as saying, as he paced around Ernst's music room, pausing to place an arm gingerly over his shoulder – not a gesture that, in those days, one German man extended lightly to another. 'I am so sorry about what you are going through. But it will get better. Be patient. It cannot go on like this.' He glanced expectantly at his friend for signs of optimism, and tried to discuss other subjects, especially their daughters: neither his headstrong daughter Lexi nor the rebellious Ursel had fitted in well at school but both were now thriving. Indeed, Ernst could be very proud, Alvensleben said, of Ursel's job at a theatre in Bremen that she'd secured so quickly after graduating from the acting academy of Ilka Grüning.

Though Alvensleben, a cultured man of deeply conservative instincts, wasn't especially interested in music, he knew what it meant to his friend and before his visits he usually took care to inform himself about the latest concerts at the Philharmonie, which Ernst could no longer afford to attend: my mother's meticulously kept booklet chronicling the concerts she had heard since she was a small girl stops precisely in April 1933.

Each time he came, my mother said, Alvensleben would leave my grandparents' home silently, thoughtfully, appalled.

6

The operation on Lenin

Ernst's visitors helped restore his faith in himself, at least as *pater-familias*. When he returned from seeing them off at the door only to be confronted by his daughters' confused despair, he would sit them down for history lessons that recalled the flourishing of German Jews in his own lifetime. Those people you used to see in the Philharmonie – Albert Einstein, Fritz Haber, Artur Schnabel, Carl Flesch – he would explain, his voice finding a new buoyancy, were celebrated in Berlin, whereas only a few decades earlier they would have been lucky to be eking out a living as a menial toiler.

Not just celebrated. Many of these Jews had Aryans working for them as devoted assistants, deputies, researchers, and students; they dispensed promotions and salary increases, their stature commanding fear and awe. Ernst drew particular hope from the case of Professor Moritz Borchardt, a pioneering neurosurgeon who was one of his oldest friends – and whose daughter Luise was my mother's school-mate and, decades later, my godmother. Moritz was descended from a family of 'poor tradesmen', he would emphasize, and rose to become head of surgery at the Moabit Hospital, a university clinic, and was made a *Geheimrat* – a privy councillor – by the Kaiser. When Moritz arrived at the hospital each morning, the doorman would telephone the wards to warn the doctors and nurses and junior surgeons – most of them non-Jews – that the boss was in the building; and they would at once rush to make sure the tables were spotless, the floors shining like mirrors, and the curtains tied back at the same height on both sides of the windows. He would say to his younger staff, 'Don't even think of marrying yet! As long as you work here you are married to your work and to your duty!' And when he left in the evening, his assistants would run out into the street in front of the hospital and stand respectfully in a line as he got into his taxi.

It was in the 1980s, half a century later, when I first heard about Borchardt's stellar career up to and, amazingly, beyond 1933, from his daughter Luise. He was, she said, a celebrity in Berlin, who had operated on Paul Loebe, the president of the Reichstag, a bevy of top German generals, and many other powerful people, including Lenin, whom the Kremlin had secretly asked Borchardt to treat after the Soviet Union's best doctors had failed to understand the mysterious brain disease that was disabling the prophet of world revolution.

My mother often talked about the operation on Lenin. She was still talking about it into the second decade of the twenty-first century, nearly one hundred years after the event. It wasn't just Borchardt's fame that thrilled her; nor was it only the heights that German Jews had been permitted to attain. It was, above all, the trust that had been placed in this Jewish surgeon. Trust: the one thing that was denied to Jews wherever they were, but in the end the only thing that mattered. Everyone suspected, my mother said, that the Kremlin was lying when they claimed that Moritz had gone to Moscow in 1922 in order to remove a bullet that had lodged in Lenin's neck during an assassination attempt four years earlier. But within its walls the Kremlin had confronted the truth about Lenin's illness. And the truth had taken them to Borchardt. Russia and Germany – two of the world's greatest powers and two of the world's most anti-Semitic nations – had both needed and welcomed and celebrated Moritz Borchardt.

Ernst was sure that his own career, like Borchardt's, had been made possible by the bumpy, sometimes retracted, but ultimately hugely progressive steps that had transformed Jewish fortunes since 1812, when Kaiser Friedrich Wilhelm III had reluctantly approved an edict granting the Jews of Prussia full citizenship. Despite the suspension of that edict not long afterwards, the reality, as he saw it, was that Jews had mostly begun the nineteenth century as paupers and outcasts and ended it as well-educated and prosperous. In 1871 his hero, Bismarck, had sponsored an emancipation law that abolished all restrictions on political and civil rights; and in 1875, the same year in which he was born, mixed civil marriages between Jews and Christians were legal throughout Germany for the first time. Jews became prominent power brokers in the regime, adopted Germanic names, increasingly married into high bourgeois non-Jewish families, and excelled in almost all areas of cultural and intellectual life.

Of course, there was still much anti-Semitism in practice, especially after the stock market crashes of 1873 and 1929, for which Jewish deviousness and greed were naturally blamed. Yet for all the lingering problems, vast progress had been made since 1743, when the great Enlightenment philosopher Moses Mendelssohn, trailblazing a path out of the ghetto and later known as 'the German Socrates', reputedly found that he could enter Berlin only through the gate reserved for cattle, swine, and Jews.

Surely, Ernst told his anxious family, such advances in the position of Jews were an irreversible historical achievement with deep roots in the egalitarian ideals of the eighteenth-century Enlightenment – roots that couldn't be destroyed by government decree and motley bunches of stormtroopers. Millions of Germans had so profited from the Jews' enthusiastic contribution to the nation's life that he was confident they wouldn't support a policy and a government that deprived the country of legions of skilled doctors, scientists, weapons designers, engineers, architects, and lawyers. Though Hitler had blamed the Jews for Germany's humiliation in the First World War, the reality was that many of them had celebrated German war aims as ardently as the most jingoistic non-Jews.

But, for all his love of Germany and German culture, Ernst despised that jingoism. He cringed, my mother said, at those highly cultured Jews who paraded their zeal for war as if it were a natural extension of their infatuation with *Kultur* and *Bildung*, rather than its antithesis. He loathed the popular songs written by Ernst Lissauer, a Jewish poet, such as 'Song of Hate Against England' ('*Hassgesang gegen England*'). And he would certainly have recoiled from Arnold Schoenberg's xenophobic roar when the great Jewish composer compared the German army's attack on what he saw as decadent France with his own will to overturn an ossified musical tradition, represented by the music of Bizet and Ravel:

'Now comes the reckoning! Now we will throw these mediocre kitsch-mongers into slavery, and teach them to venerate the German spirit and to worship the German God!'[5]

7

The hopeful case of Moritz Borchardt

To his family's astonishment, Ernst's conviction that the Jews' contributions to Germany's national life would force the Nazis to rethink their anti-Semitic madness appeared to be spot on – and much sooner than he had thought. He was out of work for only a few weeks before his clerk notified him that he would be welcome to return to the court. He knew that this *volte-face* was hardly due to an ideological change of heart by the authorities. Nor was it likely to have been prompted by a generous interpretation of the rule exempting Jewish First World War veterans from the expulsion order: he had heard that plenty of them were being thrown out of their jobs, while younger Jews whose specialist knowledge was needed were being called back. It was, he felt, simply that Berlin's courts must be grinding to a halt after losing so many of their best lawyers. Clients, including high Nazis, would be bereft of advocacy, and clamouring for the return of their attorneys. Divorcing couples petitioning his court would be unable to rid themselves of each other. Libelled Aryans wouldn't be able to sue their persecutors. Deals would be left unconsummated. All of which was likely, given that almost 50 per cent of the lawyers in the city were of Jewish origin.

Ernst was reassured by how many of his friends were also returning to their old posts. One was Professor Artur Nussbaum, a distinguished figure at Berlin University's law faculty, who had been allowed into the classroom again to help his students prepare for their summer exams, and in whose apartment a few minutes' walk from Blumeshof my mother had had many sleepovers with her close childhood friend, Nussbaum's daughter, Marianne. And there was the remarkable Dr Richard Calé, a wiry, intense, fast-talking poly-math, whose eldest daughter, Susanna, tutored my mother in ancient Greek. Calé was not only a great lawyer but a fine amateur violinist and composer, who hosted chamber music evenings attended by outstanding musicians of the day. After a brief period in which some of his non-Jewish clients had felt obliged to boycott his private practice, he was busier than ever.

It was the same story in the medical profession. Expectant mothers were demanding the attention of the senior Herr Doktor, whatever his race. Aryan babies were not refusing to be born because Hitler had issued edicts against Jewish gynaecologists, such as another family friend, Dr Alfred Loeser.

But, for Ernst, the most encouraging case of all was, again, Moritz Borchardt. Unlike most Jews, he hadn't been fired and then hastily reinstated; he had retired in the normal way, on his sixty-fifth birthday, only twenty-four days before Hitler became chancellor, and despite the anti-Semitic frenzy in the air he had been given a sumptuous send-off by his largely non-Jewish staff. He was expecting to enjoy some rest and devote himself to his literary interests after decades of gruelling work, but soon after the Nazis got into power he was called out of retirement and offered a position at an exclu-sive private clinic. Lavish resources were made available, including Aryans to work under his absolute command, just as in the good old days. Far from destroying his career, Hitler seemed to have resurrected it.

Nor did anything immediately change for the Borchardts on the home front. They continued hosting dinners at their apartment in Dörnbergstrasse, attended by the highest figures in German society and their five brilliant and Teutonically-named children: Dietrich, Gustav, Eva, Luise, and Albrecht. Everything about their life continued in its rigorous, settled way.

Over lunch at his golf club in Buenos Aires in 2006, Albrecht Borchardt, who had emigrated there with his parents shortly before the outbreak of war, told me how his father had worked undisturbed in Berlin until and beyond the horrors of Kristallnacht, the night in November 1938 when Jewish businesses, schools, homes, and synagogues all over Germany were wrecked and many Jews beaten to death. Professionally, he was unaffected, Albrecht said; he operated right up to the spring of 1939.

'Could he continue working at the private clinic?' I asked.

Albrecht said that, yes, he could, until the authorities closed it down in 1936 – adding nonchalantly that he then moved into the clinic of Professor August Bier, where he practised medicine as normal, even operating on senior Nazis.

There was no way that the authorities could have failed to know this. Bier, a non-Jew, had been president of the German Surgical Society and nobody would be able to work with him secretly.

It was all so matter-of-fact in Albrecht Borchardt's retelling of his father's story. Everywhere he went after 1933, the necessary facilities and assistants were provided, up to his own demanding standards. The idea that the greatest catastrophe in Jewish history might have been gathering pace outside Moritz's operating theatre remained imperceptible in his son's telling of the story seven decades later.

Like my parents, Albrecht appeared never to have left Germany. Though he had emigrated at sixteen and married a Brazilian Catholic with whom he had Spanish-speaking children, he seemed to have remained a German who couldn't accept that he now belonged elsewhere.

Immediately after the war, he had been the representative in Buenos Aires of a German company, which gave him the opportunity for regular trips to its headquarters. The company would put him up in one of the best local hotels, where he was given his favourite room in a part of the building that had survived the Allied bombing, with a view over mangled girders and pulverized stonework. He had been exhilarated, he told me, to contribute to the miraculous rebuilding of German industry after the war. Which other country could have managed this? What a privilege it had been to witness such creativity, to assist at the rebirth of this great nation.

Had Hitler, I asked, changed his views of Germany? Had the abrupt dismissal and emigration of his father in 1939, Moritz's despair in exile, the depression and silence into which he had sunk in Argentina, and then the violent stroke that left him almost completely paralyzed for the last seven years of his life compromised the son's love for Germany? No, Albrecht said, not at all. Why should it change? Hitler boasted about embodying the German people, but he didn't. No, thank goodness, he didn't. Anti-Semitism was the province of the common man who had never met a Jew; but it had never been in the DNA of the people at large.

As we surveyed the vast golf course in the gentle late-spring wind and chatted away about the wonders of the Teutonic mind, what a home it had provided for the Jews, and how great and warm-hearted the majority of German people were, I realized again how completely I identified with Albrecht's feelings for Germany – and with how love, if it is sufficiently great, can persist even if the loved one tries to destroy your life. And yet I was struck by how his love for Germany seemed to have immunized him against any doubts about the country, doubts from which few non-Jewish Germans would be free; how, despite it all, not least his father's terrible last years in Argentina and his brother Gustav's deportation to a concentration camp, his passion for his homeland had remained steadfast. Unlike my mother and her sisters, he evinced no recognizable suffering, let alone trauma.

Or perhaps the trauma was screaming at me precisely from out of his frozen loyalty; and I, locked into the same loyalty, lacked the ear to hear it.

8.

Ernst's death

For those less illustrious than Moritz Borchardt, ideology and race hatred were quickly to triumph again over the clamours of marooned clients, sick patients, and stricken businesses. The remaining scales fell from Ernst's eyes soon after he had been 'reinstated', when he was abruptly confined to office work, out of public view, and no longer permitted to appear in court. More restrictions followed, until he was forbidden all direct contact with clients. He had become an invisible reject, without rights, whose role could be further shrunk at any moment – and he felt it bitterly. Outwardly he resumed his daily routine, walking to work in his suit and starched collar, greeting colleagues in the corridors, and conferring, as if normally, with 'his' clerk. On Mondays he was particularly hopeful that they would get accustomed to him once more, and that habits of collegiate courtesy would win out over the commandment to hate; but then the sense of doom overpowered him again.

Clearly, he was there only for as long as he could be of residual use, and until Hitler rejected once and for all the pleas for pragmatism that the nation's saviour so despised. Ernst may have been in his old court, but, for his colleagues, for the authorities, and for Germany, he was already dead. They were palpably uninterested in his patriotism, his Protestantism, his professionalism, his love of *Parsifal* – or his First World War medal. His conviction that he would

soon be unable to provide for his family wore him down. The horror
that the Jewishness he thought he had assimilated out of existence
had become a catastrophic liability to his young wife and daughters
now haunted him day and night. The reality that his brilliant career,
in which he had smoothly risen from humble provinciality to a
position of responsibility in the capital of the Weimar Republic, had
been shattered overnight, and that he was now discardable, reusable,
and again discardable, all at whim, overwhelmed his modest but
proud personality. Over the next few months he became increasingly
depressed, brooding on the destruction of his life by his still-beloved
Germany. On returning from his customary walk before lunch with
Emmy on 17 December 1933, he collapsed and died of a heart
attack in his wife's arms, outside his own front door.

'*Sei froh!*' – 'Be glad!' – my mother said to Emmy that evening. 'It
was for the best. He couldn't have coped with this. His death is a
blessing.' Ernst had been laid out on his bed, where Ilse repeatedly
photographed the corpse.

Sei froh? My mother didn't just say it that evening; she never
stopped saying it, even forty, seventy, eighty years later. Ilse said the
same thing. Only Ursel couldn't be drawn on the death. Though my
father's death gripped her, she never spoke to me about *her* father's
death. Had it never taken root in her? Or had it taken root so firmly
that she couldn't commemorate, let alone imitate it?

As I heard this story over and over again from the other two
sisters, I was besieged by questions. Did Ernst die so quickly and
was the shock so calamitous because he had severed himself from
his moorings in the ancient faith of his ancestors? Had this closing
down of a whole area of innate sensibility and cultural memory
fatally weakened him? Wasn't that certificate, stamped by Department
9 of the Royal Prussian District Court, in which he had repudiated
five thousand years of belonging, also a suicide note – part of a
dying that had already been going on for many years and was not
yet complete? And how weary did all that fighting against himself
make him?

Or is all this fidelity to roots dangerous nonsense? Isn't identity fluid, revisable, multiple, and determined at least as much by our own experiences and choices as by our inheritance of a past? Haven't cultural traditions adapted, merged, been lost, found new sources of life, 'assimilated', ever since human beings first lived in communities? Rather than finding himself enfeebled by his abandonment of Judaism, wasn't Ernst's catastrophe that his most treasured end – to be at one with, and to contribute to the best in, German culture – had been debarred to him almost overnight? That the door to the only world that made sense to him had been slammed shut? That, for this beloved world, which gave meaning to everything he did in his life, he no longer existed?

And even if we cannot flourish without fidelity to our roots, surely we can't live out *everything* we are? Some parts of our mosaic of identity speak to us with such familiarity and intensity that all our other roots seem insipid by comparison. I know people with one Jewish grandparent – there are some, like Ruth in the Bible, with none – who claim this heritage as their chief identity and become Orthodox Jews and feel they have finally found a home to which they are unequivocally called. And I know others with the same heritage who, to this day, loathe and repudiate it and crave nothing more than its final extinction, so that they and their numberless descendants need never more be burdened with its curse.

But what happens when you don't just loathe and repudiate this root or that, but go for your oldest – and try to *kill* it? When you try to wipe a major part of the slate of your own heritage clean and start again? Isn't there something here of the spirit of those social experimenters who thought that human beings could be made *tabula rasa* and then re-constituted, free of the despised past? Don't we know from those experiments that, even given titanic will, nature and history refuse to go quietly?

Ernst has bequeathed to us, his descendants, the task of facing these enigmas. And, even when I think I have faced them, I know that I am still fumbling.

PART II

Three Sisters, Three Destinies
1933–1945

9

Next stop: Catholicism

From 17 December 1933, in the early afternoon, my mother, it seems, was neither happy nor unhappy. A sense of suspended animation, of swathes of life being on permanent hold, emigrated with her to London, and became my inheritance to grapple and live with.

Were there family dinners, or weekends on the boat moored on the shore of the Wannsee that Ernst had bought just a couple of years earlier? Did she see loyal friends and colleagues – Alvensleben, Krämer, Hackwitz? Did she eventually go to concerts again? How long did her mother continue living at Blumeshof 12?

No memories.

Did she attend her father's funeral? Where was he buried? And who came, apart from 'everybody'?

No memories.

About politics and Hitler and speeches and rallies and signs against Jews she also can't recall anything, though until 1938 she was regularly in Berlin. Family members whose Jewishness was not a matter of debate or concealment – her father's mother and his brother Theo – now vanish from consciousness. Though the three sisters had dropped in on their grandmother almost every Saturday afternoon for years, none of them can remember when she died or whether she was deported. They can't even remember her name, though she was the relative they saw most often. They do know the

name of their other grandmother, Emmy's mother, the supposedly
Aryan grandmother whom they seldom met because she so despised
Ernst. She was called Adele. They can remember the names of family
friends, even distant ones, but not of Ernst's mother, their favourite
grandparent. How were she and Theo, her younger son, faring at
this time? Not a clue. Did they ever see them after December 1933?
It seems not, except for one accidental encounter between Ilse and
Theo on a street corner, but that was years later, near the end of
1941. Theo lived in Berlin until he was deported to Sachsenhausen
concentration camp in 1942, the date at which he comes alive again
in the three sisters' memories.

What do they vividly remember of the years from 1934 up to
the beginning of the war? They remember their dramatic conversions
– the most wonderful moment of their lives, they told me, at least
until they had children. All three became fervent Catholics after
Hitler came to power, my mother first, in 1934, then Ilse, and finally
Ursel. They remember their studies and then their nascent careers:
Ilse the photographer, Ursel the actor, Marianne the violinist. And
they remember where they lived: Ilse stayed in Berlin, where she
opened an atelier on the Budapesterstrasse, which flourished beyond
the beginning of the war, counting many Nazis among its clients.
Marianne, my mother, moved to London in 1934, following her
violin teacher Max Rostal, another former student of Carl Flesch,
with whom she had started lessons after Josef Wolfsthal suddenly
died, aged thirty-one. Rostal had been dismissed from his job at
Berlin's Hochschule für Musik in April the previous year, and had
then made a living teaching at the home of one of his students,
Marianne Imberg, a close friend of my mother; but when the Imbergs
left for New York and his other Jewish students trickled out of the
country, he had finally been forced by penury to emigrate.

Meanwhile Ursel already had her job at the theatre in Bremen,
performing mainly classical roles, though that came to a sudden end
in the summer of 1934 after the Reichstheaterkammer – the 'Reich
Theatre Chamber', a professional organization under the ultimate
direction of Propaganda Minister Joseph Goebbels, to which all
actors had to belong in order to be permitted to work – demanded
proof of Aryan parentage, which at that time she had no idea how

to secure or invent. After repeatedly warning Ursel that she wasn't providing the necessary paperwork, or even paying her dues – which she was withholding to give the impression that the missing paperwork was the result of slovenliness rather than ethnic evasion – she was finally expelled in 1936, which meant she was banned from acting.

And so, returning to Berlin, she looked for casual work in dance halls and cabarets that Goebbels hadn't yet brought under his control or closed down – a world of satire perfectly suited to her talent for mimicry and to her spellbindingly labile body; a world that, my mother used to say, with a knowing chuckle, was far more to Ursel's taste than the worthy German classics that she had been obliged to perform in Bremen.

Here in the demi-monde, she forged what was to be a lifelong friendship with Isa Vermehren, a singer, accordion player, actor, and daughter of a Protestant family from Lübeck, who became a Catholic in 1938 and who would turn out to be key to Ursel's own conversion. Isa's switch to Catholicism was more dramatic, for it would take her all the way to the nunnery. Catalyzed by her, Ursel became a Catholic between Kristallnacht and the outbreak of war, the last of the Liedtke sisters to make that momentous decision.

The sisters' conversion to Catholicism, about which they were passionate, must have been a huge step to terra firma. So many, at least in Berlin and elsewhere in Protestant north Germany, had used Protestantism as a stepping stone in the journey from Judaism that it had probably lost its magic as a mask. As an emblem of assimilation it was hackneyed; and in its Lutheran shape it was surely too local, too German (precisely what had made it attractive until the rise of Hitler), to afford a sense of protection from the fires of blood-and-soil nationalism. Whereas, even in its German hue, Catholicism was a universal rather than a merely national church. In the Vatican it had a ruling power base outside Germany that was willing – at least in principle and up to the extent that the Church's own interests were safeguarded – to protect its flock, no matter what their ethnic heritage or where they lived.

No less important for the three sisters, I think, Catholicism had sensuality and drama, especially in the cult of the Virgin Mary and the vivid lives of the saints – a drama that numbed pain and, for all its focus on suffering and death, was somehow life-giving. Or so I experienced it in my youth. Seeing them in church, I was gripped and disturbed and moved – all at once – by their agonized yet ecstatic, tormented yet swooning, expressions in prayer. They often seemed on the point of breaking into weeping, and sometimes did break into weeping, not only for the tragedy of Christ's own suffering – which, from everything they said, they felt with shattering intensity – but also for the vast redemptive hope that it promised. When I dared to ask my mother about this, she appeared possessed by a power of imaginative insight into Christ's condemnation and crucifixion that few priests, with their routine sermons, could match. And, thrillingly but fleetingly, a shaft of light was cast into her mysterious inner world, and its alchemy of identities, which I had been ordered to inherit.

Back in the 1930s, how could spartan, self-reliant German Lutheranism possibly compete with this new religious haven? In those violent times, in which a family and its world were being destroyed, this mix of the sanctuary offered by a cosmopolitan Church and a rococo sensibility of dramatic intoxication and redemption through suffering was overwhelmingly seductive, promising to liberate someone with both German and Jewish heritages from the ever-increasing difficulty of belonging to either.

And yet.

Catholicism clearly offered no guarantee of ethnic concealment, least of all in Hitler's Germany. More drastic measures were needed; and, as I see it, these had to bore further and further into one's own soul rather than merely hide one's origins from hostile outsiders. What had to be changed was not just how other people saw you but also – perhaps above all – how you saw yourself. Who you felt yourself to be. And even, to some extent, who you actually were.

By the 1930s, the path to Christianity had been well-trodden by German-speaking Jews for well over a century. Hitler was in no way its instigator; nor were my family its pioneers. The composer Felix Mendelssohn, grandson of Moses Mendelssohn, was baptized in 1816. Karl Marx was baptized in 1824, following his own father's conversion. Since the early nineteenth century, many other Jews had become Christian, including the poet Heinrich Heine, the writer and creator of an illustrious Berlin literary salon Rahel Varnhagen, and the composers Gustav Mahler and Arnold Schoenberg.

I knew several other German-Jewish families who had converted from Protestantism to Catholicism in the 1930s, but none of them seemed to have attempted, let alone succeeded, to extirpate an entire heritage so that it no longer figured, except perhaps sporadically, in their self-identity.

The remarkable and puzzling thing was this: with the aid of their Catholicism, the three sisters had so transformed their inner world to purge it of Jewish life and cultural memory that, even decades after the war was over and the Nazis and their race laws were discarded, their belonging in any way to the Jewish people seemed to them unreal and absurd – a sense that they conveyed to lifelong friends, colleagues, and in-laws, many, perhaps most, of whom had no idea that the Liedtke sisters had Jewish ancestry.

This was a sense of unbelonging that I, in turn, inherited and that took me decades to begin to throw off. No matter how clear the facts, or how vividly I tried to imagine the reality of my Jewish origins, they seemed stubbornly incredible.

How a Jewish identity gradually came to feel plausible to me, then legitimate, later still vital, and finally thrilling, I still do not know.

10.

'Life is continually shedding something that wants to die'

After their father died, Ilse, Ursel, and Marianne, aged twenty-three, twenty-one, and nineteen, found themselves thrust into a disintegrating world from which each would be excluded in her own way. From now on, I think, this inner ethnic purging could no longer be a collective enterprise, but became a matter of what suited each of them best. Life, as Nietzsche once said, is continually shedding something that wants to die. And that, it always seemed to me, is what they took themselves to be doing: shedding, ever more decisively, something that they were sure wanted to die.

It was a dying that I inherited whole. But in my life it took the form of a mandate to die, rather than something I myself willed. For me, the purging of Jewish heritage and consciousness was not a liberation; it was an evisceration – a great emptying of my inner world, an emptying that, for many years, I did not feel at liberty to reverse wholesale and without inhibition; for to open the doors to Jewish life would be savagely to betray my mother and all the suffering it had caused her. And even after I began to defy the mandate by letting that life seep tentatively back in – from my early teens through close friendships with Jewish classmates; in my early twenties by going secretly to synagogue services – I still found it preposterous to think of myself as a Jew. Merely to entertain the thought was to be enveloped at once in a cloud of guilt and impossibility. Even worse, it was to feel an impostor – as if a fake Jew was the only kind I could ever genuinely be.

Of the three sisters' stories, Ilse's remains the most extraordinary because her means of concealment from the outside world were the most economical. She lived in Berlin through the twelve years of the Third Reich with a confidence in her safety founded not in reckless bravado but in utter self-assurance. She told me many times, without betraying any wonder that this was possible, that throughout the whole Nazi period she had never felt frightened. Not after her father had been evicted from work, nor after he had collapsed and died at his front door. Not after Kristallnacht. Not after her uncle Theo was deported and murdered. Not after people started disappearing in their thousands. Not after the Allied bombing began in earnest. Fear, she said, only set in with the arrival of occupying Soviet soldiers in Berlin following Germany's capitulation in May 1945.

A year or so after Ernst's death, Ilse became engaged to Harald Böhmelt, an up-and-coming conductor, composer, and Nazi Party member who had joined Hitler's party as early as 1932. He was a colourful and successful composer of film music, who would become best known for writing soundtracks for hit movies like *Kleiner Mann – was nun?* (*Little Man, What Now?*), as well as for Nazi propaganda reels.

The engagement had been difficult while Ernst was alive; according to my mother, my grandfather disapproved of his prospective son-in-law, whom he found uncultured and uneducated. But, protected by Böhmelt and probably by friends of his who were higher up the Nazi hierarchy, Ilse thrived throughout the 1930s and into the war. She lived openly and freely, and was often to be seen dancing away the evening at Babelsberg, the Hollywood of Nazi Germany, with Böhmelt and a ballroomful of Goebbels's favourites.

At the same time, together with her close friend Christabel Bielenberg, who was married to a dissident German lawyer called

Peter Bielenberg, she helped run a secret network in Berlin that hid
Jews throughout the war. Did this courageous work enable her to
feel that she herself did not belong to the people whom she was
hiding? In concealing these Jews was she also hiding the Jew in her?
Not just from others, but from herself?

Ursel, for her part, was closing in on the aristocratic world into
which she would eventually marry. After five years in the wilderness,
without the necessary permission to work, she managed within less
than twenty-four months to gain official acceptance as an Aryan in
late 1941, to rejoin the theatre at Bremen in September 1943, and,
in the same month, to become a high-ranking countess, a '*Reichsgräfin*'.
An astonishing triple feat.

Meanwhile, Marianne was in north London, immersed in the
parallel world of German-Austrian refugees, where she saw herself
as a lone 'non-Jew' in an otherwise entirely Jewish universe. She
had emigrated to England, aged twenty, only because her Jewish
teacher of violin, Max Rostal, had gone there. Otherwise, according
to the dominant version of events promulgated by the three sisters,
she would have had no reason to leave Germany.

All this subterfuge had been directed at the Jewishness of Ernst,
whom the Nazi state had already outed and dispatched. But what
about Emmy, their mother? After all, her maternal grandmother,
Bertha Hecht, had definitely been Jewish, and so, probably, had her
grandmother on her father's side. Of the grandfathers, both of whom
had died young, 'too little was known'.

For some reason, my grandmother Emmy divulged this information
only to my mother, sometimes as fact and at other times as rumour.
Or, perhaps, of the three sisters only my mother could bear to
remember it. In any event, it was a dead letter for Emmy. Though
she despised anti-Semitism and evinced no trace of it, she took herself
to be an Aryan – and was accepted as one. So when, in 1939, a Jewish
textile business called J. Eichenberg AG in which she and Ernst had
invested back in 1924 was 'Aryanized' – compelled by law to be sold
to non-Jews – she was the only shareholder in the roster of the soon-
to-be-dispossessed by which the racial affiliation '*arisch*' appears.[6]

What prompted those unpredictable moments when my mother's labyrinth of vagueness about Emmy's maternal grandmother would give way to decisive clarity? She was then so quick to recall not just the full name of this woman but her place and approximate year of birth that, when, already in my thirties, I finally forced her to search for this ancestor who seemed to hold the keys to our Jewish identity, she needed just a fortnight to track down the necessary proof.

It came in the form of a handwritten document, dated 8 June 1841, from the city archives of Braunschweig, near Hannover, proving Bertha Hecht's membership in its Jewish community. All it took to confirm her identity, and so Emmy's Jewish identity, was a call to the city hall and payment of a small fee. In return, the archivist dispatched a photocopy of the original document – and in the process restituted my fourth Jewish grandparent.

But that is all it would have taken for a Nazi official to unearth the document and blow Emmy's cover. Just a phone call. She was lucky that nobody made that call or checked on her other grandmother, who bore the name Zander, also typically Jewish. But the trick here wasn't the accident of official documents with fishy names remaining undiscovered. Nor was it to get false papers, or hide in cellars, or sleep with the enemy, or not divulge your identity to outsiders – or even to your own children. Many others did all that, only some of whom survived. Again, the harder trick was deceiving yourself so deeply that not even you remembered – or could believe – who you were. Ernst might have had a stab at this; but in truth he had barely begun. His wife had done better, and by the late 1930s their three daughters were well on their own way.

11

Great-uncle Helmut: priest, philosopher, boxer

The origin of this self-ethnic purging within our family was decades before anyone had heard of Adolf Hitler; and it was far advanced before he took power. Emmy's mother, Adele, reviled Jews, rigorously denied that her own mother was Jewish, and would never forgive Emmy for marrying a Jew. Or so my mother lamented, adding that Adele refused to address Ernst, her son-in-law, except with the formal '*Sie*', and openly disdained him. To which he was resigned, without bitterness.

In fact, the only public honesty about Emmy's Jewish roots came from a most unlikely source: *Der Stürmer*, a violently anti-Semitic newspaper that announced itself as a weekly 'dedicated to fighting for the truth' and, among other propaganda, ran semi-pornographic caricatures of Jews and accusations of blood libel. The occasion was an article about Emmy's brother, Helmut Fahsel: philosopher, amateur boxer, model railway enthusiast, lover of fast cars, devotee of St Thomas Aquinas – and Catholic priest.

Helmut, my great-uncle, was a celebrity cleric. His great gift was oratory: he could take complicated themes, such as divine omnipotence and the problem of evil, and explain them in speeches that attracted crowds of hundreds. As late as 1977 he was still spoken of as 'Germany's most famous Catholic orator' of the period between the late 1920s and the early 1930s.[7] He also loathed the Nazis and was courageous enough to speak out against them in such prestigious venues as Berlin's Philharmonie; so it was hardly surprising that he came to their attention.

It was screamingly obvious, *Der Stürmer* reported in August 1931, under the banner headline '*Judenkaplan Fahsel*' ('Jew-Chaplain Fahsel'), that he was an agent of subversive Jewish forces who were cunning enough to deploy one of their own in the guise of a Christian:

> When we saw him with our own eyes, this priest, Fahsel, when we listened to his oily guttural sound, his countenance, and his way of talking with his hands, it became immediately clear: Fahsel has Jewish blood. His father was a Jew who had been baptized a Protestant. After his death, young Fahsel came into the home of his rich Jewish uncle. Ten years ago he was baptized a Catholic. And today he, the baptized Jew, is the famous chaplain of the secret Jewish string-pullers. Fahsel's task is to sow confusion and discord among non-Jews and to preach forgiveness of the Jews. Reconciliation with the descendants of Christ's murderers. If the Jew would preach these sorts of things as a rabbi, he would have no success. He therefore sends the Jew in the form of a priest. The really dumb ones fall for it. The bright ones know. They tell their neighbour: beware, look around you, the fox is among you![8]

Der Stürmer's staff had mixed up only a few of their facts. Helmut's father, Georg Johannes Wilhelm Fahsel, who was the editor of the *Norddeutsche Zeitung* in Hamburg before his death in 1898 aged thirty-six, had been born a Protestant. But his mother, Maria Friederike Zander, had probably been born a Jew and then been baptized as an adult, sometime in the mid-nineteenth century.

It was also true that after their father's early death Helmut and Emmy were adopted by their 'rich Jewish uncle', Arthur Rosenthal, who was married to their mother's sister, Emma. Their mother, left destitute as a widow, had given her two children to the Rosenthals, who brought them up in a mansion with staff, works of art, embroidered tapestries, chinaware on display in large mahogany and glass cabinets, and other trappings of bourgeois life.

Rosenthal and his wife were childless and doted on their two adopted children. He added his name to theirs – my grandmother became Emmy Fahsel-Rosenthal – and as they grew into young adults he was generous in financing their education and developing ambitions. He found Emmy the best singing and piano teachers, and sent her to one of Montreux's elegant 'finishing schools' when she was sixteen. He bought the scholarly Helmut every book he wished for, in the finest editions, supported his studies in the classics, and when the young man resolved to learn Catholic theology he co-financed those studies, too, with a close friend, to whom he introduced Emmy after she returned from Montreux and whom he hoped she would eventually marry: Ernst Liedtke.

That Helmut's path to the priesthood had been supported by two Jews was unlikely to have escaped the attention of *Der Stürmer*.

It wasn't just the Nazis who suspected Jewish contamination in Helmut. So did many of his fellow Catholics. Fahsel's biographer and one-time landlady, Henriette von Gizycki, born Salomonski, herself a Jew who had converted to Catholicism – and who would perish in the Holocaust – laments that these co-religionists also saw his Jewish origins as a 'blemish'.

Nor can it have helped Fahsel that one of the encounters that shaped his religious life and pushed him towards Catholicism was with Rabbi Leo Baeck, an illustrious scholar and the leader of progressive Judaism in Germany. Or that he publicly attacked anti-Semites who repudiated the Old Testament and denied that Jesus was a Jew. Gizycki reports a meeting in the Philharmonie in about 1928, where Helmut confronted the Nazi author Arthur Dinter, whose bestselling novel, *The Sin Against the Blood*, declared that an Aryan woman who had once had sex with a Jewish man would inevitably have polluted offspring, even if they were fathered by an Aryan:

The excitement in the hall was so great that Fahsel couldn't be heard at all. With a great command 'Quiet!' he achieved complete silence. As a Catholic priest he defended the importance of the Old Testament. As a result he lost the sympathy of all those in his audience of a völkisch, anti-Semitic disposition.[9]

What *really* baffled Fahsel's biographer was how such rumours about his Jewishness could possibly have been spread when they were evidently groundless. To 'honour the truth', she quotes the following sentence from Fahsel's own notebooks:

> A journalist later mentioned the rich Jewish uncle and gave vent to the erroneous and absurd opinion that I had Jewish parents who had been baptized. Anti-Semites should calm down [about that], but they should also know that I have experienced from Jews acts of the highest kind-heartedness and loyalty, free of any falsehood and arrogance.[10]

Me, a Jew? Fahsel's sangfroid, just like Emmy's and Ilse's, is masterly. Crucially, he believed his own story. Like Ilse's courage in hiding Jews, Helmut's generous feelings for them, his recognition of their virtues, his affirmation of the Old Testament, and his denial that they exhibited the vices of anti-Semitic stereotype – falsehood and arrogance[11] – were extended from his impregnable conviction that he was not one of them – and that any idea to the contrary was absurd.

But Fahsel had another side to him that drew some of the sting of Nazi disdain. At the same time as he was lurching towards Catholicism, he was developing a passionate devotion to the ancient Germanic and Greek heroes, such as Siegfried and Theseus. He revered what he saw as their uncompromising masculinity and their courage, loyalty, selflessness, and solitude – and despised people who succumbed to the spell of sensuous charms or to the idyll of a comfortable life.[12]

This talk was in the air. In *Mein Kampf*, Hitler portrays himself as just such a character – the lone individual brimming with bravery, loyalty, and honesty who forgoes the security of family life, guided by a higher force that has sent him to serve and save.

But Fahsel didn't just talk; he also imposed a rigorous physical exercise regime on himself, learned jiu-jitsu,[13] practised athletics, joined the Anglo-American Boxing Club in Berlin,[14] attended boxing matches at the Tiergartenhof Hall,[15] and even engaged a boxing coach called Joe Edwards.[16] He would spend long afternoons in the city's museums admiring the male physiques depicted by classical Greek sculptures, which, as he confided in his diary, awoke in him 'the youthful sense for a new rhythm and mood, for a new independence and democratic freedom'.[17] And his day would often end at parties organized by the Association for Strength and Beauty.[18]

While still at school he became, in good Greek fashion, the protégé of a cultured aristocrat who admired Helmut's body as well as his ideals of physical and moral perfection. The older man would pick him up from school and greet the boy with a reverent and somewhat mannered kiss on the hands, on one occasion even gifting him a statue of Narcissus. Though Helmut professed himself repulsed as well as flattered by this attention, it seems that on balance he tolerated the admiration.[19]

Artur Rosenthal had long been worried by Helmut's deepening Catholic infatuation and his mystical experiences before statues of St Thomas Aquinas, but his worship of pagan ideals of manhood deeply troubled the old man. The final straw was the claim of one of Rosenthal's domestic staff to have seen a breast expander hidden under Helmut's bed, and rumours in the house that he was flagellating himself in his bedroom between sessions practising at the punchbag that he had suspended from the ceiling.

Rosenthal decided to send the young man to Henriette von Gizycki's boarding house, where a dose of normal life among young people struggling to make ends meet might bring him down to earth. The effect was exactly the opposite. Released from the staid atmosphere of Rosenthal's home, with its grand dinners and servers and governesses, Helmut pursued his religious and bodily ideals more fervently than ever.

Gizycki records how, after arriving in September 1908 in an open limousine, accompanied by a butler who carried his belongings, the sixteen-year-old Helmut immediately shut himself in his room to exercise with weights, declaring tartly: 'I strive for perfection of the body.'[20] He rejected the books she gave him – titles such as *What A Young Man Needs to Know*[21] – and instead read either thrillers or else medieval philosophy. Either Conan Doyle or Thomas Aquinas.

Why, she asked him, did he feed his mind with such lightweight stuff as *The Adventures of Sherlock Holmes*? Not for entertainment, Helmut answered, but because a scholar's mind must achieve the brilliance and dexterity of a master detective.

Helmut was deadly serious about these ideals, which blended medieval Christianity with old Germanic-pagan virtues, and didn't take kindly to all the mockery that he encountered. The First World War was for him the great event that proved how vital they were to the development of a human being. Though he didn't fight for more than a few months – he fell ill with fever in January 1915 while stationed in northern France and was discharged from the army that autumn – the war, he was convinced, magnificently confirmed that only a life governed by severe discipline, loyalty, and endurance can be happy.

Yet none of this worship of 'Germania' and the military virtues allayed the Nazis' mistrust. Helmut's safety was becoming ever more imperilled until, sometime in early 1934, Hitler's deputy chancellor Franz von Papen, so my mother told me, personally telephoned to urge him to flee the country.

Papen considered himself a devout Catholic and admired Fahsel's religious writings. He didn't mince his words in his phone call: Fahsel should make sure he was on a particular train departing for Switzerland at dawn the next morning – a ticket would be waiting for him at a mutual friend's house. The alternative was immediate arrest. His sermons and public lectures were unacceptable, unpatriotic, Jew-friendly and, for all their ideals of noble manhood, smelled of decadence. Even Fahsel's views on sexuality displeased the authorities, with their edification of Eros as a window onto God and a path to ultimate truth, beauty, and goodness.

Fahsel took the advice and left for Switzerland on the train that Papen had specified, setting up near Locarno with a Spanish widow, her sister, and her Italian housekeeper. A few weeks later his library followed, with its vast collection of philosophy and theology books, along with his model railway set and his collection of boxing gloves. The Spanish widow had been dispatched to Berlin to rescue these prized possessions, which she packed to his demanding specifications and cleared for export – not an easy task to perform on behalf of a man on the run from the Nazi regime.

For almost two decades Helmut lived self-sufficiently in a wing of her mansion overlooking Lake Maggiore, studying, working out at the leather punchbag, playing with his model railway, and listening to his jazz recordings, of which he had hundreds. She bought him whatever books he needed, always in the finest editions; he began his six-volume translation of Thomas Aquinas from Latin into German; and well into middle age he continued to model his life on that of a young aristocrat in ancient Athens.

He was never to return to Germany, except for a brief and unsuccessful stint in the early 1950s as a parish priest in the Pfalz region. While there, he attempted to resume his public lectures in philosophy and religion, but his ideas no longer found the reception they had enjoyed before the war and he soon returned to his Swiss retreat.

When the Spanish widow died, another wealthy woman, a Madame Simon who lived in nearby Muralto, came to the rescue, and it wasn't long before Fahsel moved in with her. Though he took the Spanish widow's Italian housekeeper with him, the old order couldn't easily be recreated and Madame Simon began to realize that she wanted Fahsel for herself. The Italian housekeeper was an interloper who understood nothing about housekeeping or Fahsel's real needs. She had to go.

Fahsel refused to fire the Italian housekeeper. Madame Simon was

incensed by his cozy relationship with the employee of her prede-
cessor and threatened to cut off the generous allowance she paid
him for new books, knowing that this would hurt even more than
an end to his supply of fine food and wine. One day, as she was
driving him around the lake, past the gentle slopes with their blos-
soming hydrangeas, she stopped at the side of the road and presented
him with an ultimatum: if the Italian housekeeper didn't go, he
would have to. He was to dismiss the housekeeper before dinner
that evening or Madame Simon would dismiss her for him.

He dismissed her.

Ursel's World: The Aryan Aristocrat in Hiding

12

From the Liedtkes to the aristocrats

Ursel never felt at ease within the impeccable universe of Blumeshof 12, and I think I can understand why. Devoted though I am to this inheritance, its nervy, quasi-religious obsession with music, art, and learning; its mantra of 'only the very best'; and its conviction that it is exceptional can all be crushing. The exalted standards that it prizes, magnificent though they are in themselves, can feel like a carapace that holds reality at bay – a carapace inside which bubble unconquerable panic and perplexity.

In 1927, aged only fifteen, Ursel made a decision of astonishing independent-mindedness. She was going to leave her parents' home and insert herself into a new family – a family, as I see it, absolutely removed not only from the Jewish experience, but from anyone whose ideals, however noble, were sustained by marginalization, rootlessness, and the ever-present invisible chasm that made it impossible to take firm ground for granted.

Aryan wasn't enough. Aryans could worry about all those things. Nor did the passion for *Kultur* among the non-Jewish *Bildungsbürgertum* necessarily insulate them from feelings of being marooned in a world over which they were powerless. Many of them would later support Hitler as a solution to precisely such anxieties. Only one group appeared to have unshakable confidence in its roots, no matter what other sources of insecurity might beset it – not the fakery of brazen

confidence, but the calm sort, pervaded by an impregnable sense
of status; a group that wouldn't begin to recognize the particular
existential despair that plagued the Liedtke family: the aristocrats.

The answer came in the form of Count Werner and Countess
Alexandra von Alvensleben, their son, Werner, and their three daughters, Lexi, Annali, and 'Baby'. Ursel and Lexi had become friends
at the small private school to which Ernst had sent her on her return
from a six-month cure in Zuoz, in the Swiss Alps, for a minor lung
ailment. Back in Germany, Ursel found it difficult to reintegrate
into the public school system and her parents hoped that a private
education would be the answer. It hardly mattered: she was uninterested in academic study and had already discovered her talent
for acting; but she did find there the new, safer world for which she
longed. To my grandfather's distress and my grandmother's resentful
admiration, Ursel laid siege to the Alvenslebens' deliciously self-
assured life. She adopted their tastes in clothes, interior decoration,
furniture, and manners. Soon she adopted the girls' mother too,
even calling her 'Mami'.[22]

Mami reciprocated with strange intensity. She was captivated by
Ursel's cutting wit, her virtuosic jesting, and her way of seeking
out deeply conservative circles in which she would behave with
defiant unconventionality. Ursel, for her part, delighted not just in
Mami's protective care but also in eccentricities like her predilection
for cooking while dressed in galoshes, overcoat, and a wide-brimmed
hat. The two became inseparable, confiding their secrets to one
another until Mami's death nearly forty years later.

These Alvenslebens were a remarkable family who were unstintingly
benevolent to my own, from their solidarity with my grandfather
after his dismissal in 1933 to Lexi's many decades of friendship with
Ursel and kindness to Ilse. Lexi's father Werner had been one of
the very few to visit Ernst in the dreadful days after Hitler's acces-
sion to power when many others were afraid to be associated with
him. Lexi had not only been Ursel's closest friend since their school-
days but coincidentally ended up living almost next door to Ilse's
photographic atelier in the Budapesterstrasse from the summer of

1944, after moving from Bremen to Berlin in order to be near her now-imprisoned husband. And she stubbornly went on living there, Ilse said, even after bombs had destroyed a great part of her building and there was almost a clean line of vision from her apartment directly into the cellar. She was loyal, poised, intelligent, unpretentious, cultured, offbeat, and tremendously courageous.

Lexi's family really did offer Ursel an escape from that disturbingly serious world of the Liedtkes, a world shot through with the gravity that, as I see it, Ernst embodied in its most concentrated form. A German Jew like him didn't just bear the name of two peoples; he bore the burden of these two richly burdened peoples, and the redemptive dreams of both. Into him flowed two spiritual inheritances that each placed supreme value on a deep and rigorous and grounded and virtuous cultivation of the mind in the service of the true and the good – the Germans with their devotion to *Bildung* and the Jews with their fervour for study and learning and the moral law. When the vehemently held ideals of those inheritances came together, one could inadvertently surrender the joy, indeed the lightness, peculiar to each.

As a result, some German Jews – among them my own family – took their seriousness about life to extremes that were life-destroying. Every word, every act, every decision, and every non-decision could be loaded with such crushing meaning that existence itself became intractable. Life was not allowed to dance, but had to be filled with cultural hope so vast that it could swallow up the terror of ordinary reality. Exhaustion was inevitable.

If you craved escape from all this, there were at least three durable ways. Discover a world that wasn't Jewish or German in the contemporary bourgeois sense of the *Bildungsbürgertum*: the world of the Alvenslebens. Send up seriousness with satire: the world of cabaret. Or find a religion that will promise release from life's suffering in one redeeming leap: the world of the Catholic convert.

Ursel wasn't one for doing things by halves. She went, with total dedication, for all three.

13.

Ursel becomes an Aryan

In the end, Ursel wanted more than the aristocratic bolthole that the Alvenslebens could provide, the absurdist milieu that cabaret offered, or the religious solution that Catholicism had to hand. All that was behind her when, in 1941, as even half-Jews felt under ever greater threat from the Nazi state, she took the attempt to escape Jewish origins, to bail out of her own heritage, one huge step further: she had herself officially accepted as Aryan.

She set about this task by dreaming up a story that, contrary to what she had understood until then, she was not the daughter of Ernst Liedtke. Rather, her allegedly non-Jewish mother had conceived her in an adulterous fling with a similarly uncontaminated man, who was now conveniently dead and so unavailable to deny his moment of madness. As my mother recounted it, she demanded that Emmy sign a sworn statement confessing to this infidelity and identifying the mysterious lover as a certain Kostas, a Greek violinist who, on moving to Berlin, had been financed and sheltered by none other than Ernst. The unfortunate Kostas was therefore posthumously deemed to have repaid his sponsor's generosity by producing a love child with his young wife.

In fact, Kostas's only intimacy with Emmy was to play violin sonatas with her at the piano, and his main contribution to the family was to encourage my mother's passion for the violin. He promised,

1. My maternal grandparents and their three daughters on holiday in the Swiss Alps in the mid-1920s. L. to r.: Ilse, Emmy, Marianne, Ursel, and Ernst Liedtke.

2. A room in my grandparents' Berlin apartment at Blumeshof 12.

Bescheinigung.

3. Ernst's certificate of his exit from
Judaism in 1910.

Tauf-Schein.

4. Ernst's certificate of baptism,
from the same year.

5. Ernst and his brother Theo sailing from Bremen to New York on board
the *Kaiser Wilhelm II* in1909.

6. L. to r.: Marianne, Ursel, Ilse. Berlin, 1917.

7. Ernst and Emmy on the North Sea island of Helgoland in 1926.

8. The Liedtkes' boat on the Wannsee. Ernst in the peaked cap, Emmy next to him and Ilse to the left of the gangplank.

9. The final page of Marianne's concert and theatre notebook, which begins in 1924, when she was ten, and ends abruptly in April 1933, after Ernst's dismissal, with performances by Wilhelm Furtwängler and the quartet of her violin teacher, Max Rostal.

10. Ilse.

11. Ursel.

12. Marianne.

13. The three sisters as teenagers.

14. Marianne and Ursel playing violin and accordion with canine audience.

15. Ursel (r.) and probably Katta Sterna (l.) in a Berlin cabaret.

16. Tea on the Liedtkes' boat. L. to r.: unidentified, Ursel, Emmy, Ernst, Marianne.

17. Ilse and her boyfriend, Harald Böhmelt, at the Trichter dance hall on Hamburg's Reeperbahn, late 1930s. L. to r.: Peter Franke, Werner Finck, unidentified, Erich Kästner, Harald Böhmelt, Ilse, unidentified.

though, to play his new role to perfection, as Ursel's naturally brown skin was surely the spitting image of the tanned Greek's. That her complexion also bore an uncanny resemblance to Ernst's could, for the time being, be swept under the carpet.

For all Emmy's own ethnic self-concealment, she was, my mother said, agonized by Ursel's determination to secure non-Jewish status and its repercussions for Ernst, whom it would publicly strip not only of a daughter but of a marriage that had been unwaveringly faithful. The whole venture was also terrifying for them both: sworn statements about one's race that were discovered to be false could, they had heard, carry a penalty of death. Though Emmy desperately wanted to find a way of helping Ursel, for over a year she couldn't bring herself to acknowledge her marital lapse. Only when Ursel's half-Jewish friend and fellow actor, Katta Sterna, had herself obtained a certificate of Aryan origin by similar means, did Emmy agree to cooperate in turning Ursel into an Aryan.

Katta's panache had always impressed Emmy. She had a string of films to her name and was also a hugely talented dancer and cabaret artist, openly bisexual, and a habitué of smoky clubs, where she sang popular lyrics.

Katta pulled out the stops to help Ursel slough off her Jewish origins, and the two friends trawled through a list of possible fathers before deciding on Kostas. Runner-up was an antique dealer, who had generously offered to provide a sworn statement owning up to his paternity, but he was rejected on account of his bleach-white skin and, worse, the fact that he was alive and traceable. Whereas Kostas, my mother said, had the advantage of being not only dead, but also Greek – Greece being, at that time, a hard country in which to verify people's personal histories. And so Katta helped invent a story in which the Mediterranean lover and his German paramour had become so aroused by the music they were making together while the husband was poring over his dry legal files in court, that one day – just once – they had been unable to resist consummating this burning passion in the family living room, by the piano.

The next, and harder, question was how to get the new ethnic identity officially recognized. Emmy's sworn statement admitting to the infidelity needed to clear a bureaucratic obstacle course, including an examination of Ursel's case by the anthropologists at the Reichssippenamt, or 'Reich Kinship Office', the administration charged with 'hereditary and racial investigations',[23] at the end of which the ethnic status of each grandparent would be determined. This was obviously a perilous undertaking for Emmy; after all, *Der Stürmer* had aired its suspicions about her brother, and her maternal grandmother's membership in the Jewish community of Braunschweig was easy to discover. In addition, it would have been necessary to verify the ethnic credentials of the alleged father.

At first the idea was for Katta's mother, an imperious woman with excellent connections and no Jewish heritage, to pull the necessary strings; but she was compromised by being the sister of the artist Käthe Kollwitz, whose work had been banned from German museums. An alternative route had to be found. And the ideal one, they realized, was through a fellow actor who had once starred in silent films: the talented and beautiful Jola Duisberg. She was an Austrian whom Ursel had known since her student days and who had married Carl-Ludwig Duisberg, son of Carl Duisberg, one of the founders of IG Farben, among Germany's most powerful industrial conglomerates.

IG Farben had long supported the Nazi Party financially. It also supplied Hitler's military with key materials needed to wage war and would go on to exploit vast numbers of slave labourers at the IG Farben Buna plant, which was part of the Auschwitz complex. Carl-Ludwig himself retained excellent connections to the regime. Crucially, as a film director and producer, he was close to the Reichstheaterkammer, the 'Reich Theatre Chamber', to which actors had to belong in order to work – and which had expelled Ursel back in 1936.

By 1934 the Reichstheaterkammer had swallowed up the other acting unions and professional associations that remained from pre-Hitler times, and that still included Jews and *Mischlinge ersten Grades*, or 'Hybrids of the First Degree', as half-Jews were known under Nazi law.[24] It, in turn, was a division of the Reichskulturkammer, or 'Reich Culture Chamber', which had been founded in November 1933 and which eventually brought all cultural activities in the Third Reich under state control.

Joseph Goebbels himself was president of the Reichskulturkammer, which he made an organ of his Ministry for the People's Enlightenment and Propaganda, and by May 1935 he had stepped up efforts to drive out Jews and other non-Aryans. To be a member of any of its divisions you now had to provide proof of your Aryan ancestry.

To help ensure that non-Aryans were excluded from the Reichskulturkammer and all its divisions, Goebbels appointed a certain Hans Hinkel, a senior Propaganda Ministry official and an SS officer, as one of its *Geschäftsführer*, or chief executives, as such giving him high responsibility for removing Jews from every aspect of German cultural life.

It is at precisely this time that Ursel, aged twenty-three, finds herself hounded by the Reichstheaterkammer for proof of Aryan identity. She has been sent a questionnaire demanding details of her racial origins, and has repeatedly stalled when reminded to return it. Impatience at the slow purging of Jews from German theatre is mounting among senior figures, including Hitler's deputy Rudolf Hess and the Nazi Party's ideologue Alfred Rosenberg – he who proclaims that 'The Jewish question is solved for Germany only when the last Jew has left German territory, and for Europe when not a single Jew lives on the European continent up to the Urals.'[25] Finally, on 15 April 1936, a new deadline is set for all those who have not yet handed in their questionnaires. Failure to do so, it is warned, will lead to immediate expulsion.[26]

Which is exactly what happens to Ursel. She is expelled in 1936 after failing to answer a 'final reminder' sent by the Reichstheaterkammer giving her ten further days to prove her Aryan status. But seeing no way, back then, to invent such proof, she has already abandoned the world of theatre for the less regulated demi-monde of cabaret – where she has joined Isa Vermehren and begun her journey to Catholicism.

So, to resurface as an Aryan in 1941, as she will do, and to be accepted again into the ranks of the Reichstheaterkammer is an astonishing about-turn. It seems that the Duisbergs end up going, on Ursel's behalf, over the head even of the Reichstheaterkammer, to none other than Hans Hinkel, who in April of that same year has been promoted to the rank of general secretary in the Reichskulturkammer. With his parallel career in the SS and his membership of Hitler's prestigious 'Blood Order', few officials in the entire Nazi state are in a better position than Hinkel to oversee the bureaucratic task of turning a Jew into an Aryan.

Do they get his attention by going to Goebbels himself? Does Hinkel receive financial inducements from the Duisbergs? Does he have designs on Ursel? We don't know. In the state archives in Berlin there is a file containing Hinkel's correspondence with Carl-Ludwig Duisberg, including a letter of thanks to Hinkel for his condolences on the death of Duisberg's father in 1935, Duisberg's 'heartfelt' congratulations to Hinkel on his promotion to *Ministerialdirektor*, a letter of reference from Hinkel, dated 12 January 1940, attesting to Duisberg's 'personal and political reliability', and, a few months later, an invitation to Duisberg to lead a troupe of actors to entertain German troops in occupied France[27] – all of which suggest a close connection between Ursel's benefactor and the man who is in a position to save not just her career but possibly her life.

What we do know is that Ursel, a young actor with almost no experience, whose most recent work has been in cabaret venues subsequently closed down by Goebbels, who was expelled from the Reichstheaterkammer five long years beforehand, and who has survived in ethnic purgatory ever since, now finds herself invited for an intimate chat with one of Goebbels's right-hand men: a Nazi personally and professionally dedicated to ridding German culture of people like herself.

The timing cannot be coincidental. Out of the blue, in June 1941, just weeks after Hinkel is promoted to the rank of general secretary in the Reichskulturkammer, his underlings at the Reichstheaterkammer are ordered to send over Ursel's complete file. Moreover, it seems that she is now permitted to deal directly with Hinkel's officals in the Reichskulturkammer rather than only with its subsidiary theatre division.

What happens next is mysterious. Perhaps nothing happens save a wait and a documented effort by Ursel to track down proof of origin. In any event, less than four months later, on 23 October 1941, Goebbels's Ministry calmly informs the Reichstheaterkammer, without elaborating, that it need have no concerns about accepting Ursel as a member and should hasten to pass the good news to her.

The effect is magical. Ursel reapplies to the Reichstheaterkammer, and is immediately accepted. The only problem is that, as a matter of routine procedure, she has to sign a statement assuring them of that wretched Aryan ancestry. Oh, and the statement must be supported by original evidence. She seems to be back where she started. But of course she isn't. She is able to say that the 'proof' is in the powerful hands of Goebbels's Ministry of the People's Enlightenment and Propaganda.

Ever diligent, the Reichstheaterkammer writes to the Ministry informing them that they have passed the news to Ursel, though they would appreciate confirmation that evidence of her ancestry has indeed been examined and accepted:

7 November 1941.
52219 B/J/Schf.
To: Reich Ministry for the People's Enlightenment and
    Propaganda
Berlin W8
Wilhelmplatz 8-9

Subject: Actress Ursula Liedtke, born 21.10.1912 Berlin
Reference: BeKA 20303 – 19.4. of 23 October 1941
Your decision of 23 October 1941 was communicated orally
to the above-named during her appearance here in person.
On 3 November, she signed the declaration that she is of
Aryan origin. Upon request to produce documents about her
ancestry, she stated that her documents have been handed
over to you, so that an examination of them cannot be made
from here. If proof of parentage is to be checked by you, I
kindly ask you to inform me of the result in due course.[28]

Does Ursel really obtain Aryan ancestry certificates? Is the whole story of her mother's adulterous fling with Kostas, or whoever was finally chosen as her father, so lacking in credibility, or so perilous to pursue, that it is abandoned? Or does Hinkel simply produce a note expressing satisfaction with her racial credentials, perhaps with the help of an 'expert opinion' to this end from obliging colleagues at the Reich Kinship Office? That his role is crucial is suggested by a rapturous and deeply moving letter of thanks to Hinkel, written by Ursel in her own hand just six weeks after the Ministry gets involved in her case:

17.7.41

Very respected Herr Staatsrat,
    For weeks now I have been waiting in vain for my father's papers from Christburg [Ernst's birthplace]. As soon as I have received these papers, I shall call on you. For the last few weeks I have been with Frau Duisberg in Vornbach [a castle in Bavaria purchased by Carl-Ludwig Duisberg in 1938] – and you can imagine in what a great state of bliss I have been since the day I visited you. Never in my life shall I forget how kind you have been to me and I often talk about you with Frau Duisberg. I will call you immediately when I come to Berlin. Hopefully you too can soon take a few weeks of vacation and relax from your hard work. I am so endlessly grateful to you. You have absolutely given me back my purpose in life.
    I send very warm greetings and will always remain indebted to you,
    Ursula Liedtke[29]

Despite my many discussions with Ursel, it remains unclear to me why her declaration of Aryan origin was accepted and how the necessary racial proofs were furnished, if they were. Of one thing she was always sure: the Propaganda Ministry and Hinkel had conjured a miracle. Quite apart from removing all obstacles to her employment, she had heard, by late 1941, that it was getting even harder, if not impossible, for a Hybrid of the First Degree to be allowed to marry an Aryan, a mixed union that had been forbidden under the 1935 *Law for the Protection of German Blood and German Honour*, except by special permission. Far more seriously, she feared that powerful forces in the Nazi Party were agitating for half-Jews to be consigned to forced labour, and even sterilized. As she saw it back then, without Katta Sterna, the beautiful Jola, Carl-Ludwig Duisberg, and 'Herr Staatsrat, SS-Oberführer, Pg. [Parteigenosse] Hans Hinkel, Reichskulturwalter', as Hinkel is addressed in correspondence, she might have no right to a job, no right to marry a German, no right to have children – and possibly no right to live.

14.

Ursel becomes a countess

For two years, Hinkel's ethnic sorcery worked its magic. Ursel lived more or less in peace and eventually returned to the theatre in Bremen from which she had been evicted back in 1934, moving in with Lexi Alvensleben and her husband Wilhelm Roloff in August 1943. Now in her early thirties, she was entitled to think of herself once more as a genuine German and felt protected from the increasingly drastic measures that, she heard, were periodically threatened against Hybrids of the First Degree, including, from early 1942, calls for them to be deported to concentration camps. Above all, she could now fulfil the role on which, my mother insisted, she had set her heart ever since her teens: that of the aristocrat. Not just to mingle with aristocrats or to call Countess von Alvensleben 'Mami', but to gain a title of her own. Indeed, not just to gain a title, but, as she did with all her identities, to become – brilliantly, perceptively, and in her own unique way – the character she had assumed.

Her future husband, Franziskus Reichsgraf von Plettenberg-Lenhausen, had fallen in love with her when he caught sight of a small photo of her on the desk of his cousin, Elisabeth von Plettenberg. Franziskus at once declared that he was going to marry that girl in the photo and that nothing would stop him – an impulsiveness that appealed to Ursel as much as the tall, charming, and humorous man did. Now, in addition to enjoying her new identity, career, income, and safety, she could look forward to the security of marriage to a non-Jewish German. Instead of being an unemployable non-person belonging to a subhuman race, she was about to become the Reichsgräfin von Plettenberg-Lenhausen, part of a family with an ancient seat and a circle of relatives and friends that included many of Germany's most illustrious aristocratic names: Stolberg, Böselager, Lehndorff, Dönhoff.

An inconceivable distance from Blumeshof 12.

The wedding, Ursel would tell me with relish, didn't start well. Once more, certificates of ancestry were the stumbling block. Just like the Reichstheaterkammer, the people at the wedding registry wanted the original documents, and those vital papers, if they existed, had to be tracked down, or else invented. A note from Franziskus's military superior – the 'Higher Commander of the Flak Training and Replacement Regiments' – permitting him to marry Ursel and attaching his own proof of Aryan origin wasn't, of course, enough.

Franziskus was not, however, a man to be detained by petty officials, though he surely knew that permission to marry even a half-Jewish woman would, by now, almost certainly be refused. On the big day, 23 September 1943, they arrived at the civil marriage office in Hamburg, he in his Wehrmacht uniform, she in a simple dress and flat shoes, carrying a posy of flowers.

'We cannot marry you unless the lady has her birth certificate and proof of her parents' ancestry,' the official snapped. 'You should know such things and not waste this office's time.'

But he hadn't reckoned with the groom's temper.

'If you do not marry us now, and drop your pathetic zeal, I will fell you with a blow the like of which you have never experienced,' boomed Franziskus at his would-be nemesis. 'This is a time of war and the Reich needs fighting men, not bureaucrats at desks!'

The official looked terrified, then confused, and finally submissive.

'Sir, I am not allowed to—'

'You are speaking to a Count of the Reich and you will marry us now!' Franziskus bellowed at the man, whose normally infallible weapon, a little rubber stamp that bore a swastika crowned with the name of his office, was trembling in his hands. 'And do not waste the time of an officer of the Wehrmacht! Your superiors will hear from me about your obstructiveness!'

'Sir, if you and the lady come back with the necessary papers, then I will certainly . . .' And the man's voice sighed a helpless official sigh.

Franziskus's face flushed and he was about to lunge at the bureaucratic impediment. 'Get on with it, or you will not know what has happened to you!' the Count bellowed, not even giving the official time to get into his obsequious stride.

The marriage achieved, Franziskus left for military duties in the Netherlands, where he was stationed with the occupying German forces, while his bride returned to Bremen.

15

The Gestapo comes calling

Ursel's new-found security was to be short-lived. It might have been the humiliated official at the wedding registry, his suspicions aroused, checking on her racial origins or notifying higher-ups of her failure to produce the evidence. Or perhaps another bureaucrat noticed the words 'two Jewish grandparents' that were still on her Bremen resident's registration card, which nobody had looked at since she last lived in the city in 1934 but had been dug out again when she returned in August, a few weeks before her wedding.

In Berlin she had been left in peace for two years after being deemed a non-Jew. But now, just one month after the wedding that should have made her even safer, she was investigated again, this time by the Gestapo.

All we know is that someone in Bremen's official registry of inhabitants, the so-called *Einwohnermeldeamt*, scribbled a note in Ursel's resident's card, her *Einwohnermeldekartei*: 'Gestapo enquired on 21.10.43.'

Not long afterwards, a man approached her at night in a barely lit street as she was walking home after a performance at the theatre.

'We know who you are,' the voice said. 'We would advise you to disappear at once.'

With that, he walked away.

Ursel's Aryan status had gone up in smoke: for all Hinkel's efforts,

Ernst could not be eradicated. News of her extramarital paternity had clearly not reached Bremen, and the dreaded word '*Jude*' still stained her file, attracting attention to itself like a shrieking siren. All doors were about to slam shut once more.

The unknown man must have been well-disposed to her, or she might have been arrested on the spot.

She rushed back to Lexi's home, and from then on seldom ventured out. But to hide where she was officially registered as living was hardly a smart way to disappear; she obviously had to flee the city.

Where was she to go?

She told me that she toyed with returning to Berlin and somehow melting into the capital. But evading its legions of bureaucrats was improbable in the extreme, despite her sister Ilse's success in doing just that. Then the plan occurred to her: she was going to do what was forbidden to the wife of an officer, let alone to a Hybrid wife on the run. She was going to join Franziskus at the front, in the Netherlands. Once she'd tracked him down, she would demand that he desert Hitler's army. Then they would both go into hiding.

He was now in real danger too and would surely agree to her plan. If the Gestapo's suspicions about her were relayed to his superiors, he might be arrested for marrying a half-Jew without permission – and, even more seriously, a half-Jew who would almost certainly be discovered to have secured her acceptance as an Aryan, and therefore her readmission to the Reichstheaterkammer, under false pretences. And who, in the process, had compromised one of Goebbels's senior officials.

But how was she to get out of Bremen and into the Netherlands without being detected? Here, Ursel's acting skills once again came into their own. She decided to disguise herself as a boy and leave the city on foot, only risking public transport when she was well clear of it. So she cut off her hair, dressed herself in men's clothes, flattened her chest with a corset, and fled.

I am uncertain what happened next. How did she succeed in making the 200-mile journey to the Netherlands disguised as a boy but with only the identity card of a thirty-one-year-old woman to show the German officials whom she must have encountered? How did she manage to enter the garrison where her husband was stationed, or did she get him a message to meet her nearby? Wouldn't telephoning him to arrange a rendezvous be too dangerous in case of eavesdropping?

Somehow linking up with Franziskus, she demanded that he desert the Wehrmacht. He agonized over the decision for three days and three nights. It wasn't fear of punishment that inhibited him – it was the dishonour. A patriot and an officer doesn't desert. Ursel kept up the pressure. And then, with astounding courage, he acted.

He was aware that this decision might mean a lifetime on the run and danger to his entire family in Westphalia, who would likely be treated to Hitler's policy of collective punishment. If captured, death would be immediate and horrible.

For the next few months they were hidden by peasants in the attic of a farmhouse, thanks to the help of an underground organization. They learned some Dutch from their hosts – from now on they couldn't risk speaking a word of German – and they forged new identity papers. But word got around that two Germans were living there. Fearful of being betrayed by local Dutch, they moved on to Amsterdam, where they again found a place to hide.

Though it was, in some ways, easier to remain unnoticed in a city, the danger was that Amsterdam was full of German soldiers. Occasionally one knocked at their door or stopped Franziskus in the street while he was foraging for food. He always claimed to understand no German and produced his forged ID, fearful of bumping into a soldier who sniffed out the deception.

And then, on an early spring day in 1945, that moment came. Allied troops were now flooding Amsterdam and, in their wake, Franziskus and Ursel were enjoying a new-found sense of safety. Too soon, it turned out. He was searching for bread when he was stopped for a routine check. Though, as always, he spoke Dutch, he accidentally uttered a German word or two. The young sergeant noticed his perfect accent and, crucially, saw the panic in his eyes, betraying his realization that he had made a lethal error.

But the man who arrested him wasn't German. He was Canadian. Though Franziskus could scarcely believe his luck not to be in German handcuffs, his relief wouldn't last long. Incredibly, the liberators, overwhelmed by the task of maintaining discipline among vast numbers of defeated Wehrmacht fighters, not to mention the logistics of disarming and repatriating them, were handing captured Germans back to their commanders. And German court martials were continuing to try deserters under Nazi military law. For Franziskus, the sentence was a foregone conclusion.

Extraordinary good fortune was, however, to intervene – and this time to endure.

At Franziskus's trial, a colleague from his time fighting with Rommel in Africa happened to be present in the courtroom, and he saved his life. As the presiding judge – a Nazi ranting in a crescendo of fury against people he claimed were traitors and cowards eager to stab their own compatriots in the back as soon as they saw that the war was being lost – was about to pronounce sentence, the former colleague interjected: 'That man momentarily lost his reason, but he is one of our finest officers. He saved the lives of so many of our men in Africa! He is a patriot of the Reich, and he should be pardoned!'

Not long after his astonishing reprieve, Franziskus hastened to a remote estate in the north-west of Germany, near the Dutch border, that belonged to a relation of his, a Baron Knyphausen. While in hiding, he and Ursel had agreed that in case they got separated they should try to meet up there; but when he got to the estate, he found no sign of her. Was she still living in their last refuge? Were the occupying Allied forces treating her well? He knew she was pregnant with their first child. What would happen if there were medical complications?

What he didn't know was that Ursel was not hiding without help in an attic, but living it up in one of Amsterdam's most exclusive maternity clinics.

Ilse's World: Fearless in Berlin

16.

Dancing at Babelsberg

Ursel's bravado was remarkable enough, but how did Ilse do it?

Throughout the Third Reich, she lived, so she repeatedly told me, as if she had nothing to fear. She didn't go into hiding or take an assumed name. She didn't try to get herself certified as Aryan, or marry into a new identity. Emigration – with which I think Ursel briefly toyed when her former Berlin acting teacher suggested she join her in Hollywood – was out of the question.

On the contrary, Ilse continued to dwell with brazen normality at the heart of Hitler's Berlin. She worked as a photographer on Budapesterstrasse until her atelier was bombed in 1944, openly advertising her services and counting high Nazis among her satisfied customers. She spent the ever more dangerous years from 1935 to 1942 with a card-carrying Nazi, with whom she waltzed at Babelsberg while other Hybrids of the First Degree were undergoing gradual social death. She survived the war in Berlin, collecting the food coupons to which Aryans were entitled and dealing with the myriad officials who interfered in citizens' daily lives, without once being menaced by a knock on the door – all while other half-Jews were cowering in basements until a rumour, a random enquiry, or a neighbour's unusual glance forced their courageous hosts to throw them to their fate. She gave birth to a son, fathered by Harald Böhmelt, in Berlin's Franziskus clinic in the summer of 1942, a few months after the Holocaust was set in train. The worst harassment she suffered was the ogling of men or their dull proposals of marriage – of which her unpossessable beauty attracted a steady stream.

She knew about the innumerable decrees, some of them all the more gruesome for their bizarreness, such as the ban on Jews owning carrier pigeons or buying soap and shaving cream; and she saw the assembly points where knots of the doomed were awaiting deportation. But the invitations to glittering evenings never abated, even as Jewish lives were being smashed to destruction. It was as if she was hiding herself by flaunting herself.

One of Ilse's clients, a First World War fighter pilot ace called Ernst Udet, who was helping Göring build up the Luftwaffe, regularly invited her to the debauched parties he threw. Udet was a star of 1930s Berlin who moved easily between affairs of state and bohemian free-spiritedness, and felt much at home among the film producers, composers, and actors with whom Harald and Ilse mixed. He had swagger, she said, but didn't strut with the grim earnestness of Hitler's senior henchmen. His face wasn't laminated with privilege like Göring's; nor did he slyly conceal private sensual pleasures behind a public show of rectitude. He became rich at a time of economic depression from his bestselling autobiography and from films that became world-famous, packed with his low-flying stunts. One of his most daring numbers, Ilse reported, was to fly under a bridge and then snatch a handkerchief from the ground with his wing tip. Udet was his own man; he loved women and soft drugs, and he made little secret of it.

So too did another of her clients, an actor called Heinrich George, a former communist who had effortlessly converted to Nazism and entertained Party bosses, artists, and businessmen in the living room at his villa near the Wannsee, where statues of Hitler and Stalin glowered at each other from opposite corners. 'I moved over from him to him,' he would stammer, a glass of champagne listing in his hand, while his guests lounged on soft cushions, cuddled in corners, or watched films projected onto a wall-to-wall screen.

Then there were the splendid evenings at Ufa's studios in

Babelsberg, just outside Berlin, where films like *The Blue Angel*, Marlene Dietrich's talkie, had been made, and where the roaring Twenties, with their bohemian cheek and cynical humour, had found their way into celluloid – but which was now a diligent valet of the Nazi worldview. Though it swarmed with Party members and had of course dismissed its Jewish directors and actors, it seems that nobody at Ufa knew about Ilse's ancestry. Dancing on Böhmelt's arm with delicious impunity before and into the early part of the war, Ilse felt that Babelsberg was like a utopian space insulated from politics, a world unto itself of dizzying safety.

Indeed, between Kristallnacht and the outbreak of war, Ilse even found herself accompanying Böhmelt to the Führer's official residence in Berlin, where Hitler was throwing a party for a handful of favoured artists, designers, architects, and composers – no more than sixty in total. As she recounted it in her matter-of-fact manner, as if not even a moment as surreal as this could faze her, she and Harald were stunned by the opulence of it all, less because much of Germany was still suffering from grinding poverty than because it echoed the order that emanated from the Führer and that was in turn reflected in the perfection of every detail: the furniture, the carpets, the coasters, the saucers, the lampshades, the Turkish cushions, the marble ashtrays, and the clichéd sculptures of ideal male and female forms. Not to mention the caviar, which particularly impressed Böhmelt with its shiny, briny, gold-black radiance. Endless varieties of meat and vegetables and fish were laid out on Meissen dishes in the light of shimmering candles. Aromas seeped indoors from a spotlit patio as bottles of champagne and German Rieslings criss-crossed the room, carried in the grip of white gloves. Hitler himself chatted vivaciously, but his attention, Ilse reported, seemed far away. He ate nothing and drank nothing. He was withdrawn as only a god can be. Or perhaps he was bored.

At the same time, Ilse and Harald consorted with many figures unbeloved of Hitler. They were close to Werner Finck, co-founder of the political cabaret Die Katakombe (The Catacombs), where Isa Vermehren, Ursel's friend, had found work and which, Finck relates in his memoirs, he had conceived in Harald's house.[30] They spent many weekends with Otto Dix, the 'degenerate' artist, whom Ilse found cheerful, despite his stunted career. She often saw the banned writer Erich Kästner, author of such international bestsellers as *Emil and the Detectives*, who called her 'my chauffeur' because she ferried him around in her car and who enervated her with his mother-worship, his pessimism, and his back-seat driving.

Most of these people had time on their hands: Finck had seen his cabaret closed by Goebbels in 1935 and was then briefly interned in a concentration camp. Kästner, who had gone to see his own books burned in the presence of Goebbels in 1933, couldn't publish under his real name. Other writers, like Hans Fallada, with whom Böhmelt had collaborated in making the film *Kleiner Man – was nun?*, and Peter Franke, were keeping a low profile. Ilse would join groups of them for weekends in the lovely Harz mountains, or at Finck's cottage near Potsdam, or in the Reeperbahn amusement district of Hamburg, where they whiled away long evenings at the then-famous dance hall, Ballhaus Trichter.

But what none of these people knew was that, by 1941, Ilse had another life. A dangerous and almost entirely secret one.

17

Ilse, Christabel, and the 'submarines'

Ilse did it mainly at night: helping to hide and feed Jews stranded in Berlin. Her contacts sprang from a very different social milieu to the writers and artists with whom she spent so many evenings and weekends. It was the aristocratic world of Adam von Trott zu Solz, who would later become an active resister and was hanged by the Nazis in August 1944; and of the Alvenslebens, whom Ilse had met through Ursel's friend Lexi.

The aristocrats whom Ilse knew weren't hiding Jews in their own homes, but a network of people had crystallized around them to provide intermittent shelter for Jews on the run. Known as 'submarines', these Jews had discarded the yellow stars, emblazoned in black with the word '*Jude*', that they'd been forced to wear from September 1941 – on the left side of their chest, right over their heart. They'd then gone underground wherever they could find refuge – whether for one night, for one month, or, if they were exceptionally fortunate, for longer.

One member of the network was Christabel Bielenberg, née Burton, a young Anglo-Irish woman married to Peter Bielenberg, a lawyer who was later interned in a concentration camp. Christabel was intelligent, bold, resilient, and astonishingly well connected, in England and Ireland as well as in Germany, thanks not least to her uncles, the newspaper barons Lord Rothermere and Lord Northcliffe.

In her memoir *When I Was a German*, she records how Ilse confronted her with a Jewish couple who urgently needed refuge. Christabel agonized – then told them they could stay two nights, but that was it. It was the winter of 1942:

> She had a blonde woman with her that morning; rather extra blonde who, after shaking my hand, hesitated on the doorstep and seemed unwilling to come into the house. Ilse, too, seemed satisfied that her companion should stay outside and, after glancing at our telephone to see that it was not plugged in, she explained why. The woman was a Jewess. She had removed her star when the Gestapo had come hammering at the door of her flat, and she and her husband had clambered down the fire escape and had been living in attics and cellars ever since. A safe hairdresser had dyed her hair and, latterly, a priest had housed them in his attic; but some members of his flock, pious Catholics all, had recently been making discreet but pointed enquiries. Since yesterday the good Father had felt himself and his house to be under surveillance. Ilse explained that the priest had not asked his lodgers to leave, but they knew that the time had come, and now they had no place to go. She added that the woman could pass as an Aryan . . . It was a little time I suppose before my thoughts returned to the silent sitting room and I remembered to tell Ilse to ask her companion to come in, because of course I knew that outside the front door, waiting patiently beside the doorstep was something more than an unknown woman with dyed blonde hair. Whether I liked it or not, prepared or unprepared, the moment had come to me.[31]

What Ilse did was brilliantly courageous. Of the few Germans who were resisting at all, even fewer were doing anything for the Jews. And those who were, were hardly Jewish themselves. But did helping to hide Jews also buttress Ilse's belief that she wasn't one of them? That they, not she, needed hiding?

* * *

At around the same time as Ilse confronted Christabel with the two submarines, over the winter of 1942–3, she unexpectedly received a parcel containing her uncle Theo's last possessions – among them his *Judenpass*, the identity card marked with a large J that Jews were required to carry – neatly wrapped in layers of brown paper. It was addressed to her and was sent from the Sachsenhausen concentration camp, just north of Berlin, to which Theo had been deported. It seems extraordinary that any concentration camp would send its victims' possessions to anyone, and incomprehensible that the authorities, who must have known that Ilse was next of kin to a Jew, would politely return his personal effects, listed in an officially stamped inventory, instead of coming for her too. But that is what they did.

She hadn't seen Theo for a very long time by then. As she recounted it, their last meeting was a chance encounter on a street corner in Berlin in late 1941. Her uncle wears the compulsory yellow star; his eyes are sunken; he is thin, depressed, hunched, uncommunicative. He looks away, whispering to her not to address him – for her own protection.

'What a coincidence!' Ilse exclaims delightedly.

'Go away,' he hisses.

'Uncle Theo, why are you so unfriendly? Have we done anything wrong?'

Her naivety must have seemed aggressive. How could Ilse, who was hiding Jews from certain death, ask her own uncle such a question? Yet, four decades later, she reports this exchange to me in baffled tones, as if Theo didn't realize that she knew exactly what one could and could not get away with in Nazi Berlin.

'Go away, go away,' he repeats, trying not to look nervously around him.

'We miss you, Uncle Theo! I'll come and fetch you by car. Then you'll have no excuses!'

He starts to walk away.

'Theo!' Ilse calls, as she catches up with him again. 'Well, at least let's have a bite together. We haven't seen you for ages.'

She still doesn't get it.

Finally, he points to his yellow star, and murmurs, 'You and Emmy will both be in terrible danger if they see you with me. Go now.'

'Danger? No, don't be silly! I will talk to whomever I want!'

He gives her a haunted stare.

'Please, Theo, you're so elusive.'

He walks off. The encounter has barely lasted five minutes. She will never see him again.

18.

The Rosenthals and their guest

The Rosenthals were stalwarts of Ilse's network. They were, she said, two of those magnificent working-class Berliners: irreverent, quick-minded, by turns unpredictably warm and stunningly brusque, given to acerbic humour and rapid-fire observations, freedom-loving without puffing themselves up with an ideology of freedom, contemptuous of the Nazis, and unaware of the world of tact.

They also got things done. They seemed to live a plodding life, keeping themselves to themselves, but they could work the system brilliantly, and always managed to get food coupons and find heating oil for themselves and for friends, even towards the end of the war when everything was in desperately short supply. Who would have thought that they hid Jews?

In early 1943, as they were about to go to bed, there was a gentle knock on their front door. It was Ilse. Herr Rosenthal knew what it was about. He and his wife had agreed to shelter another of the submarines. With Ilse was a middle-aged man without a family. He stood proudly but matter-of-factly next to her, determined not to look piteous. Ilse sensed that his determination appealed to them.

The man spent one night in the cellar. Then two. Then a month. In the end, Ilse told me, it was nearly two years. The Rosenthals' bluff exteriors must have hidden conscience and courage and generosity of an uncommon order; but, as she described them, they weren't the type to congratulate themselves on their morality.

Herr Rosenthal and the submarine became like a married couple, which hardly seemed to bother Frau Rosenthal, who spent most of her time knitting and reading adventure stories by Karl May and keeping to her household routine as if nothing had changed in the world outside. She placed meals dutifully on the table for both men three times a day for two years, and afterwards ate quietly by herself.

The Rosenthals reported back to Ilse how they and their guest quarrelled over who would scrub the vegetables, while there were vegetables to scrub. The guest was bookish and would chide his hosts for not knowing about the great German masters of music and literature. He taught them poems by Goethe and their setting to music by Schubert. He talked about philosophy with them, or rather to them. They became friends, bonded by respect, affection, duty, habit, and much else. But not by guilt or shame. None of them acted out of guilt or shame.

Nonetheless, Ilse said, the guest started getting on Herr Rosenthal's nerves, and eventually on his wife's too. He complained about the food. It wasn't the scarcity that irked him; rather it was the preparation, and the presentation. He had lived a comfortable life before the war and had refused to leave Germany when he could have. Nor would he think of abandoning his routines: food carefully cooked and seasoned and tastefully laid out on the plate, even if there was next to nothing of it; clean tablecloths; folded napkins; and good conversation. To say that this was pointless in the terrible conditions of war was defeatist: part of a deeper succumbing to the Nazis and the barbarism they had brought about. Too many people had done that. Table napkins were a way of defying Hitler. Like the Rosenthals, their guest intended to keep going.

Eventually the Rosenthals requested a quid pro quo. It was early 1945, Soviet forces were moving westwards, and tales of rape and looting were travelling ahead of them. Everyone took it for granted that if they got to Berlin they would impose their own version of hell on the city, beginning with rape.

The Rosenthals' request was that, if Russian soldiers knocked at the door, the guest was to shield the wife by pretending to rape her.

The pretence was to be convincing enough that the soldiers would believe it and not bother to come in. They even practised the 'rape scene'. Herr Rosenthal would knock on the inside of the front door, and the guest would make for Frau Rosenthal and fake the necessary.

The guest didn't demur. The Rosenthals were risking their lives protecting him from the Nazis, so he should risk his life protecting them from the Soviets. For, make no mistake, if the soldiers were intent on raping the wife, the man they would shoot first would be the one on top of her.

The plan was ridiculous, of course. The putative rape scene would merely arouse the conquerors' lust, whether or not they killed the submarine too. Nor would the Rosenthals be assured of any safety. But the deal never got put to the test. One day, they came home from foraging for food to find their guest dead in a chair. A book lay open on the floor, face down.

For the first time, he seemed really dangerous. You could hide a living person but not a corpse, which would begin to smell. If the authorities called at the door, Herr Rosenthal might be accused of murder. And if they discovered that the corpse was Jewish they would shoot him and his wife on the spot.

Herr Rosenthal decided that the only way to make the body disappear was to burn it by night in a freshly bombed building. By now, there was hardly a lack of freshly bombed buildings in Berlin, except where he and his wife lived, in the leafy suburb of Zehlendorf. The streets around them were almost a bomb-free zone.

He waited a day or two in case the British or Americans decided to broaden their targeting policy, enabling him to dispose of the body nearby, but the bombers refused to oblige. So he borrowed the communal car that Ilse used and drove the corpse by night closer to the centre of the city, intending to leave it in the first recently struck building he saw. Approaching a blown-out door that was trying to catch fire, he dropped the submarine onto some smouldering parquet. Little flames were leaping through the far end of the corridor, licking the walls, and would surely make their way to the body.

Rosenthal ran back to his car and watched. Though the sky was streaked with red from fires all over the city and echoing with the droning of Allied planes, he decided to give it a few more minutes before making off. A building that was as badly damaged as that would soon be done for.

As he turned on the motor, he began to hear crackles of disintegration, but it was like a shower of shards; hardly a collapse. He drove out of range and waited for an hour or two as people desperate to escape the area were running by, lugging their pathetic possessions. Leaving without seeing the job through was not on.

As stubborn as that submarine, he thought, as the building refused to gut itself. As ever, his guest seemed to be having the last word.

Finally, Ilse reported, it happened. Maybe it was another bomb, or maybe it was the fire working its way through the edifice. High up, a crashing noise burst into life, releasing a storm cloud of dust into the night sky, and the fire quickly gathered pace. Furious flames rushed up to meet the dissolving masonry like two armies charging at each other. Herr Rosenthal made off. The submarine was no more. He was certain of that.

19.

How did Ilse do it?

How did Ilse hide in plain sight, so calmly and for so long? Whenever I asked her about it, she couldn't say why she had felt so 'safe' – so confident of surviving. She knew, from the earliest deportations, about the concentration camps. She witnessed the bone-numbing fear of the submarines. But she was never afraid. She felt protected, she always told me, despite the fate of her father and uncle; and despite finding the parcel from Sachsenhausen with Theo's last possessions at her front door.

'Felt protected by whom?' I used to persist, expecting her to give me names, beginning with Harald. But I never got a clear answer. She would pause, and the fear or confused vulnerability that so often inhabited her face, especially when it didn't have a threat to focus on, would surrender to calm, clear assurance. Strength as well as remoteness would flood her countenance at those moments, and I could imagine a room full of vicious Nazis dancing attendance on her.

One thing was confirmed after the war: Ilse's name wasn't on any of the surviving records of Jews or Hybrids. That much was clear when she applied for the rations that the American and British occupiers awarded groups who had been persecuted in the Third Reich. Half-Jewish acquaintances of hers were getting the rations, but Ilse was sent away empty-handed: her Jewish identity really had disappeared.

But there must have been more to it than that. As a Jew, or a half-Jew, you didn't waltz at Babelsberg. You didn't hang out at the Nazi-infested Trichter dance hall in Hamburg's amusement district. You didn't photograph Party officials and Luftwaffe aces, or guile-lessly approach your doomed relations in the street. You moved from cellar to cellar in permanent terror of being discovered, or else you stayed at home while your protector dealt with the outside world on your behalf – like Eva Borchardt, one of Moritz's daughters, who had married a Protestant pastor, Adolf Kurtz, and never left their home in Berlin from 1941 until the end of the war.

Ilse, I am sure, had a more dependable protector than a highly placed client who needed her services, or a kindly aristocrat who arranged for her to be hidden, or a lover with connections to the Swastika: she had the power of her own denial. To elude the Nazis as perfectly as she did, she must first have had to elude herself; to look on her old identity as once foisted on her but since disowned.

Or she might have gone further: she might have felt that she didn't have any Jewishness to repudiate; that this heritage had nothing to do with her – and never had done. If someone confronted her with the subject, she could stay serene; they were necessarily talking about others.

Perhaps this was why she helped Jews, but had no close Jewish friends; why she spoke of them admiringly but never intimately; and why she recognized Jews on television, but not when the connec-tion was more personal.

Unlike my mother, who struggled her whole life with this immense heritage, Ilse never appeared to engage with it. She didn't rationalize her Catholicism as 'updated Judaism', as my mother so often did, or evince conflicting loyalties and confused dread in the face of the long history of Catholic anti-Semitism. She didn't agonize out loud about whether Jewish origins could be reconciled with being a contemporary German, or constantly switch identities depending on whom she was with, always defining herself in opposition to them. When she was mingling with Nazis in Babelsberg it surely helped that the fiendish weight of Jewish history seemed to be, as far as it concerned her, somebody else's dead abstraction. She must have ethnically purged herself in her deepest inwardness. And it probably saved her life.

It wasn't as if she couldn't be frightened about other things. Of the three sisters, she seemed the really scared one, at least in the last fifteen years of her life when I saw a lot of her. Especially when it came to loving and being loved, her big round eyes could look haunted, terror-struck, pursued. An ordinary sign of affection might be more than she could bear. A hug, a compliment, or gratitude for the home-made marzipan that she would mail me from Berlin might reduce her to floods of tears. A cozy afternoon in her basement kitchen, talking about family and enjoying the cakes that she baked for my arrival, would become uncomfortable if I told her how deliriously wonderful it was to sit on a wooden chair in Berlin eating cherry cake with *her*; how I relished her crunchy *Streusel*, topped with a hillock of whipped cream. Once, as a teenager, I begged her to move to London and she collapsed in tears, overwhelming me with her grief.

Shortly before she died in 1986, when she was already in hospital with pain that her doctors couldn't diagnose, the past showed the first signs of decisively breaking through. She was convinced that men would come in the night and take her and all the other patients in the ward and kill them. Nobody in the hospital was to be trusted. The doctors and nurses might all be operatives of higher up, unseen forces. 'They want to shoot us,' she said. 'In the morning we will all be dead. And I will be the first they will take.' She didn't want to sleep, to lose her vigilance. 'There are bad people everywhere. They will come for us. I know it.'

In the year before she was admitted to hospital I happened to visit Berlin three or four times, and each time I was deeply shaken. She was a changed person. 'I want to die,' she kept saying. 'This world is a terrible world; and it has no purpose.' 'Why, Tante Ilse?' I would ask, but she wouldn't or couldn't explain. And she refused all consolation. She didn't want to hear that we were there for her and that she gave us so infinitely much by being alive. When I hugged her it felt like her spirit recoiled at once to some inner fortress, to which she refused all access, though she always hugged me back. She lost her avid interest in current affairs. Outwardly nothing had changed in her life; nothing recent could explain this sudden abandonment of hope. Events seemed to her to be either banal or evil, but either way not worth living for.

She had moments of joy when we went out for coffee and cake not far from where she lived, or to a restaurant nestled among the tall trees in Berlin's Grunewald. But, once we had ordered, she became morose again. 'I just don't want to go on, I can't.' 'Please go on,' I begged her, 'for our sake; you know how much we love you.' But the love that used to warm her and frighten her, now left her cold.

When we got back into her car afterwards, she usually had what seemed like a medical crisis. She was breathless, clutched her chest, and said she felt inexpressibly terrible. She said she couldn't drive. I held her, put my arm around her – enough, I hoped, to make her feel consoled but not pitied – and we would sit there, in the car, for up to an hour while she stared downwards, concerned for her heart but refusing to call a doctor. For that hour she couldn't move, as if she had had a stroke. A dam seemed ready to burst – a dam holding back a whole biography. But then, gradually, she became fine again, switched on the engine, spoke peppily, and drove us home.

Marianne's World: An Immigrant in London

20

Stateless at the German Embassy

Unlike her two sisters, who refused to emigrate, my mother escaped the gathering inferno in good time. For her, though, as for my father, it was a hesitant and much-deferred departure. When you love a place as much as they loved Germany, leaving can be painful beyond imagination, even if you have been declared subhuman.

At first my mother merely 'visited' England for a few months at a time, from 1934, for lessons with her violin teacher, Max Rostal, who had reconstituted his Berlin classes in London – to where his own teacher and arch rival, Carl Flesch, would soon also relocate.

In their routines and methods, Rostal and Flesch might still have been at the *Hochschule für Musik*; except, my mother would quip, they now had to cope with the quirks of their new teaching facilities. Wind leaking insistently through the windows and sending their students' instruments out of tune; rickety plumbing that often deteriorated further when repaired; caretakers who slept on the job and resented being asked to take care of anything. Not to mention the difficulty of finding their new addresses: 3 Smith Gardens might be located in Smith Square; number 42 might be adjacent to number 6; street names were often concealed by shrubbery, and in the case of some, like Strathray Gardens, where Rostal lived, defied pronunciation even after careful practice.

* * *

From 1934 until 1938 my mother split her time between Berlin and London for her lessons with Rostal, occasionally being refused entry by the British authorities at Dover and having to take the boat back to the continent to prepare a fresh application, but staying for longer periods each time – until, in the spring of 1938, her passport expired, and she went to the German Embassy in London to renew it.

'Your birth papers!' the refined-looking official barked at her from the other side of a wooden desk. Barking, my mother sensed, didn't come naturally to him.

She presented him with her birth certificate.

'Your parents' birth certificates!' he fired back.

'I don't have them.'

'Their race?' he demanded.

'German.'

'Don't waste my time! Aryan or not?'

'Don't shout at a woman!'

'What are you doing in England?'

'I'm a music student.'

'A student? Why does a German need to study in England? That is hardly necessary! Our education is far better than theirs!'

'My teacher emigrated—'

'And music! What do the English know about music? As we Germans say, they are "the land without music" . . . A nation of shopkeepers,' he added, proud, as my mother recalled it, of quoting Napoleon's alleged putdown.

'I'm studying with a German.'

'A German?' His glance was vicious. 'What sort of German, one can only ask. Besides, you seem to spend long periods here,' he remarked, surveying the densely stamped visa pages. 'Do you really need to be here just to study? And why do the British allow you to remain for so long if you are merely a student?'

My mother was sure he knew the answer: she could stay because of her Jewish parentage. The identity to which she confessed had been well rehearsed: to the British she was a Jewish refugee, to the Germans a non-Jewish student. Those identities had – so far – enabled her to move between the two countries.

'I must inform you,' the official said, after he had leafed through the visa pages, 'that if you return to Germany without a valid passport, for which we will need the birth certificates of your parents and grandparents, you will be immediately transferred to a special camp.' And he slapped the useless document onto his desk and fixed her with a stare of blank indifference.

My mother said nothing. When I asked her what she thought he'd meant by a 'special camp', she said she hadn't bothered to ask him, but had merely slid the elapsed document towards him, and returned his contempt with a look of disdain.

As she used to say with a defiant chuckle: 'I had finally left Germany. For good.'

21

The past cannot be predicted

Why exactly she 'finally left Germany' was to be argued over for the rest of her life. Ursel insisted that my mother had merely followed her Jewish teacher, who had been forced to emigrate. Ilse went blank when the matter was raised; if pressed for an answer she said that Marianne had left for the sake of her teacher, but might also have found studying in Nazi Germany 'difficult'. My mother echoed Ursel's position when speaking to Jews. When speaking to most Germans, however, the reason was clearly her Jewish origins. Unless we happened to be visiting German families who, she worried, might not find such origins palatable.

Here, no reason at all was volunteered — my mother had left for England and that was that. Even the period of her emigration was kept vague. When our hosts enquired whom she had married, it was simply stated that my father was a 'German' who had also happened to find himself in England. What could be more natural, my mother seemed to imply, than for two Germans marooned on this alien island to seek refuge in each other?

Occasionally one of the less formal denizens of these German homes — for most seemed very reserved in those days, back in the early 1970s — would send the conversation into perilous territory by asking my mother *the* awkward question: 'Wasn't it hard for you, as a German, to abandon your homeland?'

At once the room seemed charged with menace. We all looked at each other. Who was going to answer? We children knew that the J-subject was under no circumstances to be raised by us in front of these particular hosts, even now, a quarter century or more after the end of the war.

As a child I did what was expected of me and kept silent. My silence felt cowardly, and I longed to blurt out the truth and be liberated from this infernal circus of ethnic evasion. Why did we have to go on living as if the Third Reich were alive and kicking? As if the identity of 'Jew' or 'Hybrid of the First Degree' were still a passport to social death? As if the Reich Kinship Office and its team of anthropologists were decreeing who we were or weren't? But we had to: the topic remained a harbinger of unspeakable and insoluble pain for my mother and her sisters; and loyalty to them, fear of being doused in their hidden terrors, and incredulity that this identity could really be mine inhibited me from any dash for freedom.

My mother would sometimes relieve these stilted exchanges with a matter-of-fact admission that she had been studying with a teacher who had left in the 1930s. And that she had 'followed' him. She had emigrated because her teacher had emigrated.

The menace became confused. Why had the teacher emigrated? Now she would suggest something quite unexpected. What career prospects, she demanded, did a young violin teacher have in 1930s Germany, amid the country's high unemployment and social chaos? Britain offered far better opportunities. This was the cue for her to praise everything British in terms so extravagant that the country became unrecognizable. Things went on there, she said, that made Germany seem an ineffectual backwater. Its economy? It far outstripped Germany's! Its educational system? What those children learn! You can't imagine it: at ten, my son could help his eighteen-year-old German cousin with her maths homework. The hospitals? The best and cleanest in the world. The people? Well mannered, sophisticated, and progressive, if not always neatly dressed. Efficiency? Sometimes a little wanting, but that is the flip side of a freedom-loving nature. Criminality? You hardly see any. If a youth stumbles on a gold watch in the street, they will place it considerately on a garden fence or hand it in at the nearest police station in the hope that it will be swiftly reunited with its owner.

Our hosts were visibly bemused. This was the 1970s, when Britain was known as 'the sick man of Europe'. The streets were piled high with garbage. A punctual train was as rare as a black swan. Squalid and amateurish schools were the despair of the country's own 'chattering classes'. Drunken football hooligans were not exactly advertising the refinement of British manners. The economy was in meltdown. Entrepreneurs claimed to be giving up or fleeing, as the top rate of taxation somehow rose towards 100 per cent. The whole society seemed to be locked in class war, with the middle class despising the working class, and trade unionists and business bosses at each other's throats, while aristocrats, disdainful of lower orders when they even noticed them, were living in deep complacency on their inherited assets. Inner cities were regularly on fire and some group or other was always taking 'industrial action' – in other words, going on strike. Bizarrely, England, at least, seemed to be revelling resignedly in this misery and in the orgies of complaining that it spawned – the only nation, it has been said, capable of feeling *Schadenfreude* toward itself; though, being England, it could always muddle through decline and chaos, so that everything would eventually turn out all right.

None of these realities deterred my mother from her main point: anyone in their right mind would move to Britain, whether in the 1930s or now, in the 1970s. Hitler almost seemed irrelevant to the question of why she or her teacher had ended up in London.

But we were all talking at cross-purposes. Our hosts had, I think, so little suspected any Jewish presence in their midst that they appeared to be asking quite another question. Was it not unpatriotic to emigrate? Let alone to Britain, towards which I sensed intense contempt in those days, despite residual admiration for such glories as the Beatles and parliamentary democracy. Disloyalty was what really concerned them. A German stays with their country when it is in crisis.

But in our family, to borrow a quip from the former Soviet Union, even the past couldn't be predicted.

22

Czech mates

Whatever my mother's declared reason for leaving Germany happened to be, once she had abandoned her invalid passport at the German Embassy in London she was stateless – but by no means homeless. Where Ursel had adopted the Alvenslebens and their aristocratic network as a surrogate family, my mother now had hers in the dense and intense world of London's German-speaking Jewish émigré community – a community of scientists, insurance brokers, traders, bankers, architects, artists, historians and doctors, bonded not just by exile but, above all, by music.

Here, her shifting identities – German, Catholic, student, refugee, Jew – gained another: in 1939 she was adopted as an honorary Czech. Her adopter was the Czech government then in exile in London, led by Edvard Beneš, who had been President of Czechoslovakia until Hitler annexed the Sudetenland in 1938, and Jan Masaryk, who became foreign minister of the exiled government after many years as ambassador to London.

Masaryk had a substantial budget for promoting Czech culture in the UK and was set on supporting a piano, violin, and cello trio, the Czech Trio, which had been founded in Prague in 1933, but had lost its original violinist on moving to London. Its pianist was Walter Süsskind, a native of Prague who would later become director of the Aspen Festival in the United States; its cellist was Karel Horschitz, who was urgently persuaded to change his surname to the less scatological-sounding 'Horitz'; and its new violinist was my mother, Marianne Liedtke.

The problem was that my mother not only wasn't Czech, but had an unmistakably Germanic name – not ideal at a time when Czechoslovakia had recently been overrun by her native country.

But a family as deft as ours at juggling its identities could surely rise to this challenge. She at once cabled Emmy for help. Had an ancestor passed through the area and perhaps stayed there for a few years? Or, even better, married a Czech and produced a traceable child or two? Emmy had always been good at pulling 'forgotten' origins out of the hat – and, when necessary, at forgetting them again. Nor did she disappoint this time. A faint memory of local forebears quickly assumed sharp contours, birth and death certificates were excavated from dusty cellars, and my mother was able to report to Masaryk that she had a maternal great-grandfather, Leopold Wilhelm Dütschke, who had been born in 1829 near Lissa, a small town in Bohemia, which had then been German but was now Czech.

Admittedly Dütschke had no known affinity with Czech culture – in fact, the rise of the Czech national movement had caused him to flee his birthplace and settle in Hamburg, where he died long before his home town became part of the newly formed Czechoslovakia. But, for the purposes of membership in the Czech Trio, he seemed to offer real credentials. My mother therefore resolved to change her name from Liedtke to Dütschke.

Masaryk was unimpressed. A connection to Czech lands was useless if her new name was as brazenly German as Dütschke. Dütschke was even worse than Liedtke – it seemed to be formed out of the word *Deutsch*. The name sounded like an invasion.

He hit on a simpler solution: 'Marianne Liedtke' should morph into 'Maria Lidka'. Lidka was the stuff of folk idyll: the name of countless Czech women and of the country's major chocolate brand. And Maria . . . well, one thought of fresh-faced girls skipping down Bohemian country paths on their way to Sunday Mass.

It was a sweetheart deal. The trio was a runaway success, performing all over Britain and, most memorably, in the National

Gallery's wartime concerts, as well as marking Czechoslovak national holidays, especially Independence Day. Though its programmes often showcased the German classics, they were peppered with enough Czech music to look as though Dvorak were being seasoned with Beethoven rather than the other way around. And my mother, to whom Czech music had been almost wholly alien until not long before, was now hailed as playing it as only a native can: 'Czech music played by Czechs' ran a headline in the London *Star* in March 1940. 'Bohemian music, with its strong and immediate appeal, played authentically in the national manner', wrote *The Times* in the same month. 'They graduated from the Masterschool of the Bohemians with Smetana and Dvorak on their daily syllabus', boasted the Czech Trio's publicity flyer of its young players.

But my mother didn't just get another identity with which to navigate her life. Thanks to the Czech Trio, she finally gained a legitimate income. She could now rent a one-room apartment, rather than living in a series of damp bedsits and teaching rich but untalented amateurs in return for enough cash for a day's food and a bus ticket home.

23.

Grandmother Martha May

My mother owed her income to the Czech Trio, but I owe my existence to it.

After one of its concerts in 1940, an ebulliently warm-hearted woman with blazing red hair and a kind of shuffling gait that seems typically central European – benign, cultured, strong, stubborn, cozy, and a little resigned all at once – visits my mother in her dressing room and makes an offer:

'I am a concert pianist; I was trained in Kassel and Cologne; and I'd be happy for you to try out, with me at the piano, any new music you're learning,' the stranger announces, smiling broadly at her accomplishment.

My mother is suspicious. These sorts of offers are usually made by people who are either lonely or nursing the illusion that they are unrecognized virtuosi whose time is imminent. 'Where have you performed? What sorts of concerts have you given?' she asks.

'I haven't played in public for some time, but I am a professional,' the redhead replies. 'I used to play all over Europe and in South Africa.'

Then she makes the crucial offer: 'I am also an excellent cook.'

This succeeds in grabbing my mother's attention. The Czech Trio has transformed her finances and she is now able to rent a tiny apartment, but she is hardly rich. Her feet are frostbitten from two winters living in an unheated room, which she rented from a Mrs Etheridge, a Welsh woman who lived with her forty-year-old bachelor son and had never left the shores of Britain. My mother hasn't been able to afford even the stoves that give out ten minutes of vague warmth in return for dropping a coin into a meter. Her friend and admirer, Felix Vandyl, a fellow violinist and a refugee from Warsaw, has developed a technique for lowering the necessary coin tied to a piece of string into his heater and then retrieving it once it has triggered the switch; and he inhabits what sounds like a tropical boudoir, even when a gale is blowing through his leaking windows. My mother should come and see for herself, he insists. She does, aware that his motives might extend beyond altruism or pride in his costless thermostatic device. But she never masters the technique. Your hand has to be absolutely steady or the coin will slip out of its string, and this is hard even for a violinist with a controlled bow arm.

'I also have two charming sons,' the woman adds. 'Edward is a doctor and Walter a banker.'

But this hardly interests my mother. She has more than enough suitors to keep her busy.

What my grandmother, Martha Grünthal-May, fails to tell her future daughter-in-law is that Edward, her elder son, is a formidable amateur cellist whose own musical evenings are filled with young professionals as well as more seasoned performers. Though he is a doctor, with an uncanny talent for diagnosis, his greatest passion is chamber music.

Even better, my mother discovers, he is a talented cook and master shopper who manages to procure imposing cuts of beef and lamb at a time when butchers have little more than patches of meat embedded in hillocks of gristle and fat. And he loves gadgetry of every kind: gramophones, drills, motorbikes, fast cars. Fearful that Hitler will try to invade Britain, he has acquired a motorboat that he is sure can cross the choppy North Sea and treacherous Baltic waters to safety in Sweden and, if the Nazis march there too, proceed onwards to Australia. How his tiny craft could make it across U-boat-infested waters while warships are being sunk or huddling nervously in convoys is unclear. But, in the meantime, the boat offers a delightful way of entertaining women on weekend dates from which, once underway, they cannot easily make their excuses.

Within a few months my mother has all but moved into Edward's house. Thanks to him and Martha, she has graduated from semi-starvation to gastronomic paradise in one easy step.

24.

Saved by arrest

By late 1943, my mother had a lot more to thank Eddy for than the delicacies that he continued to secure as food became ever scarcer and rationing ever tighter.

German refugees like her, still designated by the British authorities as enemy aliens, were under strict curfew; but she had forgotten to keep track of the time as she and Eddy and two of her fellow Rostal students, Norbert Brainin and Hans (soon to be Peter) Schidlof, played a Beethoven quartet, and then, at his insistence, one by Schubert, before he served an unmissable dinner. As they started the desert, she realized that it was already after curfew time. The prospect that this might force her to stay the night delighted Eddy; but she knew what that was likely to mean and decided to risk the walk home, leaving the other two to sleep over.

Hurrying through darkened streets — streetlights were turned off to make it more difficult for German bombers to locate their targets — she ran straight into the law.

'And who are you, miss?' the policeman asked, confident that he had caught a sex worker on the way back from a client. 'Your papers, please.'

But he hardly needed to see papers. The accent said it all. My mother was arrested on the spot, taken to a police station, and locked in a cell for the night. After questioning the next morning, she was released on bail, guaranteed by Eddy, and told to report to a magistrates' court a fortnight later.

'Why were you out so late when you say you know the rules?' the magistrate demanded as she stood in the dock in a borrowed dress and wide-brimmed hat. From his condescending tone my mother was sure the court assumed that she had been engaged in the sex industry – and, worse, earning money, which was usually illegal as an enemy alien.

'I was playing quartets.'

'Playing quartets?' the magistrate enquired, convinced she had quickly incriminated herself. 'How, pray, do proceedings unfold when one is "playing quartets"?' He clearly supposed that the playing in question involved some act of group sex, involving two couples or perhaps three sex workers and a client.

My mother looked confused. 'You know,' she stammered, 'string quartets: Beethoven, Schubert, Mozart . . .'

The gallery broke into laughter. Beethoven! That was an original excuse, and certainly more imaginative than the usual run of self-justifying lies.

'Case dismissed!' the magistrate proclaimed, after further enquiries about what actually happened when one played string quartets.

As my mother was about to leave, the policeman who had detained her appeared out of nowhere. Expecting an apology, she stopped to smile at him, mumbling that she had never been in a court before, though her father had practised family law in one of Berlin's oldest. Instead, he asked if she would like to go to the cinema with him one evening.

'I wouldn't dream of it,' she shot back, contemptuous of the officer's nerve to ask for a date after inflicting on her that cold, lonely night in custody, fearful of the punishment that breaking the curfew might bring.

In fact, she owed the good cop serious gratitude. On returning home the morning after her incarceration, she found that a German rocket had scored a direct hit on her boarding house, leaving a pile of rubble, a giant crater, and a vestige of facade. Neighbours said that it had struck at about 2 a.m. Eddy's dinner and her arrest had saved her life.

PART III

Newly Created Worlds
1945–1990

25.

C & A to the rescue

It was a Sunday in Amsterdam, just after the Allied liberation of the Netherlands. Ursel was heavily pregnant and still living alone in her attic. Where, she worried, should she go if she went into labour? And to whom could she safely turn for help?

She was terrified that, as a German, a harmless question could end in a lynching or even a shot to the head. Franziskus had disappeared while out looking for food, and might have been arrested and killed by Wehrmacht soldiers then still prowling the city, or perhaps by Allied forces. The locals, consumed with hatred for their former German masters, wouldn't know that she was a non-Aryan who had been on the run from the Gestapo; that her husband had deserted the German army; and that they had both been in hiding with the help of Dutch underground operatives. It was best to remain invisible.

Surely, she thought to herself, the one person who could definitely be trusted was a Catholic priest in the confessional, bound by his vow of confidentiality. It would be safest to ask for help in a whisper through the grille of the darkened cabinet, after she had divulged her sins.

She was not disappointed. The priest on duty was eager to help. His voice seemed unthreatening and his profile gentle. Could she please wait at the back of the church until he had heard the other penitents? He would come to her as soon as he was finished.

But she panicked. The priest could be an informant. The secrecy of the confessional might not be absolute. After all, it was said that priests had the right to breach it in case of confessions of murder. Weren't the Germans responsible for countless murders in the Netherlands? There would be no point telling him about Franziskus's desertion in the hope of attracting sympathy; now that the war was lost, lots of Germans were probably making up stories about deserting or being Jewish.

She fled to her attic and shut herself away.

Forced to look for food again after a few days, she crept out of the house – and bumped straight into the priest.

'Why did you vanish?' he asked.

'I really didn't want to bother you,' Ursel lied.

'But I have help to hand. Two of my parishioners, two sisters, will take care of the birth for you. I spoke to them immediately after I saw you and they'd be delighted to get you to the best clinic.'

The two parishioners were members of the Brenninkmeijer family, the owners of the C & A retail chain, and the hospital room for which they paid was like a five-star hotel. Ursel gave birth to her first child, a daughter, in even more luxurious surroundings than she had known in her youth. The baby was swaddled in the finest silks and cottons. While Europe hungered, Ursel had never had it so good.

26

Locked in the attic

In 1946, my mother returned home. During the war she had heard nothing from Ilse and Emmy after their messages, sent through the Red Cross, dried up in the summer of 1942. Attempts to contact her family in Berlin immediately following the capitulation went unanswered. The last time she had seen her mother was in 1939, when Emmy paid a flying visit to London to attend her debut violin recital at the Wigmore Hall on Friday 13 January, accompanied by Gerald Moore; and she hadn't seen Ilse for even longer, though she knew from the final Red Cross telegram that she had given birth to a son.

She was steeling herself for the possibility that her mother and sister might be dead when, one afternoon soon after the German surrender, a fellow refugee and close friend called Esther Mendelsohn, daughter of a Berlin architect who had known Ernst and Emmy, took her to visit her new boyfriend, John Burton.

They were sipping tea in John's apartment when the phone rang. It was his sister from Berlin, who was married to a German and had spent the whole war there. John, normally a model of reserve, became intensely animated when he heard her voice, and my mother picked up snatches of a story about hiding with her children in the Black Forest, while her husband had ended up in a concentration camp. She caught one or two names – Adam, Fritz – though they meant nothing to her. 'Lexi' came up too.

And then the voice said: 'By the way, a friend of mine here is looking for her sister in London. Can you help?' 'London is a city of millions,' John riposted in his teasingly superior manner. 'I'll do what I can, but obviously we'll be searching for a needle in a haystack.' 'She's a violinist and her name is Marianne Liedtke,' came the reply. 'Do you know any musicians there?' 'Oh, well, *that* will be easy,' John interrupted, with deliberate understatement, puffing languidly on his pipe. 'Now, let me think.' (I knew him well and he would have relished drawing out a coincidence like this.) 'Actually, Chris, she's sitting right here. Why don't you have a word?'

The woman on the phone, John's sister, was Christabel Bielenberg, who had hidden the 'submarines' with Ilse during the war and had begged her to find a refuge for the Jew who ended up with the Rosenthals. As Christabel was the only English-born person in Berlin whom Ilse knew, she had asked her to see if she might track down her youngest sister, who, she hoped, was still alive and traceable.

Early the following year, with the help of John's formidable connections, my mother secured a place on an RAF bomber that was flying from a small airfield outside London into Berlin's Tempelhof airport, supplying the occupying troops in the British sector of Berlin. The rattling turboprop had no passenger seating other than on the corrugated metal floor. A few proper seats up front were reserved for officers or sensitive equipment. The vibration and the din were continuous, but conditions on this, my mother's first ever flight, were smooth – until soon after entering German airspace, when clear skies turned foggy and the pilot announced that they would have to descend immediately into Hannover. It would be impossible to make it to Berlin that day.

After a night spent in a hangar, fog hung heavy over the airfield and the pilot warned that it might be at least another day before they could fly. Travelling by ground was still extremely difficult: there were few buses and trains, and permits were required to move from one occupation zone to the next. The trickiest to pass through was the Soviet zone that encircled Berlin, so it quickly occurred to my mother to abandon the trip and instead to go and visit Ursel, who she knew was at the Plettenberg family castle, which, like Hannover, was within the British zone.

As soon as she arrived, it was plain to her that country life was no idyll for her sister. Ursel relished the acceptance and warmth that her new family showed her, but found the isolation hard. She was fascinated by the tales of emotional brutality that seeped in from surrounding villages – isolated childhoods, icy mothers, cruel fathers, and the violence of self-denial, where perdition could be glimpsed in a box of stale chocolates; but she longed for poetry too. She seldom shrank from stirring pots and enjoyed the buzz of local rumour – such as about the bride in a hamlet some kilometres away who was astounded to discover on her wedding night that her husband could arouse himself only by leaping naked out of a large wooden wardrobe, smelling mustily of old oak, into their bed, preferably illuminated by a shaft of moonlight. But she was also oppressed by the claustrophobia of these lives.

When my mother saw her sister marooned here, devoid of the concerts, theatre, and dance that Ursel craved, she decided, as she generally decided in any unfamiliar situation, to make music. She would play violin sonatas in the castle. A professional pianist, Herr Kraus, was duly located, the white piano was heaved from a corner of the large living room, and the concert was about to begin.

'Where is the audience?' my mother asks Franziskus.

'What audience?'

'Well, where is everyone? You said this house is full of Germans who fled the communist takeover in Prussia and Pomerania.'

'Oh, I've locked them in the attic,' Franziskus answers matter-of-factly. 'They are tone deaf, and not one of them has even heard of Beethoven.'

'Release them immediately!' my mother orders, thoroughly enjoying Franziskus's mischievous style. 'Or I'm not playing. You're crazy, Franziskus. It must be horrible up there!'

A parade of forlorn figures soon slides awkwardly into the drawing room. One huddled behind the other, in single file, they move with wary steps, saying nothing.

'We will be playing sonatas,' my mother announces when they

are seated. 'Brahms and Beethoven, each in four movements,' she adds.

Everyone looks bemused.

'You know Beethoven, I am sure!' she says, wondering now whether Franziskus might not have been exaggerating.

An elderly gentleman tries to clear himself and his relations of the charges of cultural philistinism that Franziskus had seemingly levelled at them.

'Yes, we know who Beethoven is,' he says, slightly peeved. 'I . . . we . . . just didn't know he wrote anything for the violin.'

27.

Ilse returns to Berlin

It was the first week of May 1945, Berlin had just fallen, and Ilse decided the time had come to attempt a return to the city. She'd heard that the Russian army was seizing people's homes for its officers, as well as plundering them for valuables. The Americans would surely follow suit as soon as they arrived and she was anxious to get back to my grandmother's house in the suburb of Zehlendorf – to which Emmy had moved in 1936 to escape the memories of Blumeshof 12 – before it was commandeered by soldiers, or else by the homeless and displaced. For the first time in months, it seemed safe to venture back: recently the sound of gunfire had been sporadic rather than continuous. Nights were eerily quiet without the din of exploding bombs.

She was holed up in Babelsberg, where, the previous summer, she and Emmy had sought refuge from the bombing of Berlin in the house of a Colonel von Nordheim, who had deserted the Wehrmacht not long before and whom she had met at one of the Ufa balls early on in the war. He was an old-fashioned soldier – an embodiment of duty and discretion, but also sensitive and humane – with whom Ilse enjoyed a bond of trust and respect, as well as the sort of silently erotic attachment to a powerful yet elusive older man that, my mother said, she often sought. The moment they met, they sensed that they were on the same side, but without mentioning Hitler, military campaigns, concentration camps, Poland, Russia, or any of that. They knew little about each other: he had no idea that he was harbouring a Jewish woman and she asked no questions about his private or military life.

As the Russians had encircled Berlin, she had hoped that Babelsberg was one place where, in their haste to vanquish the capital, they might not linger. It had become a ghost district of, she was convinced, no material interest, aside from the equipment in Ufa's vast movie studios, which the Red Army had already occupied.

But not long before the capitulation, von Nordheim's house had been invaded by a ragged bunch of the *Volkssturm*, the militia that Hitler assembled in the last months of the war to defend the Reich to the death. This motley group of youths and middle-aged men had surged in, puffed up by absurd self-confidence, as if they were about to win an easy victory against a pack of tin soldiers. In fact, they were using the building for one of their 'heroic last stands' – and the Russians knew that they were in there.

Ilse was desperate. The *Volkssturm* had guns and patriotism, but no effective strategy, training, or leaders. Their idiotic defiance had turned von Nordheim's house into a sitting duck, and Russian soldiers were approaching. Fearful of being killed, Ilse hid herself, her mother, and her two-year-old son in the cellar behind piles of old clothes and books, making sure she left military uniforms and other souvenirs of the defeated regime, for which Stalin's army was known to have unlimited appetite, conspicuously outside the front door.

The shooting soon began, and went on for one relentless hour before all fell quiet. At first Ilse thought this meant that the *Volkssturm* had been wiped out. Then it started up once more, as viciously as before. After only thirty minutes, silence intruded again.

Ilse left her child and Emmy, and crept up the stairs. There was nobody to be seen. Had they all escaped, or were they regrouping elsewhere? She kept walking up the spiral staircase. As she passed an open window, drops of blood fell through the clear spring air. Eventually she saw them, dead on the roof garden. Four dozen of them. Perhaps they thought they'd have an advantage shooting from that height.

Nearby, a mass of men was crawling over the fields, accompanied by a few tanks. Ilse fled back to the cellar, praying that they would bypass the house. Which, luckily, they did.

But she was sufficiently worried about the suicidal and out-of-control *Volkssturm* to stay put at von Nordheim's even when it was said that the battle for Berlin was over and they had surrendered. She remained in Babelsberg for another few days after the capital's fall; then, early one morning, at around 5 a.m., she walked the fifteen kilometres to Zehlendorf, leaving Emmy and her son to follow when she gave the all clear. It was 8 May, the day on which Germany would unconditionally surrender. She had no idea that within hours the war in Europe would be over.

28

Geri and Eva are shot

In Zehlendorf, all was peaceful. No shooting could be heard and the early-morning sky was deserted. My grandmother's house had been neither pillaged nor occupied. A few windows were blown out, but otherwise, like most of the area, it was undamaged. In a nearby park, hundreds of Russians had set up camp. There were Cossacks with their colourful dress, unkempt and exhausted horses, and the odd tank that kept watch at crossroads. Soldiers in celebratory mood were wandering the streets drinking and singing. It hardly seemed like the end of a world war.

Now Ilse was really frightened. Any knock on the door might spell death. She could handle a Nazi, but the Russians were more unpredictable. It was certain, though, that if you gave them what they asked for they would smell treasure and come in for more. If you refused them, they would kill you. Everyone knew that the booty they coveted wasn't just material. They wanted to rape and kill women too. Stories were emerging about three generations, from grandmothers to their pubescent granddaughters, being treated in this way.

She and Emmy, who had returned home a few days after Ilse, decided that, in the event of a knock, the older woman was to walk audibly towards the front door, while Ilse slid herself and her son under a bed, feeding him the cookies that she had baked to keep the child quiet at precisely such times. The Russians might rape Emmy, but they would be less likely to kill her than they would younger prey.

How wrong Ilse was. A week or two later she heard unusual songs from her neighbour's house, which belonged to old friends, Geri and Eva, both of them professional singers who had been Emmy's teachers. In place of *Lieder* by Schubert and Schumann, the strains of *Ochi chyornye, ochi zhguchie, Ochi strastnye I prekrasnye* and other Russian folk music could be heard. A balalaika was moving into a higher gear. Peals of male laughter and some forced female twitters drifted across the garden fence. There was stamping and clapping. Then a gunshot. But the music continued. Someone screamed. Another voice seemed to get hysterical. Two more gunshots. And there was silence.

Ilse and my grandmother froze. They bolted every lock, placed money and cigarettes near the front door in case the Russians broke in, and hid themselves and the child under beds. Retreating steps could be heard. People were speaking animatedly in the street. Then all was quiet again.

They lay under their beds until it was dark. Ilse crept out of the back of the house and into Geri and Eva's. They were both lying dead by the fireplace, together with the body of a young woman who was naked except for her bloodstained bra. The parquet reeked of vodka, and cigarette ash had been trodden into a rug. Otherwise nothing had been disturbed, except that the toilet in the downstairs bathroom was jammed full of potatoes. Ilse hurried back, leaving the bodies.

The next day there was more coming and going next door. After that, nothing stirred for several days. Something had to be done about the bodies, Ilse thought. But what? Sure that Geri and Eva's house was empty, she stole over. As she entered, she froze. A soldier was smoking a cigarette by the fireplace as he rifled through papers.

'What are you doing here?' he snarled. When Ilse heard the American English, she felt that a death sentence had just been lifted.

'I live next door. I'm an old friend of these people.'

'Go bury the bodies in the park,' he ordered her. 'Oh, and clean those potatoes out of the toilet!'

'What are they doing there?' Ilse asked.

'Don't you know?' He chuckled. 'Those Russian boys from behind the Urals, they've never seen a toilet. They think you use it to hide valuables. You push things down the pipes and that way other people can't get at them. I'll bet you there are a lot more potatoes stuffed into the piping behind the bowl.'

The American soldier surmised that the boys had tried to rape Eva and the younger woman and that the three of them had been shot when Geri attempted to protect them.

Ilse wrapped each of the corpses in a carpet and dragged them, one by one, to the park, then hurried home for a spade, and dug their graves.

A few days later, the same thing happened to other neighbours, a few doors away. They, too, had been forced to invite in some Russian soldiers, who raped a mother and shot her son, before raping her again.

At first, Ilse said, the Soviet high command seemed to tolerate and even encourage the raping, as if their troops were entitled to a spot of revenge after the horrors they had endured at the hands of the enemy. Many had survived the inconceivable brutality of battles such as Stalingrad as well as that special discipline supposedly ordered by Stalin, which I'd once been told about by a Red Army veteran on the night train from Moscow to Riga: any soldier who hesitates for a moment is shot by a comrade behind him. That was one way, he said, in which the dictator forcibly kept up their fighting spirit. Now the war was over, they were bored, weary, and consumed by hatred for the conquered nation.

But soon they were called to order and told that rape would be severely punished. At least in this part of Berlin. Eventually their liquor store was closed. A Russian officer even called on Geri and Eva's household to offer his condolences. Nobody was there, so he called next door at Ilse's. When Emmy opened the door, she feared the worst; but slowly she understood from the officer's few words of German and her smattering of Russian that he was reassuring them that Soviet order would prevail.

Ilse decided to move into Geri and Eva's empty house to protect it from another occupying force prowling the streets of Berlin: the abjectly poor and the displaced, who were sleeping rough, living off rats and other street animals, and looking for shelter as well as anything to grab and sell. Their daughter, Monika, had fled Berlin with her husband during the bombing for the relative safety of a small town in Westphalia, and without a guardian the house would certainly be looted. Ilse set up her photographic studio there with the equipment she had rescued from her old studio in the Budapesterstrasse after it suffered a direct hit, and settled into her new home with her son, leaving Emmy to keep watch next door.

29.

'I love shopping'

In July 1945 the Americans formally assumed control of Zehlendorf. The victorious powers were dividing up Berlin into zones of occupation, and now the Russian troops gradually withdrew to their own sector in east Berlin, replaced in Ilse's neighbourhood by a bunch of equally restless GIs.

Under the Americans, Ilse said, life for the locals was a lot less frightening – and a lot less comfortable. The US forces weren't prepared to live in tents in the park, relieving themselves at night in the rain-sodden mud, as the Soviets had done, while the enemy they'd vanquished luxuriated in comfortable beds.

Within days of the new regime taking over, Ilse found a note, on US Army notepaper, pinned to her front door. All Germans out! Within seventy-two hours!

Where she was supposed to go with her mother and a small child at such notice was not the victors' problem. Ilse's first idea was to live in one of the tents that the Soviets had abandoned in the nearby park. She packed a few of the lighter valuables to take with them, including some of the family silver, a candelabrum, and an ivory pen holder; and buried whatever else she could – pictures, cutlery, antique vases, porcelain, wine glasses – in the garden, wrapped in sheets. The three of them then left to claim a tent.

But the Americans were about to issue another order. My grandmother's road, the whole park, and all the streets in the surrounding area were to be cordoned off for the exclusive use of military personnel. Again, you had seventy-two hours to leave. So the trio moved on, this time to an apartment beyond the exclusion zone that belonged to friends of friends.

The next day, Ilse was out for a walk to search for other places to live, in case she was evicted again or quarrelled with her new hosts, when, pausing to read an advertisement seeking vegetables, a man tapped her on the shoulder.

She jerked around in terror.

'Do you speak any English?' asked the young American soldier. 'I need someone who can develop fifty-three rolls of film. My captain needs the photos by the day after tomorrow. Do you know anyone who can help me?'

'I can help you!' Ilse exclaimed euphorically.

'By the day after tomorrow?'

'Only if I can gain access to my house – or rather, my neighbour's house. I have the necessary equipment for developing films there. It's in the exclusion zone, so I'll need a permit.'

'That will be impossible,' the soldier answered.

'I'll do a perfect job for you. I'm a professional photographer.'

'Well, maybe we can get you a permit, but only at night,' he relented. He must have been worried about the precedent – about discipline breaking down if other Germans saw Ilse moving in and out of the zone with impunity.

Within twenty-four hours, Ilse had a permit for a single nighttime visit to her street, and only to work. She would have to develop the photos and then leave at once.

Beside herself with excitement, she returned to Geri and Eva's house as soon as night had fallen; but she couldn't resist going to see hers first. Though it was an absurd risk to take – returning to your requisitioned house was forbidden – the front door was ajar and strains of the 'Charleston' being played on the piano were leaking into the melancholy air outside.

As she approached the entrance, she passed several pieces of my grandparents' furniture that had been dumped on the pavement, stamped with the words 'US Army Property'. Ilse knocked and, without waiting for an answer, crept into what had become her almost unrecognizable living room.

'Well, hello!' came a Southern drawl from a corner. 'What do you want here?'

A young priest with, Ilse reported affectionately, the politest manner emerged from her mother's bedroom. She wasn't frightened; he hardly looked the type to lead the charge in a rape scene or even to try gentle seduction.

'Chaplain Sellars,' he announced. 'Lieutenant in the US Army.'

Ilse's relief at seeing this considerate house-sitter was tempered by the pink, purple, and yellow walls and the clunky furniture that filled the place. The priest was charming, but his taste in interior decoration was awful. The place looked like a dilapidated bordello.

'My furniture?' she enquired. 'I know I'm not really allowed in here, but I did get a permit to return.' And she told him about the encounter with the soldier.

'I'm so sorry,' he interrupted, 'I just don't like all that wood. Your furniture is out on the street.'

'I saw – can we put it in the garage? To protect it from rain and theft?'

'Sure, ma'am. There's more in the back garden.'

The back garden! Of course, she had buried those heirlooms there, and in the park. Hopefully they wouldn't discover those.

'As you know, ma'am, we can't return the furniture to you,' Sellars added, concerned that he might have given Ilse the impression that it was still hers.

'But you don't want it anyway,' she pleaded.

'Ma'am, we aren't allowed to give requisitioned property back to Germans.'

'But we aren't really German.'

He looked puzzled.

'My father was Jewish; he was persecuted,' Ilse stammered. (As Ilse tells me this story, I realize it is one of the very few times she has ever spoken to me of such things.)

'Are there Jews left here?' the priest asked, surprised.

'Of course there are! Especially mixtures, you know.'

'How about the photos?' Sellars added. 'You've only got a few hours.'

'Yes, the photos! The equipment is all at our neighbours' house, next door.'

He couldn't hide his disappointment that she had to go.

'You used to play this piano?' he asked. 'Next time you're here to develop photos, it'd be nice if you'd play something for me.' It seemed like the rules allowed him to engage her to entertain him, provided this was categorized as a service and not as friendly contact.

Ilse shrugged. 'I can't play very well.'

'I love shopping,' Sellars said. 'In fact, I'm a shopping addict.'

'Shopping?'

'Yeah, that guy who wrote all those lilting mazurkas and waltzes. You say you play the piano and you don't know shopping!'

It took a moment for the penny to drop. 'Oh, you mean Chopin!' she exclaimed. 'Far too hard. No, I can't play Chopin for you.'

As she developed the fifty-three rolls of film, she found herself dwelling on this charmer of a priest. *I wonder if he's Catholic or Protestant?* she mused to herself. *He must be Catholic,* she decided.

30

Ilse's Nazi flag business

The soldier was so delighted with Ilse's work that he commissioned her not only to develop more films but also to photograph American troops within the exclusion zone. Soon she had a thriving business and was being paid in exotic fruit like oranges and bananas, as well as in coal, wood, and coffee, and sometimes a packet of cigarettes that she could sell on the black market. She shared these bounties with her friends, paid her rent with them, and quickly became one of the most sought-after tenants on the edge of the zone.

Then she had her big idea. The Americans kept asking where they could find souvenirs of the defeated regime. Nazi flags, helmets, boots, Wehrmacht uniforms, and – fetching a premium price – SS knick-knacks. Ilse put the word out among her contacts. Within weeks she was inundated with memorabilia. Of course, there were lots of fakes among them. One man turned up with what he claimed was Hitler's personal telephone, which he had retrieved from the bunker where the Führer had committed suicide with Eva Braun. The story was improbable, as the Soviets, who had got to the bunker first, wouldn't have missed a trophy as good as Hitler's telephone. But, back in Kansas or Utah, who would know? Nobody was asking for authentication anyway. The telephone from which Hitler had supposedly dispatched his ever-loonier orders for the last stand in Berlin fetched good money.

Demand was far outstripping supply, even after Ilse stopped weeding out the worst fakes. But the gory stuff, which was the most profitable, was hard to come by and even harder to manufacture. Sewing one of those fearsome black SS jackets was a big job. Ilse tried etching the SS motto '*Meine Ehre heißt Treue!*' – 'My honour is called loyalty!' – into knives and daggers she picked up in ruined buildings or from friends who'd been in the army, but it didn't look right. Then she realized that the symbol most obviously identified with this bizarre regime that had boasted it would rule over a racially purified world for a thousand years was the Nazi flag. So she found first one tailor, then two, then a whole production line of them, and ordered them to make Nazi flags.

'But we have no material!' was their obvious protest.

'I have material,' Ilse replied. 'My street, our whole area, was occupied by the Soviets and there are flags with the hammer and sickle everywhere. In the centre of Berlin, near the Reichstag, if you look into cellars and storerooms you will also find Soviet flags – thousands of them.'

It was a superb business model. There was a limited supply of Nazi memorabilia. The Soviets had hauled a lot of it off when they looted the ministries and homes of Hitler and his henchmen. But there was a practically limitless supply of red flags, as Stalin had ordered his troops to flood the defeated capital with them, to rub in his heroic victory. The flags were already cut to size and attached to wooden staffs. All that remained was to find the dyes to turn them into Nazi flags. Geri and Eva's house, which Ilse had occupied with her photographic equipment, now became a centre of operations for a lucrative business.

In return, the Americans gave her not just any food and cigarettes, but rarities like liver pâté and Marlboros, as well as nylon socks and good coats. Some of this she bartered for fresh meat and vegetables, with which she fed her family and a dozen friends. She herself hadn't eaten better or enjoyed classier cigarettes for a long time.

31

Chaplain Sellars

Ilse's nocturnal permits to visit her studio in Geri and Eva's house were eventually replaced by day passes, and then, as restrictions on Germans were eased, she was allowed to return home.

Well, not home, because Chaplain Sellars was still occupying my grandmother's house, now with another US army chaplain. Home had to be at Geri and Eva's, next door, where she lived for over a year, until early 1947, when Monika returned with her husband and their young daughter from Westphalia, to where they had fled as the endgame approached in Berlin.

There had been a buzz between Ilse and Sellars from the moment they met. Though Sellars knew that he wasn't allowed to give back my grandmother's furniture, one night he whispered to Ilse from across the garden fence that he wouldn't object if she removed everything from the garage. Anyway, she could always pay him in Nazi flags if necessary; then the transfer would be a sale, not a restitution. Or, better still, she could replace the furniture with old beds and chests of drawers that she might find elsewhere, so that it wouldn't look as if hers had been returned. With the Marlboros she'd earned, she could buy a lot of used furniture.

Ilse's friendship with Sellars deepened. They couldn't be seen going in and out of each other's houses, but they could simultaneously have dinner in their adjoining gardens. He shared things with her that she couldn't find on the black market – things like canned spam and whisky. She cooked with his ingredients and passed the dishes back across the fence. And Sellars was very kind to her son, whose father, Harald Böhmelt, had broken up with Ilse after she'd refused to marry him, and now lived in another German city. Sellars took the boy on excursions to nearby lakes in the Americans' big military vehicles and to parties for the GIs' kids. Most importantly, he got Ilse fresh commissions to photograph the troops.

It was more work than she could manage, at least with the equipment she'd rescued from her atelier in the Budapesterstrasse. She had left the best behind; it was too heavy to carry and hopefully it would be too heavy for the city's looters. So Ilse did what few Germans could have done: she convinced Sellars to take the risk of persuading some GIs to fetch for her whatever they could load onto a US Army truck.

Soon her surviving cameras and dark-room tools were set up in Geri and Eva's house. Sellars also put her in touch with the buyers at one of the special shops for American soldiers – the so-called 'PX shops'. It was a privilege for a German to supply one of those shops. You didn't only get an income and the occasional goodie; you were also recognized as an insider. And this earned you the trust to be allowed to move more freely around the city. As well as a little envy from less fortunate Germans.

One of them, whom I met in Zehlendorf in 2006, remembered Ilse from those far-off days. 'Ilse was smarter than the rest of us. She looked better-fed. She was a Big Fish. She had contacts with the Americans. High-up ones.'

'How did you know about her contacts with the Americans?' I asked her, as we sat drinking tea, almost exactly sixty years later.

'I worked as a cashier in the PX shop where she used to bring her stuff to sell,' the woman replied. 'The quality of the things she brought for the GIs kept getting better. You could tell that she was popular – with both her sellers and her buyers. She seemed particularly well in with one American, a priest.'

'Oh really?'

'Yes, one evening as I was walking home after work, I passed a house and saw Ilse standing by the front door, chatting with a pastor with a dog collar. *This woman looks so much more relaxed and healthy than the rest of us*, I thought. Then I said to myself: *But that's the same woman who sells things to our shop. This must be her house. Or else the priest is her boyfriend!'*

By 1955, the house was no longer pink, nor did the inside look like a dilapidated bordello. The American Army paid for it to be redecorated before finally returning it to my family, a decade after Chaplain Sellars had moved in.

32

Ilse in the parsonage

If you had survived the war as a Jew or half-Jew in Germany, and you *still* didn't want to be saddled with that heritage, you either had to keep remembering to forget who you were, or you had to escape to a place like America or Britain where the word 'Jew' didn't trigger in your fellow citizens the insolubly complex feelings, the almost physical shock, that history has ensured it so often does in post-war Germany.

As I see it, Ilse had always been masterful at forgetting herself. But since there was no longer an enemy out there with jackboots and Final Solutions, she now had to be the pursuer as well as the pursued. With the Nazis gone, she had to flee from her Jewishness all the more decisively. Abandoning her professional photography in 1948 in order to live with two priests in a Catholic parsonage might have been part of that flight.

By then she had another reason to want to leave her old life in Berlin. Her Elysian relations with the US Army, her access to products to sell to the PX shop, and the dinners across the garden fence with Chaplain Sellars were threatened by the atmosphere of emergency in the city. It was rumoured that Stalin wanted the Western-held sectors for the Soviet Union, and that he was going to blockade them into submission. As a result, the Americans were now on high alert and there was a run on food and fuel.

The parsonage where she found a job as housekeeper was in the northern port city of Kiel, and it boasted lavish parties and excellent food. Ilse was its only live-in woman and quickly attracted the attention of the senior priest, Pastor Rudolf, a larger-than-life gourmet, wine-lover, and womanizer, who filled his salon with musicians and writers. As it happened, this flirtatious Epicurean in a cassock was known to our family already, having met Ursel while she was still engaged at the theatre in Bremen. His seduction ritual, she reported, was charming, witty, and almost irresistible.

For the most part, Rudolf's brand of Catholicism suited Ilse well. Despite Germany's social chaos after the war, people still had time to frown on single mothers and their 'illegitimate' children; and in this Catholic refuge Ilse found unquestioning acceptance of her position. As important, she also found in Rudolf a mentor for her Catholicism, which had become ever more ardent during the course of the war.

Ironically, this ardour might have made her a single mother. When, in late 1941, she discovered that she was pregnant by Harald Böhmelt, and Harald hoped this would finally force her to agree to marry him, she declined in advance. This wasn't because of his membership of the Nazi Party, or because she feared having to produce Aryan credentials at a wedding ceremony; rather, she demanded, as a condition of marriage, that he, a Protestant, commit to raising their child a Catholic. When he refused, pleading for the child to be given a choice at thirteen, Ilse abandoned their relationship. That and not the Nazi race laws, it was said by some in the family, was the real reason why she never married him, even after the war.

Or was it? There was also the fact that Harald had fathered a second child with someone else at around the time that he made Ilse pregnant. A daughter was born to this other woman in 1942, a few weeks after Ilse gave birth to her son. At last, it seemed, the real reason for Ilse not marrying Harald had come to light.

Or – again – had it? Ilse seemed happier without a man about the house; Catholic priests, who were forbidden to marry, suited her better than a husband. Ursel insisted that Pastor Rudolf and her sister had enjoyed a steady relationship, but my mother doubted that was what happened. It is true that she was close to him and would also later go on holidays with his handsome deputy; but though both priests became her confidantes and friends, that, my mother felt, was where Ilse would have wanted it to stop.

Whatever happened in the parsonage, the reality is that, apart from the four priests – the two Americans in Berlin and the two Germans with whom she lived in Kiel – this sensitive, generous, and loving woman was not known to have had any intimate relationship with a peer between 1942 and her death in 1986.

33

The Jewish altar server

The Nazis were history. In Germany, Jews were safe. In Britain, Germans had long ceased to be 'enemy aliens'. Yet, even before I was born, my parents were quarrelling over my identity.

The only thing they agreed on was that I was to be raised neither as a German nor as a Jew. Speaking German to me or giving me any form of Jewish education were therefore out of the question. It also went without saying, but was repeatedly said, that I was under no circumstances to think of myself as British. Though I would be born, raised, and educated in Britain and have English as my mother tongue, to regard myself as British would be a 'betrayal' of who I was – whoever that might be.

The big question was whether I should be raised a Catholic. My mother said yes. My father said no. Though he came from a line of devout Bible scholars, he had no detectable attachment to the Jewish faith and kept none of its festivals. But he had abysmal memories of Catholics in his native Rhineland, of being chased down alleyways by Jew-baiting classmates, and of the standard-issue taunting about his family's sacrilegious thirst for the blood of Christian babies.

Besides, he thought he had made a big enough concession to Catholicism already: he had reluctantly agreed to my mother's demand to marry in a Catholic church, and, to that end, had undergone investigations by clergy uneasy about marrying her to a divorced Jew.

It wasn't the Jewish bit that concerned the Church; it was the divorce from his first wife, Hilde. My parents were astonished to learn that the Catholic Church regarded even the divorce of two non-Catholics, whom it didn't marry, as illegitimate. Any marriage, they were told, is a binding decision in the eyes of God, whether or not the parties to it believe He exists; and so an atheist or a Jewish or a Buddhist marriage may no more be undone than a Catholic one.

It seemed like an impasse – until my father had an inspired idea. He was Hilde's second husband; she had been briefly married to a German she had met while holidaying on the Spanish Riviera. The Church had to be consistent about its doctrine. If he had married a divorced woman, *his* marriage was surely illegitimate in its eyes. Which meant that he was still technically a bachelor!

He had barely seen Hilde in the years since she had abandoned him and their two sons and returned to her native Switzerland, but now it was time she did something for him. He needed her first marriage certificate. He would show that to the Church and it would realize that he was not, after all, a divorced man.

Hilde was delighted to help. If he married my mother he would no longer be the forlorn ex-husband, pestering her to return. Even better, their sons' upbringing could be subcontracted to a step-mother. And the Church duly accepted him as an unmarried man who was taking a wife for the first time.

Oddly, my mother and father wanted to marry in Germany, though at that time they still professed to despise it. They settled on a church near Freiburg, recommended by Dr Gertrud Luckner, an old childhood friend of my father who had saved hundreds of Jews during the war, been captured on a train in 1943 as she tried to smuggle money to those left in Berlin, and survived incarceration in Ravensbrück concentration camp.

Luckner was the one person who could persuade my father that there was another sort of Catholicism, one that turned its back on anti-Semitism not because the times now demanded it do so, but out of moral and theological conviction. She was the only witness at their marriage.

* * *

My parents' quarrel over my religious identity was eventually resolved in a deal: I was to be raised without religion until the age of thirteen. Then I could choose what I wished to be.

The deal had one proviso. Both religions demanded a rite of initiation soon after birth. The Catholics had baptism, without which I would have no guarantee of salvation if I should die in infancy. And the Jews had circumcision, which got more painful the longer you waited. So I was both baptized and circumcised – in the same week. A priest officiated in the one case and a rabbi in the other.

Though I would occasionally be allowed to 'keep Mummy company' at Mass while my father prepared our Sunday lunch, the deal was essentially respected until his death – after which it was immediately abandoned.

I was then brought up a pious Catholic, going to Mass every Sunday, receiving weekly religious instruction, having my first Communion, and enjoying outings with the kindly friars at our local church-cum-priory.

At the age of eight or nine, I struck up a friendship with one of these friars, Brother Albert, who was invariably waiting for me after Mass with a bar of chocolate that he had secreted inside his robes. I would dash to the back of the church, where he was chatting to departing parishioners, and fish around for the piece of kindness that I knew he hadn't forgotten.

I wondered what a friar's body looked like beneath all that protection. It would surely be hairless and lacking a penis, with the smooth patina of ivory or marble that had somehow softened into flesh, like the statue in Ovid's *Metamorphoses* that Venus transforms into a living woman. It would also be of mixed gender or none, as well as uniformly gentle in all its nooks, as if cruelty had departed him of its own accord, without having to be brought under control.

Sometimes, on a Saturday, Brother Albert took me to a nearby cafe, where he ordered a cup of tea and poured so much milk into it that it turned an iridescent shade of beige. How could he enjoy it? Was he so unspoiled by sensuality, or were his appetites so useless to him, that he could still taste the delicious tartness of tea leaves through all the beigeness? He would buy me a plain Danish and chuckled when I asked if I might indulge in a cream cake instead.

My gastronomic venality seemed charming to him, though he seldom joined in. When he did, he remained impassive, and the mildness that usually leaves a face when it is in the throes of joy at a cream cake never left his.

It was bliss to be the focus of Brother Albert's solicitude and to know that it could shine even outside his church. But these occasions were also awkward, as, alone with him, he and the mysterious piety of the priests, who were by turns severe and benign, would feel alien – a universe away from the microcosm of our German-Jewish home – and a frisson of fear would course through me.

One day Brother Albert suggested that I might like to become an altar server, a vote of confidence in my person that thrilled me.

'Come and see me in the sacristy before Low Mass next Sunday,' he told me.

Low Mass was a short affair, with little music, a bullet-point sermon, and a small attendance that seemed exclusive and intimate.

Father Paul was going to take it. He was businesslike, with the air of an accountant in holy vestments. I recognized him from the confessional, where, despite its darkness, I could identify the priest on the other side of the grille from his profile or his voice or both. And this unspoken intimacy we had on account of his knowing and forgiving my sins – those I had genuinely committed as well as those that I had invented – made my forthcoming debut as an altar server less intimidating.

Brother Albert kitted me out in a cassock of my own and told me what to do when. It was particularly important to remember to ring the bells before the priest consecrated the bread and the wine, and never to lose any crumbs from the plate bearing the Communion wafers, as, after their consecration, they were the body of Christ.

As I left the sacristy following my induction, I took a handful of unconsecrated wafers from a pile that I saw stacked on a golden plate, and stuffed them into my mouth.

Brother Albert erupted in anger.

I was mortified. Less at having eaten Christ's potential body several times over than at being shouted at by a friar whose only weapon, I had imagined, was benevolence. But my attempt to apologize got stuck on a first grunted syllable: the wafers lost their crispness on contact with saliva, and their glutinous mass was sticking my tongue to my palate.

I never lost my fascination with those Communion wafers. How extraordinary that unlimited numbers of them could become Christ's body in a trice; and that the miseries of the world might be redeemed merely by swallowing them with due piety. My favourite task as an altar server soon became to hold the golden plate under each congregant's chin as they received Communion. Brother Albert had explained to me that it wasn't easy: since I would stand to one side of the priest, I needed to take care neither to touch the worshipper's chin with the plate, nor to hold it at an angle at which crumbs of Christ's body could fall off.

But what came to intrigue me most were the congregants' expressions. Each one was so different, and so was each tongue. Some tongues were grainy, others were smooth; some glistened, others were oddly matt; some had pointed ends and others were almost semi-circular. Most exciting of all was my mother's. I hoped that, if I studied it in its sufferingly outstretched, receptive position, it would disclose the secret of who she was beneath her truculent, brilliant, coping self, vehemently dedicated to her twin religions of music and Catholicism. And so, perhaps, it would also disclose the secret of who *I* was – and might become.

34

The promised land of Switzerland

There was a type of despair peculiar to the German Jew of my grandparents' and parents' generations that I am convinced had struck deep roots long before Hitler. In the case of the three sisters, fervent devotion to German music and later on to Catholicism was undoubtedly experienced as redemption from that despair: as ways of channelling its formidable energies towards what they took to be sublime ends of ultimate meaning and value.

But such devotion didn't just redeem despair. The exhaustion it brought about also intensified the despair it was aimed at alleviating. And, for all the riches it imported into one's inner world, the way it shut out the rest of life also left a space there that was barren and haunted.

So what was at the root of this unpacifiable spirit of gravity, which had so captured my mother, Ilse, and Ursel – and by which I, besieged by it as I was growing up, felt at once inspired and oppressed? It didn't, I think, have obvious causes. It wasn't merely the result of anti-Semitism, or of unrequited love for Germany. Nor was it a product of the suffering intrinsic to life, to which all three sisters were unusually sensitive. It couldn't be alleviated by fleeing to a place of safety. It was strangely unnameable and therefore intractable.

If I can say anything about it, it is this. There is a pain that can be worse than being rejected or hated: the pain of being unable to feel wholly at one with what we most love. The insoluble dilemma of many highly assimilated German Jews was to have found, in Germany, a culture that became the supreme source of meaning for them, yet which had dimensions of inwardness – such as a romanticism that was at once cold and voluptuous, sentimentally pessimistic and morbidly optimistic – that they found alien. As a result, this German world, which flowed in their veins and which some German Jews mastered to the point of becoming its unsurpassed exponents and creators, *also* seemed insuperably foreign and unreal. And to that extent life, which, for them, could thrive only in and through this world, came to seem insuperably foreign and unreal.

I have often encountered Jews of my parents' and grandparents' generations from, say, Poland or Ukraine, and, though they might be broken in other ways, they seldom displayed this particular despair – which would be instantly obvious in many a refugee from Berlin who had escaped in good time with her family and possessions. The Polish or Ukrainian Jew, however profoundly she loved and embodied and reimagined the culture of her country of origin, still had the memory of expulsion written into her DNA and, to that degree, at least, still felt an outsider. Whereas the assimilated German Jew's joy and torment was that she felt that in Germany she had found her only possible spiritual home, even if she suffered social exclusion; yet this home that felt so indispensable also retained an unassimilable, even repellent, element.

There was one infallible antidote to this despair. The Alps, and specifically the German-Swiss Alps. Here, a deep calm took hold of the émigré German Jew's soul, which briefly stood still and was filled with happiness – and with wonder that such calm was possible.

It began as soon as we crossed into the Promised Land of Switzerland, usually by car. In those moments of transition we felt like hostages who had walked through a magic curtain into another realm where, incredibly, we could be wholly at ease.

What was this narcotic that German Switzerland offered? It wasn't the order, balm to the soul though that was. It wasn't the safety, though that too was blissful. For order and safety could also be found in the French and Italian parts of Switzerland, or in Scandinavia, or in Japan. It was the Alps; but only the German-speaking Alps. The French-Swiss mountains might be as beautiful, but, to us, they didn't speak the same language; the Austrian were complicit in the menace of an unresolved Nazi past; and the French and Italian were positively alien. Only in the German-Swiss alpine world could we inhabit beloved depths of the German spirit without being in Germany. Only here could we step on land that felt hospitable to all the greatness of Germany, while being unburdened by all the evil. Only here could we be free.

Deluded it might have been, but so great was the redemptive hope that we invested in these Alps, so great was our need for them, that we made the pilgrimage at least twice a year. Each time, without exception, the journey from the Swiss border was a progression of euphoria, as the foothills first came into view, and beyond them ever steeper slopes, and then in the distance the first, ecstatic sightings of snow-capped peaks, until we were winding our way upwards, past the gushing of brooks and the serenity of glacier-blue lakes, along routes flanked by pine trees with healthy lichen caressing their trunks. Climbing higher and higher, we finally reached our destination and stepped out of the car and took our first breath of bracing air; and Mother would quote Ernst and Emmy, who had loved this journey in the same way, and exclaim, '*Ach Kinder, die Luft! Atmet!*' : 'Oh children, the air! Breathe!' And my brother and I would inhale noisily and deeply and repeat in unison, half mocking our mother's reverent, ecstatic tone but knowing that we meant it no less earnestly: '*Ach Kinder, die Luft!*'

Here, too, memory was unchained and truth could be spoken. Ursel's enactment of my father's death would have been far more upsetting in London than it had been in the little kitchen in Gsteig. In this landscape, we felt held and protected, rather than compelled to construct the ground on which we trod. Our souls no longer squinted, to paraphrase Nietzsche. Mother seemed less reliant on Catholicism, less strenuously pious in general. Music was made more freely, emancipated from the task of providing either release from earthly suffering or a source of value so vast that it could dwarf all fear, especially of an anchorless world. There was no need for such strenuous faith, for we were in a place where nothing could be destroyed. However vast human rage, it seemed impotent beneath these eternal peaks, which stood guard over those who loved them but were otherwise blissfully indifferent to mortals – never having us in their sights.

We also noticed that those who were not of German-speaking descent didn't seem to have the same relation to the Alps. They, too, might relish the peace and order of Switzerland, or the hiking, the skiing, and the air. But there was no metaphysics in it, or at least not in the same, urgent way. The idea that this mystical terrain was the *only* true home in the world would have been, to most of them, incomprehensible and absurd.

Around the time my brother and I hit puberty, my mother decided to switch from Gsteig, with its gentle pastures, to the altogether more challenging atmosphere of Sils Maria, which lies at six thousand rather than four thousand feet, and is surrounded by vegetation and valleys and lakes that somehow seem to pose questions of life and death at every turn.

Here, in our hotel, there were no Anglophones except the heavily accented German and Austrian refugees, their children and their children's children. I still remember some of the names: Lotte Hammerschlag-Bamberger, from New York; Lilo Kantorowicz-Glick, who had been a student of Max Rostal in Berlin together with my mother and had then lived with her in the same unheated room in London, repelling the same stream of suitors, before moving on to America; Walter Herz, from Brussels, who, we discovered one evening, had been a near neighbour of my father in Cologne. And when we were all clustered after dinner in the salon of the hotel, where the three of us shared a room, I was seized by the fantasy that this is how life might have tasted had we remained in the country of our ancestors.

There were some non-Jewish Germans there as well. The excitement as well as the trepidation of sharing these holidays with them was bracing. In a small room off that salon, we children would escape our parents' vehement opinions and reminiscences to play with the slot machines without limit by reusing a coin suspended from a piece of string, just as my mother had tried to get free heating from the stove of her freezing bedsit back in the 1930s. There, my brother and I met two German sisters of about our age, twelve and thirteen, a lot less awkward than we were and with picture-perfect blonde hair. One evening, we got them to sit on our laps, and it was thrilling to be close to such lovely forbiddenness, to communicate in our few words of German, and to anticipate the moment when we would kiss, which never happened. I still remember the delicious weight of the older sister on my lap and the tenderness of her cheek as it accidentally, or not, met my own. And I remember a thrilling but nonetheless deeply embarrassing stirring in my pants, which I very slightly shifted her away from, hoping that she hadn't noticed but also hoping she had and was as thrilled and embarrassed as I was about it, and that it might lead to deeper intimacies.

And it was almost as exciting – and profoundly liberating – that there was no talk of Germans and Jews, and to imagine that perhaps they'd never heard of Auschwitz and could relate to us in a fresh, unburdened way. Until the evening when our mother walked in to tell us that playtime was up and threw a furious glance at the girls encircled by our desirous arms, and then at our sheepish faces, and afterwards, up in our bedroom, told us this was unacceptable. We didn't know the ancestry of that family; we didn't know what the grandparents had done; this mustn't happen again. We had managed to get their phone number, but we were bereft and humiliated and never called them.

In this way, for a few treasured weeks each year, the golden rule that the refugee must never arrive was suspended – only to snap back the night before we left, when, after the last dinner, suitcases would be packed with pained reluctance, far less carefully than on the way out. And every time we were about to drive out of Switzerland, my mother would say the same thing when we reached that place in Basel, not far from the frontier, where the ways part: Germany in one direction, France in the other – and, beyond France,

England and then America. 'You cannot imagine,' she would tell us, 'how unnatural it is to be heading away from Germany.'

And every time her feeling would find a precise echo within me. It was unnatural but right. We were, we told ourselves, trading home for liberty.

35.

Central Europe in London

The world of Jewish émigré London could not have been more different to my upbringing as a non-Jewish, non-German, non-British Catholic. On Sundays, after church, we would do the rounds.

It was the 1970s, but it felt like gatecrashing Jewish central Europe in the 1920s. English was hardly spoken in these homes, or appeared only as an interloper in sentences that began and ended in German and occasionally in Czech, Romanian, Hungarian, Russian, or Polish.

The immigrants hung a defiant 'thou shalt not' over us, their British-born children, which said: 'You shall never leave the world that your ancestors loved.' But, of course, we *couldn't* leave their world; we didn't know how to and were terrified of trying lest we fall into an abyss of total unbelonging. How could we possibly say goodbye to all that treasure, to all those people, and to all those memories?

The overriding challenge we faced wasn't how to assimilate to the culture of our British hosts; it was how to build a life in a German-Jewish world that, beyond its powerful presence within our homes, had long ceased to exist.

No matter how vertiginously the German-Jewish émigrés climbed the ladders of British society, or how successfully they adopted British manners and mannerisms, none that I knew ever felt they had succeeded – or wanted to succeed – in becoming British in

their innermost sensibility. Unable and unwilling to have one foot
in each world, they remained, until their deaths, German Jews
transplanted into an alien land.

At the same time, they were fervent British patriots, however
bemused by British ways: ferociously loyal to a country to which
they felt they didn't culturally belong. The German émigrés, in awe
of Anglo-Saxon tolerance and the rule of law, were perhaps the most
overtly patriotic of all the central-European refugees. They would
rigorously refer to 'we' and 'us' when speaking of their adopted
country and were so much more diligent than the natives about
fixing 'GB' bumper stickers to their cars that, it was said, a car with
those letters almost certainly identified its owner as German-Born.

This patriotism had a source more resilient than any official inte-
gration initiative or citizenship ceremony: gratitude. For all the
hardships of arrival, when they had been designated 'enemy aliens'
and refused permission to work, and for all their sense of not
belonging and even of not wanting to belong, this gratitude for the
sanctuary and opportunities they had been given remained impregnable. I remember my mother's exclamation when she was
automatically awarded a state pension on turning sixty. 'You mean,'
she protested, 'that they saved my life, and now they want to pay
me as well!'

Our first stop on those magical Sunday-afternoon tours of refugee
north London was the home of Adela Kotowska, a pianist who had
been a child prodigy in Lwów, then in Poland, and her husband
Efraim Sznajderman, known as Felix Vandyl, a native of Warsaw.

Adela's teas were uninhibited cholesterol fests: the table at the
centre of the all-green kitchen – the walls were painted bright pea
green, the shelves of the cupboards were lined with shiny green
paper, the table cloth was green, and her apron was green – was
laden with toasted smoked-salmon sandwiches, cholla with chopped
liver, cheese blintzes, two and often more large cakes, and a canister
for spraying whipped cream onto anything one wished. In the adjacent living room, various musicians would be chatting.

Norbert Brainin, a violinist who posed severe competition for the most fattening parts of Adela's teas and who, she claimed, had been deflowered by my mother under her piano as German bombs dropped on London, was a regular. So, too, was Władysław Szpilman, a Polish pianist who had been a close friend of Felix since their youth and whose memoir of surviving the Warsaw Ghetto, thanks to an SS officer who spared his life because he enjoyed his piano playing, was later made into a film, *The Pianist*. Unlike Brainin, Szpilman did little damage to the food, was private and reticent, and never, as far as I can remember, played for us. He would sit in a big armchair smoking his pipe, offering occasional comments in his mischievously sad voice, and protecting himself with a bone-dry sense of humour and staccato sentences that gave little away. He would abruptly get up and retire to his bedroom – he generally stayed with Felix and Adela on concert tours of the UK with his Warsaw Quintet – and not emerge again. It wasn't that he was reluctant to talk of his wartime experiences. On the contrary, he would talk freely about all that, if you asked him about it. As I remember, his map of Warsaw was organized around his most horrific memories. 'The best bread shop in the city – it's still around the corner from the local SS headquarters'; or, 'The new junior school – right on the spot where they shot thirty Jews before my eyes.'

Though the Nazis had murdered all eight of her siblings, Adela loved Germany. After the war, she even thought of returning. Her formative years had been in Berlin, from 1928 to 1936, studying composition with Paul Hindemith at the Hochschule für Musik and earning a living accompanying the students of Carl Flesch. In Flesch's classes, first in Berlin and then in exile, she had played with many of the great violinists of the twentieth century, among them Ida Haendel, a fellow child prodigy from Poland, and Josef Hassid, whom she regarded as the supreme talent of them all, but who she said had played his last concert at twenty-one and died in a British asylum for the insane after being lobotomized at twenty-six.

'I am more German than Polish, perhaps because we were for so long part of Austria-Hungary,' Adela would say of her home town,

Lwów. 'We, at least my family, were never just Polish. We were à
la Polonaise.'

It seemed that, for her, Poland was associated with a rejection that
she had never experienced in Germany. It was harrowing to hear her
stories of the anti-Semitic rampages she had witnessed as a child – the
night sky illuminated by the blazing Jewish village that thugs had pillaged
and set alight; the bestial hatred that overcame ordinary, decent people,
who were kind to their neighbours and polite to shop assistants, but
wanted to murder when they heard the word 'Jew'. And in the next
breath: 'You know, Lwów was called *Klein Wien* – Little Vienna. It
smelled and felt like Vienna. I was forced to come to England by Flesch.
If he hadn't emigrated, I would have stayed in Berlin.'

Stayed?

It wasn't so bad in the first two or three years of the Nazi regime,
Adela insisted. Jews couldn't work in the state-owned academies, but
they could do private work – cabarets, accompanying silent films,
playing in clubs and revue bars. She maintained that she'd never heard
an anti-Semitic remark in those places. Goebbels even used to come
to one of the clubs. Once or twice he tried to flirt with her. He was
an ungainly, ugly man, she said. Disgusting. 'But Hitler – he had
charisma.' One day, she arrived at a local station somewhere near
Berlin, and there was this huge commotion; and it was because Hitler's
train was going to stop there on its way through. She was in the
women's toilet when she heard that. The attendant in the toilet wanted
to talk to her, though she seemed to sense that Adela wasn't German.
She couldn't control her euphoria. 'He is our hero, he is a great and
good man, and he will save Germany,' Adela reported her as saying.
While the attendant was still swooning, the train pulled into the
station. 'We both rushed up the stone steps to the platform,' Adela
said. 'The toilet attendant held my hand for support; she was a little
older and besides she was breathless at the arrival of the Führer. The
atmosphere up there on the platform was unbelievable. It was a
mixture of carnival and reverence – as if the Messiah had been
announced. And then he peeked out of the railway carriage. Just for
a moment. He peeked out of the window. His eyes twinkled severely.
He waved. A moment later, he withdrew into the darkness of the
train. And then he was gone.

'The toilet attendant was still holding onto my hand, almost gripping it. As the train withdrew out of sight, she turned to me, still in her reverie, and said: "He is so tall in reality! I never knew he was so tall. Like a knight!" And I said to her, laughing, "How could you see how tall he is? You could only see his head leaning out of the window! Actually, he's quite short!" She stared at me blankly. I don't think she even heard what I was saying.'

After we had eaten our fill of Adela's tea, there would be music. It took some effort; the vast quantities of sugar had made everybody restless and a little confused, but one after another the guests would play. Usually Adela could be persuaded to toss off a few nocturnes, waltzes, or polonaises by Chopin. She did this reluctantly, but once dragged from the kitchen, where she was constantly resupplying the tea table, to the piano, still in her green apron, she would become absorbed into this world of which she was a master exponent — until she abruptly had enough. 'That is all you will get for today,' she would announce as she shut the piano lid with theatrical finality. Or: 'This is no good at all. I never practise. Now, one of you, come on, take out your instrument and play!'

Everyone looked lazily around them, hoping that somebody else would volunteer.

At this point, Brainin might dash off a movement of the Beethoven violin concerto, with Adela, back at the piano, playing the orchestral part, or jokingly imitate one of the great virtuosi and their mannerisms: Jascha Heifetz with his poker face, his teacher Max Rostal with his twitching nose and glaring eyes, Carl Flesch with his Buddha-like stateliness. Or Felix, who had been a professional violinist before he started dealing in old musical instruments, would ponder out loud what he was going to perform and which of the magnificent violins that he kept suspended from coat hooks in a wardrobe was best suited to the music in question; and he would move us all with the powerful Hassidic passion of his playing.

'OK, Karl, now it's your turn!' And Adela would summon Karl Wongtschowski, a retired orthodontist born in Berlin. Karl was a passionate amateur violinist whose life spanned three centuries: he was born in 1898 and he died in 2001. Though his orthodontic practice had flourished and he had successfully embarked on a new career as a psychotherapist in his late seventies, his first and greatest love was music. Two or three times a week, whatever the weather, he would go by bus to a concert – until the age of 101, when his girlfriend and musical companion, Lotte Herzfelder, died. He studied musical scores – of which he had an enormous collection that I was privileged to inherit – with ferocious diligence, often in the rain at bus stops; one did not go to hear something performed, he insisted, without acquainting oneself with the score beforehand. Back in the privacy of his apartment on Willesden Lane after the concert, he would play the first violin part of a string quartet or the solo of a concerto that he had just heard, to the accompaniment of a recording minus the leading part.

These electronic companions were, however, employed *faute de mieux*. He was nostalgic for the war years when he had played with refugee musicians such as Brainin. Often, he had played first violin, relegating these luminaries to second fiddle. This chutzpah worked for one reason only: money. Denied a work permit by the British government, they were grateful for income that was cash in hand and wouldn't get them arrested; whereas Karl was allowed to practise his profession without restraint. The immigration authorities had deemed dentistry a necessity, but music a luxury.

In later years, he resigned himself to playing for the only captive audience he could find: his patients. Marooned almost horizontally on his dentist's chair, they were unable to protest when he announced, in the middle of a complex procedure, that he had recently been making progress with Bach's *Chaconne* and could prove it to them. He would unpack his violin, tune it up, check that his bow hair was tight enough, and play to his charges, with closed eyes, furrowed brow, and an occasional beatific smile at a modulation that he considered he had perfectly executed.

Karl would stop precisely at the point in the score to which he had practised, put his violin tenderly back into its case, and exclaim:
'You know, I have to say it myself, I've never played that better.'
He would then explain why.

Hiding the crucifix

Every day of the school year, from my first day at six to my last at seventeen, I crossed an international border. In the morning, I departed the 1920s Germany of our home in 1960s and 70s London for the life of a country teeming with sensibilities that never ceased to feel insuperably foreign – not only because they were, but also because I felt duty-bound to regard them so.

And, each evening, I returned, never forgetting that I was a native of one and a visitor to the other – that to feel any other way would be murderously to betray my ancestors and myself.

Once home from school, there would be a strict routine. Tea and cakes were awaiting me at precisely 4 p.m. They were cleared away thirty minutes later, whether I was finished or not, after which there was piano practice for two hours before dinner, which took place at precisely 7 p.m., and was always of the utmost simplicity: bread and cheese, or else chicken rissoles or fish fingers and potato croquettes, heated up from frozen, followed by a dessert such as reconstituted crème caramel prepared by dousing a yellowish powder with boiling water. Or Mother would open a tin of ravioli, which were factory-cooked to a state of limp near-disintegration and slid, in a single cylindrical mass, into the saucepan with a gentle plop that I never ceased to find reassuring and comical.

After that diversion from more serious matters, we would usually repair to the living room to play recordings of great musicians, sometimes listening to the same composition in two or three different interpretations, after which it was obligatory to compare and contrast their respective merits. Finally, there was homework for a couple of hours before lights out.

Television was prohibited. This was at my insistence, my mother claimed, because I thought it 'a complete waste of time' – a conviction to which she stuck adamantly even when we visited her friends and I at once vanished into their television rooms for the duration of the evening.

Almost nobody who wasn't from 'our world' ever entered this sanctuary. Even professional services came straight out of *Mitteleuropa*. Our family doctor, Ernst Lucas, who had played chess with my father every Saturday, was from Cologne – and had the air of a saviour because the family of his wife, Lilly Reifenberg, had afforded my father protection and employment in one of their many businesses after he was evicted from his job at the Dresdner Bank in 1934.

The pediatrician, Kenneth Samson, from somewhere else in Germany, was a genial figure privy to the family's foibles and furies, sometimes visiting as a friend, when he was relaxed and informal, at other times calling on us in a professional capacity, when he assumed a grave demeanour and his voice descended from a baritone to a bass.

Our dentist, Walter Nuki, and his wife Gina, both from Vienna, often visited to play string quartets.

Carl Flesch Jr., son of the violinist, who first met my mother when she was a teenager in Berlin and who continued to be known as 'the young Carl Flesch' into his nineties, was the family's insurance broker.

Jupp Dernbach, a fine artist who designed our music room, was from Meyen, near Cologne.

A Dr Hell looked after our pictures. Enormously erudite, he was a restorer at the Royal Collection in Buckingham Palace as well as at the National and Tate galleries. Born in the ancient German-speaking community of Romania, he had studied and worked in Berlin before fleeing to London with his wife.

The few non-émigrés who managed to enter our fortress of the displaced were either colleagues of my mother, or else students from the Royal College of Music, where she was a professor, dropping in for a supplementary lesson.

Other intruders were schoolfriends of mine, though I didn't dare to invite anyone whom my mother would consider 'alien'. Not that asking my Jewish schoolfriends home was without its complications. For one thing, they would be startled to see crucifixes hanging over our beds. There were occasions when the difficulty of explaining our Catholicism was too excruciating for me to summon the necessary nonchalance when they caught sight of this idolatry, and I might guiltily hide my crucifix in a cupboard or under my mattress until my friend had left.

So many of my mother's fellow refugees were nominally Christian, or at least knew how common it was for German Jews to convert, that for a long time I assumed that *all* Jews were familiar with and even relaxed about conversion. I imagined, or hoped, that fellow Jews would take this bold step of my mother and grandfather in their stride – and perhaps even admire it for its open-mindedness, or, failing that, as a sign of canny self-preservation.

I couldn't have been more misguided. The astonishment verging on hostility of those my mother referred to as 'English-speaking Jews' – Jews whose ancestors had arrived in Britain or America three of four generations previously and who no longer harboured a lost European homeland – when they discovered this treachery, was overt, uncomprehending, and profoundly humiliating, throwing me into a crisis of self-presentation that often spiralled into terror.

It wasn't so much a crisis of identity, for as I entered my teens I thought I was sure in which direction my identity lay: I was a German Jew whose family history had caused me to be born and raised in England and in the Catholic faith; the core of my world was defined by the warmth and musicality of the guests at Adela Kotowska's Sunday teas; and its elaboration in contemporary terms would be vouchsafed by science, philosophy, and submersion in 'Europe'. But how was I to explain this to those Jews who saw our fudged identity as a vile combination of cowardice and betrayal? In fact, the latter numbered not a few German Jews, despite the myth promulgated by my mother that they were infinitely understanding on this question.

One of these German Jews was the father of Samuel, whom I had met at my junior school. Friendship with the whole family blossomed after an end-of-year concert where I had played the piano in a Mozart duo with the school's violin teacher, who lost her place in the score so badly that I began to convulse with laughter, and soon no longer knew where we had reached in the music either. Cacophony ensued before we managed to recover. After this shambles had ended, a man at the back of the audience boomed, with magnificent inappropriateness, 'Funtustic! Vunderfool!' The German accent was unmistakeable. And at once, with that tribal recognition which is second nature to the immigrant, I swivelled towards the voice that so clearly issued from the heart of our universe. It belonged to my friend's father – another refugee from Berlin.

It wasn't long before we, as a family, were invited for a Friday-night dinner at Samuel's home, an evening that would turn into a nightmare.

Who were we? And how were we to explain who we were? As soon as we arrived, I realized that we were on the spot. Next to each place at the dinner table, except two – those reserved for my mother and for Samuel's – were kippas. And Jewish prayer books. We were going to have to have a 'proper' Friday evening, with singing, prayers, kiddush, the works. Since I had almost never been to one, I had no idea what to do. In fact, this was not long after I'd enrolled as an altar server at the local Catholic church.

Luckily, we had a short time before we sat down for dinner when we could talk about, to us, normal subjects like music. My friend's father was an avid amateur pianist and seemed thrilled to have discovered musicians with whom, he immediately announced, he was expecting to play. I fervently hoped that this bond might take the edge off the appalling embarrassment that was imminent. Surely, I told myself, music would decisively trump any religious or tribal heritage for our host; and so our fidelity to Beethoven would stand an excellent chance of redeeming, or at least masking or otherwise distracting from, our betrayal of Judaism. A betrayal that he and his family had not yet uncovered but inevitably would.

I sensed, though, that my hope was futile. Our pre-dinner discovery of common delight in music felt like a moment of reprieve when we could still keep secret our insolubly conflicted identity; and they could continue to assume, as I was certain they did, that a family of refugees from Hitler would be, at the least, secular Jews.

Then something terrible happened, about which I still cringe. As we sat down and the father began reading in Hebrew and his sons joined in and then they all modulated into song, out of synch with each other and grunting more than singing, I began to laugh. Uncontrollably. Loudly. I was shaking and getting redder and redder.

At first they ignored me. Perhaps because my reaction was incomprehensible; perhaps because they were absorbed in the liturgy. Presently I was thrown some perplexed glances, which became worried, then irritated.

I fought against my hilarity by imagining my father's grave and the funeral I hadn't been allowed to attend, but to no effect. I was able to stop only when the prayers were finally over and the kiddush wine was passed round – which gave me the opportunity to take a sip that I hoped would convey a sense of togetherness, and of knowing after all what I was supposed to do, and also of apology. For what pained me then, as now, is that they might have seen my laughter as mockery, though it was anything but. So I felt the greatest relief when their housekeeper, a Spanish woman, wheeled in the food, and I was able to be comforted by the familiarity of a meal. And the insoluble embarrassment of not knowing the prayers, or of how to present whoever I was, which had stoked my nervous laughter, did eventually trickle away.

Each time we visited this family, the Spanish housekeeper was so pleased to see us, not only because we loved and praised her food but also because after that first dinner I had confessed to her, in the privacy of her kitchen, that we were Catholic. It was a joy, she said, to have fellow Catholics in her home for once, especially on an intimate family occasion like a Friday evening.

Banished to the car

My mother always used to say that families where a German Jew had married a British or North American Jew were very different in atmosphere to those where both spouses were German Jews. In the first case, the two cultures could meet, even if they might struggle to converse, and the children could learn to move more easily and naturally between these vastly different worlds. She maintained, for example, that it made all the difference that Samuel's mother was English-born. He seemed to have an easier time of being a Brit.

Not that an entirely German, or Austrian, Jewish home would necessarily be any more relaxed. Dinners with Ernst and Ilse Gombrich, for example, he an art historian, she a pianist with whom my mother had played in their refugee days, were riven with tension, but for entirely different reasons. It was the need to maintain a regimen at all costs. After arriving and a few minutes of acclimatizing chat, we would sit down to listen to recordings – usually of string quartets, trios, and other chamber music. A favourite was the Hungarian Quartet, which was, by their common consent, the supreme master of the genre.

On one of those occasions, I was in the middle of revising for my high school exams and wanted to begin writing a practice essay. Soon after the first movement of Beethoven's opus 130 quartet opened, I reached for my satchel, fished out some paper with such care that not a crackle could be heard, and started making notes.

Unceremoniously, Gombrich arose from his chair, went over to the player, and stopped the music mid-phrase. He then swivelled to face me. 'One cannot both listen properly and work properly,' he announced. 'Which do you intend to do?'

I muttered something about having to revise, and promised that I would work quietly.

'It isn't a matter of noise,' he riposted impatiently. 'It is a matter of distracting those who wish to listen. And, as I said, of not being able to do both things properly. Which do you want to do?'

'I had better work,' I said. 'Shall I go to the kitchen?'

'We have dinner prepared in the kitchen and the table is laid.'

'Then I will go outside and sit in my mother's car!' I said.

'Excellent idea,' he replied. His countenance was unchanged: with his finger poised on the 'stop' button, he waited for me to leave the room. He was not going to start again until I had left.

'Be back in fifty minutes, at seven o'clock, when we are having dinner.'

I returned forty-eight minutes later. The music was over and a warm smile broke over his face as I walked into the living room.

'Did you make progress?'

'Yes, I wrote three pages.'

'Three pages! That is fantastic. *I* could never write three pages in just forty minutes.'

'Fifty minutes.'

'It doesn't matter!'

'But they were just revision,' I protested. 'Stuff I already knew. It was nothing. The things you write about are much more complicated and also they are original,' I stammered, embarrassed that my trivial homework, repeated by hundreds of thousands, millions, of schoolchildren all around the land, could be included in the same breath as his path-breaking works.

'Irrelevant!' he shot back. 'To write three pages in that time is admirable.' And he extended his paw of a hand round my shoulder and led me into the kitchen.

*   *   *

It is hard to convey how happy I was in this world filled with strict but deeply warm-hearted people of astonishing cultivation and modesty. Modest in everything except the standards to which they held themselves – and others.

Gombrich himself had written many successful books; and yet he, like us, lived in the type of small, nondescript, suburban house that my mother affectionately called a '*Hundehütte*' – a dog kennel.

Others, no less distinguished, were equally unassuming. Visits to the home of Peter Gellhorn, a conductor and pianist from Breslau, whom my mother had known since her student days in London, both romantically and professionally, and who had been chorus master at the Glyndebourne opera house and a conductor at Covent Garden, were no different. There would be a few minutes to catch up on what had happened since we all last met; cursory discussions of politics and literature; and then there was music. But with Peter it took a different form. Each time we visited, he would run through an entire opera at the piano, singing all the major parts himself – and when there were duos, trios, or quartets of singers, highlighting each leading voice sequentially.

This made for very long evenings when the opera in question was by Wagner. As it often was: he must have taken us through all ten main operas of the master, from *The Flying Dutchman* to *Parsifal*, at least twice over the years.

Peter's devotion to music was absolute. Only the best was adequate. Just as among those audiences who came to our own home for my mother's trio evenings, music was more than 'the meaning of life'; it was life itself, the voice of being, the Creator's self-revelation. One didn't need to be a professional musician; but without deep musicality no other vocation could truly live.

Along with this perfectionism went unpretentiousness and discipline. Dinner after his exposition of an opera was always simple: soup followed by bread, cheese, and cuts of cold meat, possibly with a glass of wine. Again, you just had to fit in with his mania for order, or face the consequences. A guest's coat could be hung only on a certain hook, and not on another. Larger coats must be behind smaller ones. Failure to observe the rules would result in Peter rearranging all the misplaced items himself, accompanied by a look of thunder. A spilled salt cellar would evoke an explosion if you tried to clean up the mess yourself, which he insisted you could not do properly. With fierce concentration, he would wipe the grains off the edge of the table into his cupped hand and discard them in the sink, returning to the table to repeat the exercise, though there was no longer a grain to be seen. The job had to be completed meticulously – once, and then again.

The European Union as saviour

By the time Karl Wongtschowski, the orthodontist and amateur violinist who used to turn up to Adela Kotowska's Sunday teas, celebrated his hundredth birthday, in 1998, he had moved to a care home. It was a small gathering: Adela was there with her two sons; so was Karl's girlfriend Lotte Herzfelder, my mother, and a few other refugees or their 'children', some of them already in their seventies.

Whenever one of us tried to make a speech, Karl waved us down, indicating his aversion to eulogies, which he found pointless. He had reached this birthday and that was that. A message from the Queen lay on a table next to a large cake and a disorderly pile of congratulatory cards.

Though he had bought the cake, everything else was prepared with his own hands. The one thing he could no longer make himself was what he most wanted: music. And the care home boasted an out-of-tune upright piano in its communal room. Joy finally flushed Karl's face when my mother announced that we were going to play Beethoven's *Spring* sonata for him, her on the violin and me on the piano. After that Adela would chip in with her incomparable Chopin, though as usual she wouldn't decide what to play until she sat down.

It had happened since I was ten or eleven: being called on to perform duos with my mother – or trios with her, and my brother on the cello. We often did it at home, when a group of her friends came over for a musical evening and a thoroughly rehearsed programme of chamber music unfolded in a ritualized way; a buffet supper was served afterwards, cobbled together by the three of us; and there would be earnest discussion on the merits of our performance until, much to my mother's relief, the front door would be shut behind the last guest. And on Sundays we'd sometimes play at the two care homes in London dedicated to German-speaking Jewish refugees, their large halls filled with dozens of old people listening reverently – an audience for whom music was the most perfect way of experiencing, articulating, and celebrating the world.

Yet on many of these occasions, as at Karl's birthday, I would feel something very different to the delicious joy of belonging, which émigré circles normally evoked in me. Instead, I could be overwhelmed by claustrophobia and melancholy. A world that had been destroyed, however magnificent and true it had been, couldn't be a home for a person born into a different epoch. In the face of cultural devastation, there is no return. I became convinced that any meaningful future in exile had to somehow – but how? – bring the great values and sensibilities of that lost world into real relationship with the present one. Otherwise the result would be inner chaos: talents floundering in a void and incapable of being enjoyed.

From my teenage years onwards, my own refuge was immersion in science, and later in philosophy. The more contemporary, the better. At first, and to my cost, I refused history. Naively, I didn't want to hear about what thinkers had thought in the past, in case they dragged me back into dead or dying worlds; I was interested only in what they had to say today.

And in part because surrender to England was so unthinkable – another recipe for floundering because we could never belong there – I developed lifelong passions for German philosophy and for European unification; for the creation of a great, integrated family of nations under the rule of supranational law, a family that together would overcome the destructive evils of self-exaltation and self-loathing. Here, I wouldn't be faced with confinement to a nation state – or else with rejection of any loyalty to a polity, which would also throw me back into the void. 'Europe', with its immense cultural variety, was the perfect anchor for a life with problematical local roots.

Ironically, this self-Europeanization was exactly what Germany craved. It, too, was set on discovering a contemporary identity through a home that was supranational. I devoured the memoirs of Jean Monnet and the other founding fathers of what became the European Union, and saw this ideal as the nucleus of a new order that would not only hinder any repetition of the nationalist crimes of the past but, far beyond that, create a new kind of national identity grounded in a deepening intimacy with the otherness of neighbouring peoples and countries, rather than in insular defensiveness against them. European unity, I was and remain convinced, is among the West's greatest post-war ideals.

PART IV

The Past Cannot be Restituted
1990–

39

Love declaration to Germany

Since my childhood, every visit to Germany has been a homecoming to a world of uncanny familiarity. Germany is *Heimat*: the spiritual and cultural world to which I am most naturally attuned. A place where almost everything feels recognizable, even if I have never encountered it before: the depth in people's faces – and their complexity, which seems more insoluble than other nations'; the abrupt mood swings, especially in Berlin; the pleasure in a voluptuous hopelessness that is ultimately a source of hope; the extremes of humanity and detachment, and of sensitivity and hardness; the intense confidence abutting awkward insecurity. No nation sees deeper and no nation is more naive.

Germany, including no doubt its vices, is in my genes; in my mother's deep musicianship; in my father's fury at seeing two unmatched socks; in my own love of German philosophy; in the joys of spraying whipped cream onto my aunt Ilse's *Zwetschgentorte* in her Berlin kitchen. No Nazi history could quell my love for this people, perhaps because none of us can help loving what we take to be the source of our being. Is it really so difficult to love those who have hated you if they define your existence?

So I can imagine why my great-uncle Theodor, Ernst's brother, insists on staying in Berlin until the Gestapo come for him in 1942, though he is considered racial refuse by the nation that he holds dear and though he has to avoid seeing Emmy and Ilse or any other family member, for their own safety. Even after he is no longer allowed to work, he continues to live in the Bavarian Quarter of Berlin with his mother and their devoted housekeeper, Hedwig Kuss, who now finances their needs with the money she has saved over many years in their employment. A lifelong bachelor, Theo has lived there since they arrived in Berlin from their home town of Christburg in West Prussia, early in the twentieth century.

It is a happy household. Until Ernst's death in 1933, he and Emmy visit on Friday evenings, when the Shabbat candles are lit; and on Saturday afternoons my mother and Ursel, and less regularly Ilse, drop in.

My mother will remember those visits all her life. While she fools around with Hedwig, Theo sits there and chuckles, gentle to the point of defencelessness.

From the mid-1930s, Hedwig has implored him to emigrate. Perhaps he would have left if Ernst had lived; Theo was always the less decisive of the two and, since childhood, had been taken under his elder brother's wing. He knows that Ernst once had a property in Croatia, which he bought with a second cousin called Heinz, and that he had toyed with the idea of emigrating there. But that refuge, my mother said, vanished when Heinz secretly sold it and made off with the proceeds to Shanghai, a city to which many German Jews fled in the late 1930s as doors began to shut in the West.

Theo takes this betrayal of trust badly, which might be one more reason why he feels he has nowhere to go. Fundamentally, however, he finds a non-German existence inconceivable, even after the horrors of Kristallnacht. As the orgy of Nazi destruction intensifies, so does his passivity. He isn't just depressed; he is sinking into the sort of inertia that seizes people when they cannot imagine any alternative to a dead end. When he does finally leave Berlin, in 1940 or 1941, it isn't because the Nazis have tipped the scales for him; it is because Hedwig forces him to go.

She presents him, she tells Ilse after the war, with a small suitcase and directions to an address in Hungary.

'Why there?'

'Friends of mine,' she says, pointing to a ticket, a map, and the coordinates of his hosts.

I see him standing silently in the apartment's windowless corridor, his profile obscured by its shadows. To summon the energy to emigrate and make his way to a minor town in Hungary seems beyond his powers. That night, I imagine, he doesn't go to bed, but sits in the old armchair in their living room, not exactly brooding, not exactly sad, but numb as thoughts meander through his mind, then fizzle out before they can offer him their conclusions. The next morning, he leaves – less frightened than dazed.

Somehow, he reaches the Hungarian border but never crosses it. Overcome by homesickness and the menace of Magyar hieroglyphics, he halts before an alien land and language.

A fortnight after his departure, as Hedwig is going about her chores, she hears a shy knock at the door. There he stands. She is appalled and frustrated. He enters silently, avoiding her questions. He sleeps on and off for days. Hedwig continues to cook for him, do his laundry, and address him respectfully as '*der Herr*', as she has always done. Above all, she makes sure that nobody knows of his existence. On one of the few occasions he dares to venture out for fresh air, he has that chance encounter with Ilse in the street.

A few months later, Hedwig has another go at making Theo vanish. She gives notice to the landlord of their apartment and moves into a one-bedroom place, rented in her name. There, she hides him for almost a year, though she has heard that giving refuge to Jews is now punishable by deportation to a concentration camp – as, my mother said, happened to my father's friend Gertrud Luckner – and she earns money for them by cleaning other people's homes. He is still the boss, but now she is paying herself to work for him. Theo, she hopes, will officially disappear.

Nobody knows why the Gestapo comes in late 1942. Hedwig guesses that their downstairs neighbours have informed the police that they can hear the footsteps of two people in the apartment above and, seeing only one person come and go, are sure that Hedwig must be sheltering someone.

Theo is taken to Sachsenhausen concentration camp, just north of Berlin, where, Hedwig reports, he dies a few weeks later, after being forced to undertake hard labour. He is not a man to survive such circumstances, and so, for his captors, he is dispensable. Maybe, she hears, he died from exhaustion or disease, or maybe by lethal injection, or with a single shot to the back of the head.

Extraordinarily, she finds out about the hard labour by visiting Sachsenhausen with a food parcel. She thinks it is the sort of prison where you can drop books, groceries, and fresh clothes for inmates. That the priority of a concentration camp is not to punish its Jews but to destroy them isn't a reality in which she is prepared to acquiesce.

And that is the last that anyone hears of Theodor Liedtke, until Ilse finds the parcel from Sachsenhausen, neatly wrapped in brown paper and tied with a string, on her doormat, addressed to her. Inside, she finds a pile of folded clothes, some books, a squashed hat and a *Judenpass*. In a separate envelope is a list of the contents, stamped, and signed off with a '*Heil Hitler!*'

Except for his *Judenpass*, which Ilse hides in a drawer with her most private papers, Theo's remaining chattels will not survive the American occupation of her house after the war. He has left nothing behind in the world except the identity that the Nazis had foisted on him.

Or so we all believed.

40

The blessings of procrastination

Procrastination is an art in which I claim formidable expertise. I am seldom unable to find new ways of putting off until tomorrow what I'm desperate to accomplish today, and never at a loss to justify the joys of doing so: important tasks cannot be rushed; ideas come when they come; I need to be on top form, which I'm not at the moment; a break will give me new energy; I am delaying out of perfectionism, not sloth.

What I hadn't realized until one day in early 2006 was that avoiding the task in hand could also have life-changing consequences. Instead of reading up on the latest scandals of the US president or seeing what ex-girlfriends were up to, I googled Yad Vashem, the Holocaust memorial in Jerusalem.

I entered the name 'Theodor Liedtke' followed by 'Berlin' and hit return. Up popped the record of my great-uncle, including details of his last addresses. This was Theo's permanent memorial in a faraway land that he had never visited. I marvelled at the survival of so much information on a salesman in a vanished department store whose remains had probably billowed from an incinerator into a scattered grave in the sky.

Then I stumbled across something completely unexpected. In a section of Theo's memorial marked 'Personal Testimonies', I found

a witness statement by Theodor Liedtke's 'grandson', Klaus Meltzer
– as well as his address in Cologne.

Grandson? Theo had definitely been childless, according to Ernst,
Emmy, my mother, Ursel, and Ilse. No member of my family had
ever seen him with a woman, never mind come across evidence of
offspring.

It was a stunning discovery. Not just to find this as yet unknown
close relative, but, even more poignantly, to have a fresh connection
to Theo and so to Ernst – whose living realities had so far depended
entirely on the testimony of the three sisters.

Within minutes, I am speaking to Herr Meltzer. I hear a drawled
'Hallo, Klaus hier' as the phone is answered, and I get to the point
right away. 'Hello Klaus . . . Herr Meltzer. I'm calling from London.
My name is Simon May. It's about Theodor Liedtke. I am his great-
nephew and I think you are . . .'

At first I hear nothing but sobbing and aborted attempts to speak.
Nobody has ever called him about Theo before, he eventually stam-
mers. The name hasn't come up in the thirty-five years since Klaus's
mother died. She was, he says, Theo's daughter.

I want to be sure, though, that we are talking about the same
person. Does Meltzer's information about Theo's life – when he
was born, his education, his occupation, the Berlin neighbourhood
where he lived, when he died, where he died – match what I have
heard from my mother and Ilse and Ursel? The answer is, almost
entirely, yes.

Then I ask him the obvious question: who was his mother's
mother? His voice freezes. 'Yes,' he says enigmatically. 'That would
be a question!' he mumbles. I ask again, more casually. 'Yes,' he
answers again. 'Are there any clues?' I finally venture. 'None at all,'
he replies. His mother always refused to talk about that subject. She
died when Meltzer was twenty-eight years old, in 1971, and never
spoke about her own mother.

All she said was that she, Ellen, lived with her parents in Berlin
until her mother died in 1933, when she was fourteen. The death
was accidental: her mother had been hanging curtains in their living

room when she fell off a ladder and suffered a fatal concussion. After the tragedy, Ellen continued to live with Theo until the end of 1936, when he sent her to 'finishing schools' in Garmisch-Partenkirchen in Bavaria and then in Montreux in Switzerland. Soon after returning, she met Herr Meltzer's father – and the rest was history.

That's it. There are no photos of Theo's alleged wife or lover; no letters; no stories of family holidays, of this woman's interests, or of her background; no clues to her name or when she was born. Some years after Ellen died, Meltzer's paternal aunt divulged a couple of other fragments about the mysterious woman. One was that the real reason she died wasn't concussion from falling off a ladder while hanging up curtains, but rather an infection that she had caught from Ellen, who had been wracked by guilt her whole life for, as she saw it, killing her mother. The aunt also told Meltzer that Ellen's mother had been raised a Protestant, though she was almost certainly of Jewish descent.

One thing was sure: Ellen never mentioned the apartment in the Bavarian Quarter where Theo, according to my mother, lived a bachelor life with his mother and Hedwig Kuss.

41

Did Great-uncle Theo
have another life?

If Theo was living a double life, he was making a tremendous fist of it. Ernst, Emmy, Ilse, Ursel, and my mother as little suspected Ellen's existence as she did theirs. My mother and Ursel were visiting Theo at his mother's apartment on Saturday afternoons for tea and cake in exactly the years when he was supposedly living with Ellen and her mother: from around 1924 — when Ellen was five, my mother ten, and Ursel twelve — well into the 1930s. So where was Theo really living?

Buried among my mother's memories of those Saturday afternoon teas were two clues. One was Hedwig's excitement whenever Theo arrived back at the apartment he shared with his mother. 'Hedwig was devoted to Theo, she adored him,' my mother used to say, 'and, when he got home and rang the bell down at street level, she would always cry excitedly, *"Der Herr kommt, der Herr kommt!"'* — sir is coming, sir is coming! — 'and then she would throw open the front door as he was still a floor or two beneath them, and stand ready to take his coat and hat and sit him down for tea and cake.'

If he had merely been returning from the shops or from a morning at work, Hedwig's excitement each time he arrived back might have been a little overwrought. Perhaps on those Saturday afternoons he, too, was a visitor at his mother's flat?

But there was a second clue that Theo might have had a secret life outside his mother's apartment. Family lore had it that, though he had never been known to have a girlfriend, he had long been in love with Emmy's aunt, confusingly named Emma, who had adopted Emmy and Helmut after their father's death left their mother, Adele, on her own. This meant that Theo was reputedly in love with his brother's wife's aunt.

She couldn't have been the mother of Theo's child; she would have been around sixty when Ellen was born. But her husband Arthur Rosenthal had died five years earlier, in 1914, and as a rich and childless widow she might have become Ellen's sponsor or even adoptive mother. Someone with means must have been behind Ellen's affluent upbringing. Theo's salary as a salesman at Tietz's department store would hardly have financed the villa where Ellen was raised. Most Berliners, including well-off people like Ernst and Emmy, lived in rented apartments. To own a large house with a dozen rooms was the preserve of the rich. Nor would he have been able to afford her private education in Garmisch-Partenkirchen and then the finishing school in Montreux. And, of course, the same *Tante* Emma had sent her own niece and adopted daughter, my grandmother Emmy, to a finishing school in Montreux.

The oddest thing of all was that Theo, Meltzer said, had transferred ownership of the villa into Ellen's name in 1938 or 1939 – precisely when Jewish property began to be systematically expropriated and when J. Eichenberg AG, the textile business in which Ernst and Emmy had invested, back in 1924, was Aryanized. What point could Theo have seen in transferring the villa from his name into his daughter's: from one person stripped of property rights to another?

It was this question that took me to Cologne in April 2006 to meet my newly discovered cousin and, through him, to delve into the enigma of Theo's life before the war. I would soon find myself in murkier historical waters than any I had yet encountered in my immediate family.

42

The Nazi and the Jewish woman

In 1937, a few months after returning from her Swiss finishing school, Klaus's mother met a young Nazi Party member called Walter Meltzer at a tea dance in Bavaria. Ellen, then eighteen, was coquettish, quick-witted, and Jewish. Walter, twenty-two, was a fervent Nazi, committed to Hitler, and hungry for war. He had been chairman of the National Socialist *Oberschülerbund* at his Berlin high school and had jubilantly hoisted the Swastika onto the school's roof on the day of Hitler's ascent to power in January 1933. His burning ambition was to join the SS. Theirs was the rapturous attraction of strangers.

Klaus was proud of his tumultuous conception. When I first met him, he was in his mid-sixties, dressed in sneakers, baggy trousers and a frayed T-shirt, with wisps of white hair and a beret that adhered to the right side of his head as if defying gravity. He spoke slowly, tortuously seeking his words; then seemed unsure whether they were the ones he really wanted.

'We Jews are complicated people, aren't we?' he said, gesturing at the wooden wall behind him in his tiny living room in a predominantly Turkish neighbourhood of Cologne. On a shelf there was a menorah and a copy of the Old Testament in Hebrew. On the wall adjacent to it hung a kippa and a framed certificate of his father's promotion to the rank of captain, signed by Hermann Göring,

supreme commander of the Luftwaffe. On the floor stood a small
leather box which contained his father's award of the German Cross
in Gold, also signed by Göring, a congratulatory note from Field
Marshal Albert von Kesselring, one of Hitler's top generals, and
photographs of Walter with clusters of bright-eyed SS men. At the
bottom of the box were the leather flying gloves that had been
recovered from Walter's body after a Luftwaffe plane that he was
test piloting mysteriously crashed. They were thick and shiny, as if
new. I made to touch them, but recoiled.

'My father was an honest patriot,' Klaus said in a voice that was
at once defiant and anguished. 'His first love was Hitler, his second
my mother!'

Klaus's parrot, Gregor, an attention-seeking bird with an ener-
vatingly persistent shriek, seemed to echo the word 'Hitler'. The
parrot was named after one of Klaus's heroes, a former communist
politician from East Germany called Gregor Gysi, who became a
member of the Bundestag after German reunification.

'Did your father stop loving Hitler?'

'No, never.'

He paused, and I thought he was going to start crying. 'Maybe
he did after he saw the atrocities. But that was only in late 1942.
Before that, he had been a pilot in France, then in Africa. He was
usually in the air. So he didn't always see what was happening on
the ground. And he didn't go to the worst places of Nazi mass
murder, like Poland and Russia.'

'What happened in 1942?'

'He was on his way back to Germany from a mission, I think it
was in the Balkans. The last part of the journey was by land, through
Croatia. What he saw there broke him. The corpses hanging from
trees. The children lying dead in ditches. He was so nauseated that
he ordered his driver to stop the car, jumped out, and threw up in
the gutter. Those few days in Croatia placed the whole Nazi dream
in question for him. He still loved the Luftwaffe. He still loved his
comrades. But perhaps he started having doubts about Hitler. He
was broken.'

'And your mother? Where was she while he was in Africa?'

'She was in Berlin. She looked after the villa until Theo was deported in 1942. Thanks to Walter, Theo managed to transfer it safely into her name three years previously. My father took a risk for her. You have to leave him that.'

So maybe that was why Theo's villa wasn't forcibly sold after Jews were no longer allowed to own property. Perhaps he had also claimed that Ellen's mother wasn't Jewish.

'Quite apart from the Aryanization of property after 1938,' Klaus continued, 'it was just as well that my grandfather gave the villa to my mother. You see, he was arrested soon afterwards for theft; and as an indicted criminal he would have had an even harder time selling it for a decent price.'

Arrested? Theft? An indicted criminal? This was an even more bizarre dimension to my great-uncle Theo's mysterious life.

As soon as I was back at my hotel, I telephoned my mother to ask if she had heard any rumours about her uncle's indictment for theft, but she dismissed the whole story as quite impossible. 'It's total nonsense,' she said. 'They are making this up or confusing their facts.'

'So what happened to Theo's house?' I asked Klaus.

'After the war, my mother sold it. Not for the money, but because she wanted to get away from the memories.'

It seemed possible for a Nazi like Walter Meltzer to protect a Jewish woman in this way — just as, perhaps, Harald Böhmelt had protected Ilse. Ellen hadn't only kept the house; like Ilse, she remained unharassed for the whole war.

I asked Meltzer how his father's parents had reacted to their son falling in love with a Jewish girl.

'They treated her like a little princess. Especially my grandfather, Christoph: he had a crush on her, no doubt about it. She was so petite and flirtatious, and she had this contagious laugh that charmed men.' Walter's father, it seemed, enthusiastically supported his son's match with this lively young woman. He even went to see a friend in a ministry about getting her declared an Aryan, but was told that this would be impossible.

'And Walter's mother?'

'She knew that her husband liked Ellen and she was an obedient wife. But she loathed Jews and didn't want her for Walter.'

In the case of Else Meltzer, Klaus's grandmother, some jealousy of her husband's affection for the little princess might also have been at work. So, too, might resentment of Ellen's better education – especially those finishing schools which, she rightly suspected, made Ellen look down on her new family, with their homespun nationalism, love of military marches, and brash ditties in praise of Hitler.

The Jewish thing can't have been an absolute sticking point for Walter's mother because she adored Theo. She doted on him; warmed to his gentlemanly bearing and shy nature; worried that he was undernourished; and insisted that he visit as regularly as possible, until, for the sake of his daughter, he no longer appeared in public with her – and soon after that no longer left his home.

'So, did they protect Theo?'

'No.'

'Did they discuss his precarious situation?'

'No, that was never mentioned.'

It seemed that Theo would sit there for hours in 'his' chair, sipping tea, eating Frau Meltzer's cakes, or participating in a family dinner, yellow star affixed to his jacket and *Judenpass* in his pocket, while the portrait of the Führer stared down from the wall and the bookshelves groaned under the weight of Nazi literature. The words 'Jew' or 'Jewish' arose only when Ellen left. Then Frau Meltzer, Klaus said, would be unable to contain her revulsion at Theo's daughter. 'Keep your hands off this dirty Jewess!' she would snarl at her husband, though never at her son. 'You are bringing misfortune on us all.' But Christoph would hear nothing of it and quietly reminded her that Ellen gave their son so much happiness. Besides, couldn't one love the Führer *and* enthusiastically support one's son's decision to marry a Jewish woman?

Walter had suffered a terrible blow shortly after meeting Ellen. His application to join the SS was turned down. The reason given, so Klaus recalled his mother telling him, was his physique: at 172 centimetres – about five foot eight – he was too short. In addition, he might have had too many fillings in his teeth. With Ellen's help, Walter attempted to appeal the decision, but all he got was another rejection. He had a good body, they said, with excellent stamina; his loyalty to the Führer and his esteem for the lofty calling of the SS were not in doubt; but, at 172 centimetres and with all the fillings, he didn't make the grade.

Ellen helped him through the depression that followed the rejections, but Else Meltzer pinned the blame entirely on her. Her son's inadequate height had nothing to do with it, she said. Ellen was a spoilt girl from a big villa, who had ruined her son's discipline and resolve. The SS interviewers had seen him and smelled the degeneration, and that was the work of the Jewish virus.

But Ellen was too besotted with Walter to worry about an anti-Semitic future mother-in-law heckling from the sidelines. She assured him, Klaus said, that the SS selection panel were bureaucrats who couldn't recognize superlative manhood; and she predicted – accurately, it would turn out – that the highest commanders of the Reich would recognize what she had known all along. Inspired by her support, he dedicated a photo to her, showing him heaving away at a construction site with a group of other young Nazis, and on the back of it he scribbled:

'We – yes, we! – are the *real* SS!'

43

Just ask the Führer

Ellen's confidence in Walter was not misplaced. He was drafted into the Luftwaffe, where he quickly rose to the rank of *Staffelkapitän*, commanding a squadron of pilots. At first, he was stationed near Berlin, so it was easy for him and Ellen to be together when he was off duty. In his longer periods of leave they repaired to special Luftwaffe holiday homes in Bavaria and Saxony. Hitler was Walter's world; and Ellen's life was blissful within it.

Sometimes, Klaus said, his jingoism was too much for her, such as when he returned from his first mission in France and placed the bloodied helmet of a dead French solider triumphantly on the kitchen counter. She was not going to tolerate that vile trophy in their home and threw it out. But he was with her only briefly before he was sent to Italy and then to Rommel's army in North Africa, where he was transferred from combat operations to flying transport planes for resupplying ground forces.

In a way, Klaus said, his father would have preferred to remain in combat. Destroying enemy planes and watching them spin out of the air was indescribably exciting. But flying clunky transport aircraft was dangerous too: three times he was shot down, and three times he survived.

Recognition was swift. Walter was awarded the Iron Cross Second Class, the Iron Cross First Class, the Honour Goblet of the Luftwaffe, and then, on 27 March 1942, the German Cross in Gold, which I had seen in the leather box in Klaus's apartment.[32]

Although the campaign in North Africa was heading for disaster, Walter was one of its young heroes. In December 1942, the Knight's Cross of the Iron Cross[33] was added to his list of decorations. Three months later, Ellen told him that she was pregnant. And, on 21 July 1943, Göring promoted Walter to the rank of captain.

It had been a heady twenty-four months, the cascade of joys interrupted only by Theo's deportation to Sachsenhausen, which Ellen had witnessed when she went to the assembly point where he had been ordered to report and, from a safe distance, watched him disappear. Through it all, she continued writing Walter love letters of undiminished freshness. As the war progressed, the shortage of paper forced her to write on toilet paper in lipstick, but though she had to be briefer she was no less ardent.

For Walter, the Knight's Cross of the Iron Cross and the promotion to captain didn't just bring military glory. He was now entitled, so Klaus's mother reported, to ask Hitler for a personal favour, through one of the Führer's representatives.

Without a moment's hesitation, he knew what this would be: he would request permission to marry Ellen, who was now four months pregnant. He rushed to tell his closest friends in the Luftwaffe. 'I am going to ask the Führer for permission to marry my girl! That is all I want of him!'

'But why do you need permission to marry?' they asked. 'Are you mad? Anyone can get married! Ask for something that only he can bestow!'

'But this is something only he can bestow,' Walter answered. And he explained that Ellen was Jewish.

The others were stunned. They had never suspected it of him – how could such a convinced Nazi choose a Jewish girl? Most dismaying to them, though, was the danger he was prepared to put himself in. 'You've lost your mind, Walter! The Führer says he will grant any wish, no matter what it is. But he would never grant *that* one. Instead, he will have you both executed.'

Walter's comrades would gather round him when others were out of earshot to dissuade him from this absurd idea; but his indiscretion had almost certainly been his death warrant. One of them must have ratted to higher authorities, perhaps accusing him of wider disloyalty too.

His superiors reacted with brutal speed. Walter was discharged from active service and assigned to test piloting, which was notoriously dangerous: you were trying out planes that had been rushed from design to prototype. And the loss of prestige was devastating. Instead of being transferred to a new front line or a position on Göring's staff, Walter found himself sidelined to a role where heroic defence of country was no longer possible.

His morale had already been deteriorating before his latest promotion. Ellen had noticed that he started getting strange after the trip back from the Balkans through Croatia. The brutality he witnessed there was no longer heroic; this was savagery, delight in inhumanity, the abandonment of all rules of warfare. It broke his will – and possibly his faith in the Nazi cause.

Ironically, when Walter was promoted to captain he wasn't only told that Hitler guaranteed to bestow on him a favour of his choosing. Göring's grandiose certificate announcing the promotion with effect from 1 August 1943 also declared that the recipient 'could be assured of the special protection of the Führer'.

Two weeks later, on 15 August, the prototype that Walter was ordered to fly fell out of the sky, soon after take-off from Berlin's Schönefeld airport.

He died instantly.

44.

The Jew and the ex-monk

It was never clear whether such crashes were due to mechanical failure or sabotage – or even whether they had happened at all. If the authorities needed a heroic explanation for the death of someone whom they had decided to kill, or who had embarrassingly committed suicide, the crash of a test flight, or some other accident, might be cited.

Ernst Udet, one-time client of Ilse's photographic atelier in Berlin, was a case in point. He was a hero of the First World War and one of the creators of the Luftwaffe, but he had gradually fallen out with Göring; and when Udet buckled under the pressures of bureaucratic infighting and his boss's contemptuous treatment of him, and then committed suicide, Göring's office issued a sombre announcement regretting that he had died while testing a new weapon. The regime even put on the spectacle of a state funeral. Who knows whether Walter Meltzer was really in that aircraft that took off from Schönefeld?

Whatever the explanation, Ellen could no longer delay going into hiding. Walter had probably been her great protector, and with him gone she decided to vanish. The last time Walter's family saw her was at his funeral. Though it was a sweltering summer's day, she showed up in a large fur coat with which she tried to conceal the bulging evidence of Walter's *Rassenschande*: the 'racial disgrace' of sexual relations between an Aryan and a Jew, which were prohibited by the 'Law for the Protection of German Blood and Honour'. She disappeared as soon as the coffin had been lowered into the ground.

That evening, she made for the remote countryside near Janowitz in Silesia, where, Klaus said, friends in the circle of the rebel cleric Pastor Niemöller had arranged for her to be hidden and to find forged identity papers. Four months later, she gave birth to Klaus.

Ellen never loved anyone as she had loved Walter. In losing him, she lost her own life too; she became severely depressed, started drinking, and by the end of the war was an alcoholic.

Then, in 1946, she met Friedrich Edelman. It certainly wasn't more of the same. Far from being a Protestant, a Nazi, and a German, Freddy was a Jew, a Zionist, and an American. He had been born in Austria, fled to the United States when Hitler marched into Vienna, and was now back in Europe with the occupying US Army. But he didn't intend to stay long in Germany. He wanted Ellen to move with him to Palestine, soon to be the State of Israel; and, in a striking reversal of the direction of travel in our family, he insisted that Klaus be raised as a Jew and no longer as a Christian.

Ellen craved a new life after losing both Walter and her father, but not quite as new as this. Unhappily resettled in Haifa, she was soon reversing the reversal: while Edelman steered Klaus towards Judaism, she, at the same time, prohibited him to learn about it. She demanded that Klaus leave the room any time a Jewish celebration was about to start, even one as routine as lighting the Sabbath candles. Only when it was all over and the prayer books had been locked away was he allowed back in. In fact, she wanted him to avoid not only Judaism but Jews – something of a challenge in Haifa – and encouraged him to look on their Jewish neighbours as strangers.

Edelman quickly made plans to return to America, ostensibly to start a business, but possibly because he was finding life with Ellen unendurable. She was missing Germany terribly and had never found in Edelman the vertiginous sense of safety that Walter and his family had inspired in her. In 1952, she departed with Klaus for Munich.

*   *   *

A few months after arriving back, Ellen met Heinrich Seidel. He was neither a Protestant nor a Jew, but a former Roman Catholic monk with a weakness for women and westerns. He made only one demand of her: Klaus had to convert to Catholicism.

The ten-year-old boy was duly transplanted from German-Jewish Haifa to a conservative Catholic orphanage in rural Bavaria in which Seidel worked as an orderly. There, he made friends with children who had lost their parents in the war and received his first Communion and his confirmation. Like me, he became an altar server.

The new family had some happy times, in particular at Christmas. Ellen would send Heinrich and Klaus out to the cinema while she prepared the crib under their Christmas tree, laid a festive dinner table, and cooked a goose. When they got back from the cinema, they would put on their best suits and wait patiently in the corridor of the small apartment until Ellen rang a bell that summoned them into the living room. In the middle of dinner, Heinrich would stand up and read the story of Christ's birth from an old Bible that she had had bound for him in pigskin.

At Christmas, birthdays, or sunny weekends, the storm clouds over Ellen's life would briefly part; but otherwise she was increasingly dogged by fears of persecution, and her alcoholism became crippling. She began to shut herself off from the world and often didn't know which country she was living in. Like Ilse towards the end of her life, she became convinced that Nazis were encircling her and would turn her home into a killing zone. From the mid-1960s, she was barricading herself in her apartment and closing all the curtains 'in case the Gestapo find us'.

One day, Klaus found her standing on a chair, pointing frantically in the direction of a skylight. 'They are going to come through there; they are on their way to get us; they are going to deport us,' she screamed. As soon as she woke up in the mornings, she reached for the bottle. She was screaming in her sleep and she was screaming by day. In 1971, she died of alcohol poisoning, aged fifty-two.

The Nazi, the Jew, the ex-monk: Ellen had been least troubled with Walter. But her letters to the young *Staffelkapitän* and the photos of them together seem to reveal something beyond delight in Walter for his own sake: namely, her euphoria at the primordial safety that she believed he could vouchsafe. His allure must have intensified as Theo became more isolated and depressed, unable to work, stripped of all civil rights, and finally deported and murdered.

Walter's passion in those letters and photos feels more subdued. His happiness appears inflected with unease, even doubt. Perhaps he was naturally reserved; but was he also concerned at the almost godlike safety that she craved from him? Did her love become a burden when he realized the power of that craving? Did he worry whether its fearsome appetite could want anything about him that didn't satisfy it?

45

The parrot and the bulldog

Klaus has been telling me all this in his attic bedsit, while we drink coffee and eat Turkish cakes and leaf through old photos, interrupted repeatedly by Gregor the parrot. But after two days searching for a third dimension to my great-uncle Theo beyond my mother's portrayal of the kindly bachelor living his blameless life with his mother and Hedwig, I badly need a break from talk about Jews and Aryans, the SS and nervous breakdowns, Göring and the German Cross in Gold, the Luftwaffe and the Sabbath.

Occasionally Klaus and I try to change the subject and tell each other about our own lives. I discover that he is a judo black belt, a photographer, a painter, and an educationalist; that he has been a candidate for the far left in local elections; and that he is a tireless supporter of immigrants and minorities, especially Turks and Iraqis, in his Cologne neighbourhood, and has founded a community centre for Turkish women. Yet our conversation circles back compulsively to the heritage that has brought us together. And after so much immersion in that heritage, and its source in Theo, we are both worn down. He needs time alone and I decide to do some sightseeing, determined to leave history behind me.

*　*　*

Schneckelchen 1 9 39 Schnuckelchen

18. Ellen Liedtke
(nickname
'Schneckelchen'),
putative daughter of
Theo Liedtke, and her
fiancé, Walter Meltzer
('Schnuckelchen'),
in 1939.

19. Walter Meltzer
(bottom middle) with
comrades in Nuremberg
during the 1933 Nazi
Party rally.

20. Ursel (r. standing) with Maria 'Baby' von Alvensleben (r. seated), probably Lexi von Alvensleben (middle seated), and their mother, Countess Alexandra von Alvensleben (l. seated), at the yacht club Klub am Rupenhorn, Berlin, 1931.

21. My mother, Marianne, with violin.

22. Marianne playing in a wartime concert at the National Gallery in London. On the reverse of the photo she writes: 'The concert was moved to the basement as a bomb had just fallen upstairs.'

23. A Czech Trio programme from 1941. The Trio was sponsored by the Czech government-in-exile in the UK and provided my mother's first legitimate earnings as a refugee.

24. Ursel's letter of thanks, dated 17 July 1941, to SS officer Hans Hinkel, one of Joseph Goebbels's senior officials, who was key to her achieving Aryan status.

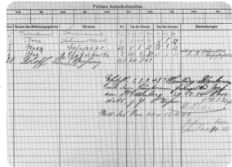

25. The resident's cards on Ursel in Bremen City Hall, 1931–43. Directly underneath an entry recording her recent marriage to Franziskus an official writes: 'Gestapo enquired on 21.10.43'(r.). On the other card (above), she is listed as having two Jewish grandparents, despite having been accepted as an Aryan two years previously.

26. A letter of 17 September 1943 from Count Franziskus von Plettenberg's military commander permitting him to marry Ursel and enclosing his medical certificates and proof of Aryan origin.

27. The bombed idyll of Blumeshof 12 (r. foreground) in 1945.

28. The ruins of Ilse's studio at Budapesterstrasse 43, Berlin, in 1945. Behind it the destroyed Hotel Eden, famous for its 5 p.m. jazz teas, which had been frequented by Marlene Dietrich, Otto Dix, Bertolt Brecht, and the young Billy Wilder.

29. Ilse's temporary studio in 1945, with her portraits of US soldiers. On the reverse of the photo she writes: 'On the walls a gallery of handsome men.'

30. The temporary graves of Geri and Eva, Ilse's neighbours, shot in their home by Soviet forces and buried by her, Berlin, 1945.

31. My father, Walter May, in London in 1958.

32. My mother, Marianne, my brother, Marius (r.), and me (l.) in 1959/1960.

The buzz of non-European languages by the great cathedral feels liberating; but it isn't easy for me to flip out of the past. As I pass a cafe, I spot a display of chocolate truffles in the window. I look closer to see what they are, then freeze in horror, hardly able to believe my eyes. '*Pralinen Mischling*', a little sign announces: a racial hybrid of pralines! I double check. Of course, I misread it. '*Pralinen Mischung*', it says: a *mixture* of pralines.

I walk on, heading towards the Wallraf-Richartz Museum. Rather than bringing me into the present, the hubbub of tourists is only drawing attention to the vast vacuum that Hitler's war still leaves. What on earth are they coming to see? A bomb site hastily rebuilt, much of it an eyesore? Copies of buildings that were reduced to rubble by one night's air raids? How could people travel halfway round the world to wander these ugly streets and shopping arcades that are like gravestones of the old Cologne? I feel bereaved by the irreversible destruction that ripped the heart out of a great city and turned it into a necropolis – desolate at the loss of heritages that took centuries to accumulate.

The bustle in a nearby tavern where I stop for a glass of beer is like the chatter of the dispossessed. Even the cathedral, which the bombers largely spared, can't defy the irretrievable loss. The way it stands there in its stubborn vastness merely draws attention to the loneliness of the survivor in a desert of death.

I have been to other German cities many times without feeling such pain and loss. I haven't felt it as much in Berlin, that sardonic capital of guilt where, with its grime and inefficiency and cutting humour, Germany takes a break from itself. Nor in Munich, whose corpses stay more obediently in their graves than they do in Berlin. And still less in those places where ghosts seem well and truly silenced until a city hall committee orders them from their hiding places for a meticulously choreographed commemoration.

But, of course, I'm mourning the destruction of my father's world. My discovery of Klaus has brought me to the city where he was born, where he was raised and grew to adulthood, which he fled with his mother in 1937 when he was thirty-two, and in which, I've been told since childhood, no trace of him and his family remains – so no point visiting it. In my eagerness to solve the mystery of

Theo's secret life, I am simultaneously barging into the centuries-long history of my paternal ancestors in this part of Germany – and into the reality that the lives of my father, uncle Edward, grandmother Martha, and grandfather Ferdinand are as absent from Cologne as the bombed city itself.

As I follow the tourist trail across the cathedral square, I am inadvertently retracing my father's youthful tracks. For, my mother later tells me, he passed this way every day after he finished work – first at the Dresdner Bank, which had employed him since he left school at fifteen, and then, after his dismissal by the Nazis, at a small private bank owned by the family of Lilly Reifenberg-Lucas, the silent wife of our doctor, Ernst Lucas. After leaving his desk, he would become so absorbed in the paintings of the Wallraf-Richartz Museum that, my mother added with pride, he frequently had to be evicted just after closing time.

He loved the old Cologne – its mordant, wise-cracking wit; its death-on-a-plate local dishes like *Flönz* and *Himmel un Äd*; the splendid wines that are made around it in the lands of the Mosel. On his first return visit after the war, sometime in the late 1950s, he walked into his favourite cafe two decades after he had last been there, and the now elderly woman behind the counter instantly exclaimed, 'But you are young Walter May!' She embraced him tearfully, fed him and my mother with as much cake as they could bear, without accepting payment, and then sent them away laden with even more – but not before recalling that he had been Cologne's junior champion at *Skat*, one of Germany's national card games. And he had returned to the street in which his mother had lived before fleeing to England, but none of it had survived the Allied bombing.

I am daydreaming that his favourite cafe was the one with the window display where I thought I'd seen a praline *Mischling*, when, turning a corner, I stumble across an old mikvah, or Jewish ritual bath, the ruins of which appear to date back to the eleventh century and are preserved under a wooden canopy in a small piazza within the cathedral's shadow. Near the mikvah, a plaque commemorates the patriotism of local Jews in defending the town against invaders, after which the Jewish community as a whole was thanked for its loyalty by being evicted for nearly four centuries, returning only in the 1790s under French occupation.

Then I notice a woman trying to explain to her two sons, probably aged ten and twelve, what a mikvah is and that Cologne was once a great Jewish centre, but ordinary Germans sat by while these fellow citizens, who of course had their own customs but were otherwise just like you and me, were expelled or killed. She's doing her best to arouse their empathy, but they aren't interested, or else they're repelled by dark fates, or perhaps they believe that if people were evicted they must have done something to deserve it. Then one throws a pebble at the other – and, giggling conspiratorially, they flee the melancholy business of memorials and expulsions, tearing round the square, out of their mother's control.

Family legend has it that, in a house not far from here, in the middle of the First World War, two boys of about the same age were determined to do what their mother had always told them must not be done and set the family's parrot against its bulldog. The parrot had been a gift to the younger, and the bulldog to the older. The two creatures were irreconcilable enemies, and so the boys' mother had demanded that the parrot be locked in its cage upstairs, while the bulldog was confined to the living room.

The boys loved each other but were rivals, as most siblings are. And they had an ongoing argument over which of their pets was the more lethal.

'My parrot would win any fight,' boasted Walter. 'She could bite out your dog's eyes, and for all his bulldoggery, he wouldn't even be able to see his enemy, let alone jump high enough to catch her.'

'Nonsense! Can't you see that he will eat your parrot alive?' Edward retorted. 'Your little bird will be too curious not to hover close to him and will think that she can bite him and then fly away before getting hurt.'

'Bulldogs might be strong, but they're stupid,' the younger rebutted. 'They're all posture and snorting.'

The boys decided that they'd wait until their mother went out and then set the two creatures against each other.

The fight was savage. The parrot scored a first swift victory, deftly biting a piece of flesh out of the bulldog, which left a trail of blood that traced its crazed trajectory all around the room. Cleverly, the parrot had gone for the dog's rump, so it could escape before the doltish hound managed to lumber round and snap its jaws tight on thin air. Then the parrot moved in again, digging its beak into the dog's nose. But now the dog was too quick: its jaws seized the parrot's abdomen, and ripped through it. It was over as quickly as a duel between love rivals. The parrot lay dying as the stunned dog wandered over the coagulating blood, feather, and fur.

The younger boy was devastated and determined to salvage his pride at once.

'Guess what I've got in the garden!' he teased his brother, trying to distract himself from the carnage.

'A chihuahua?' enquired the older with the condescension of the victor. 'Though you can barely call that overgrown rodent a dog.'

'No, a rocket!'

They tore out to the garden, forgetting about the dead bird and the dazed dog. The younger boy scraped away at some soil and unearthed a small artillery shell.

'It's a British one,' said the little boy. 'I found it in the park. There are more there. The British can't aim! They'll lose the war, I know it!'

'Careful,' shrieked the older one. 'It could explode!'

'It's fine,' the younger admonished him. 'If it didn't explode on impact, it won't explode by itself now.' And he started to dismantle it, removing the projectile bit and emptying out the explosive material, or perhaps it was the propellant – neither boy could later recall which.

Where the eleven-year-old had learned to undertake such a delicate technical operation nobody knew. He then placed small quantities of the powder at a few points on the lawn and in the flower beds, and threw matches onto each one in turn, triggering loud bangs.

At that moment, their mother entered.

'You maniacs! What the hell are you doing? Those are obviously

British shells. What will we say if explosives are found in our possession?'

And she scooped up the powder, gathered the shards of metal casing, and ran inside, past the room where the dog was still recovering, to the bathroom, where she flushed it all down the toilet.

A few hours later, there was uproar in the neighbourhood. Yards of sewerage piping had ruptured – something inside must have burst or cut them – and the stench was unbearable. Some said it was those perfidious British: they weren't just shelling the city; they were trying to poison its water supplies as well. Others were pointing the finger at a still more insidious enemy.

'Clearly,' they were saying, 'this could only have been the work of Jews.'

46

Lech Wałęsa, the 'Jewish President of Poland'

It was only in 2016, a decade after my first visit to Klaus Meltzer's apartment in Cologne, that I overcame the inexplicable inertia which had prevented me from searching for traces of my father's family in Germany, whether in this city where he had been born, or in the small town of Trier, 200 kilometres to the south, where, my mother said, earlier generations of Mays had lived for hundreds of years.

My inertia seems inexplicable because it is, above all, my father and his German world that I crave to recover – and, through a kind of reverse emigration, to reclaim for myself. It was his death at the German Embassy in London, as Ursel had tantalizingly re-enacted it all those years ago, that triggered my lifelong quest to find a living relation to him and to what I see as the sacred inheritance of the German Jew.

Until then, the only route that seemed available to me lay through my surviving parent and her sisters: the world of Marianne, Ursel, and Ilse; of their mother Emmy; and above all of their father, Ernst, the totemic source of it all.

Though I had uncovered so much of Ernst's life and legacy, there was one remnant of it that still eluded me: his grave, in Berlin. As my mother had no memory of his funeral, except that everybody came to it, I was bereft of clues. Over the years, she and I had made numerous enquiries in Protestant, Jewish, and civil cemeteries in both east and west Berlin, to no effect.

Back in the summer of 1991, I decided that, if I couldn't track down *his* earthly remains, I would try to find the graves of his father and grandparents, who, my mother was sure, had died in the place where he was born and raised: Christburg in West Prussia, or, since 1945, Dzierzgoń in Poland. When Ernst was a child, in the 1880s, Christburg had a Jewish population of around 250 (out of a total population of just under 3,300), at least one Jewish cemetery, and its own synagogue. But the sepulchral communist-era offices where we went yielded neither Jewish burial records nor pre-war lists of residents. We should see, though, what we could find at the surviving cemetery, an official said, sketching a little diagram with directions.

We found a rectangular plot, hemmed in by forest, strewn with broken stones bearing traces of Hebrew script, and overgrown with vegetation. A few gravestones still stood, but they seemed mute and expressionless, as if they'd lost the will to bear witness to an extinct community and had allowed its secrets to flee. Desecrated by the Nazis and then abandoned for decades, this habitat of the dead had itself died. Tall trees, their trunks reaching serenely towards the sky, clustered just beyond its wall; but, far from casting a protective eye over the scattered stones, they and their colonies of singing birds seemed oblivious to them. This was a world so inert, so shockingly emptied out, that even melancholy could find no home in it.

A rustling noise by the entrance heralded the arrival of an elderly couple and, discovering that they spoke some German, we fell into conversation. If anyone in the vicinity was in a position to identify the dead in this cemetery and to tell us where registers might exist, the man said, it was him. After being forced to work as a doctor in Auschwitz, he threw in matter-of-factly, he had been a local official until his retirement; so he had some knowledge of where and how the Nazis, and afterwards the Polish communist authorities, kept records. As far as he was aware, the Germans had destroyed all archives of the Jewish community along with most of its gravestones – and of course the synagogue. Besides, he was sure that almost nobody ever asked after the Jews of Dzierzgoń, the last of whom disappeared in the 1930s; we must be the first people for a long time who'd come looking for relics, and certainly the first from abroad.

Our attempts to loosen his tongue on Auschwitz and what he had done or suffered there were unsuccessful. By now it was late afternoon, and we decided that we'd better stay overnight in the vicinity rather than drive, as darkness fell, to a larger city. Could they recommend a hotel? No, they replied, the hotels from communist times had all closed their doors, and they didn't know of any decent new ones. After all, it was only seven months since Lech Wałęsa had become the first freely elected head of state following the fall of communism. But there was a couple who let out rooms and might be able to put us up. They were old enough to have lived through the Nazi occupation of Poland, so we'd be able to converse with them in German.

After a long wait, a woman, probably in her seventies, with bright-red hair appeared and, without vetting us, introduced herself as our host for the night. 'I have a lovely apartment, which you can have all to yourselves,' she declared. Stammering our gratitude for this astonishing flexibility, not to mention trustingness, we asked how much she charged. 'Nothing,' she answered. 'You're my guests!'

When we arrived, her husband was waiting for us with a dinner of cold salads and meats and bread, along with beer and vodka. Soon, we were all sitting down to eat.

'We Poles suffered terribly under the Germans,' the wife began. 'My husband had just finished an apprenticeship in a milk shop when he was forced into slave labour.' As she told us the story, he pulled an identity card out of his jacket that had the letters 'PK' on the front, which stood for *polnische Kraft* – Polish [Labour] Force. She had seen members of her family shot before her eyes, others arrested and never heard of again.

Of course: our speaking to her in German and driving a car with a German number plate meant that she was taking us for Germans. And, plainly, my mother was of a reproachable age. Perhaps our hostess had waited decades for this moment when she could let people like us know, to our faces, what our nation had inflicted on her. Bizarrely, I felt guilty. I wanted to apologize for the unspeakable cruelty that Germans had visited on Poles.

At the same time, something made us cautious about exculpating ourselves by owning up to a Jewish origin. What if our hosts despised Jews as much as Germans? Or more? Just as in some of those German homes back in my childhood, we rolled out the official story about my mother following her violin teacher to England before the war, so that we would neither be implicated in the Nazi time nor be suspected of Jewishness. This version of events really did have its uses.

I think they understood that, though my parents were German, they hadn't been in Germany during the war. But I don't know whether they nonetheless assumed that the rest of my father's and mother's families had been innocent of Nazi crimes. It did sound like they were trying to make us realize how they had been abused under 'our' yoke – and now wanted to be asked for forgiveness.

But this was all a long time ago, they eventually said, and today's Germans were very different. They had apologized again and again; they were good neighbours; and they were helping Poland's economy.

The really unredeemable people, on the other hand, were the Jews. They would never be friends of the Polish nation; they would only exploit and extort. German crimes were in the past, but the real and present danger were the Jews.

For the first time ever, I felt relief at concealing Jewish origins, grateful for our trusty kaleidoscope of identities. Trapped for the night in this communist-era apartment with prejudices that, a few decades earlier, had been murderous, I was frightened. I understood what Ernst had feared his whole life. Instinct told us to keep my father silently in the background, and mercifully our hosts never enquired after his ethnicity.

Yes, she continued, the Jews are responsible for Poland's terrible economic problems. The inflation, the closure of factories, the imposition of brutal, capitalist, so-called 'reforms' that have created mass unemployment and forced women into prostitution – all this is the work of Jews. Their aim is to destroy Poland so that its assets can be bought up on the cheap by greedy bankers in London and New York who are in league with Lech Wałęsa, 'the Jewish President of Poland', and the 'Israelite' Tadeusz Mazowiecki.

This was giddying stuff. Lech Wałęsa, the former trade unionist who had been instrumental in the fall of communism, was certainly not Jewish, and the same went for Mazowiecki, the country's first non-communist prime minister since 1946. Besides, we attempted to explain, there were almost no Jews left in Poland. But we were getting nowhere. 'Where do you think all those people who escaped from Auschwitz went?' our hosts enquired. 'They stayed here, of course, to rob us and to live off us. Under communism they had to keep a low profile. But now they, or their descendants, have free rein. That's why we're in the mess we're in.'

Escaped from Auschwitz only to rob Poland? The accusations were so fantastical, I argued when they'd gone for the night and we found ourselves alone in the private space of these generous strangers, that it was oddly impossible to take offence.

The next morning, as we were eating breakfast, my mother announced that she'd been awake all night. She looked terse and shattered and vulnerable. Of course: it must have been horrific for her, whose life had been wracked by the destruction of the world of Blumeshof, by those terrible words, 'Get out of here immediately, you East Asian monkey!' which had sent her beloved father to his death, and by the insoluble unbelonging of exile, to experience such hate first-hand. And then to climb into the bed of the strangers who nursed it. And before that to find no trace of Ernst or his family in the place of his birth. And to encounter the doctor from Auschwitz. And to see all those smashed and abandoned Jewish gravestones – monuments no longer to lives but to the utter nothingness of a vacated world. How grossly insensitive I had been not to cut off that whole loathsome conversation.

'No,' she said, in a quietly anguished tone, 'it was none of that; it was your face last night. I've never seen such haunted grief in anyone. As your mother, it was terrible to witness, Simon.'

I was stunned. Not just because I had no recollection whatsoever of feeling haunted grief, but also because my mother never proffered intensely personal comments about how I looked.

By the time we were in the car, an hour or so later, and had found the calm to talk about it, the fierce shape of whatever she'd seen in my face had dissolved and she couldn't describe what exactly had overwhelmed her. Or else she found it too painful to disclose. But her reaction left me in shock: shock that I hadn't wanted to take the anti-Semitism seriously, though I certainly felt fear and even terror when I imagined being unable to flee; and shock at how grateful I was for the protective lie, which normally infuriated me, about my mother merely following her teacher to London – at how swiftly I'd embraced self-concealment at the merest provocation.

Before this sobering insight into my own loyalty to family tradition – loyalty which might have anaesthetized a much deeper horror that my mother had glimpsed in my face – had had a chance to take root back in the apartment, our hosts had marched in, full of fresh morning energy and I think ready for more conversation.

But by then everything felt different. We had to leave. At once.

Embracing us, they'd thanked us for our visit, which they said they had so enjoyed, and still refused to accept any payment. When their heads were turned, we'd left some money next to a flowerpot, and headed back to the safety of Berlin.

47

Finding Grandfather May

Unlike in Berlin, where I'd searched for years for Ernst's grave without success, in Cologne it took me no time at all to locate my other grandfather, Ferdinand May.

Why can we want something so badly – in this case, any trace of my father's family in Germany – and yet do nothing about it for decades?

Why could I fail to take the simplest action in pursuit of this treasured end, yet remain unfailingly diligent about including organic skimmed milk in my grocery list?

Why did I unquestioningly believe family members who insisted that nobody knew when Ferdinand died, or where he was buried, or what his last address was? Rumour had it that he had collapsed from a heart attack on a park bench in Cologne in his thirties while smoking a cigarette.

But, in minutes, everything can change. A single email, which I sent to the huge Jewish cemetery on the outskirts of Cologne in April 2016, revealed that he had died at fifty-nine, on Christmas Day 1928, at 12.45 in the afternoon; that he and my grandmother Martha had last lived together at Rachdorffstrasse 27; and that 'the master carpenter Adolf Zirker' had reported the death.

Riding the subway to the cemetery on a beautiful summer's day in June 2016, I felt an almost ridiculous sense of destiny: of heritage waiting for me at the end of a rail track, unobscured, for once, by denial, conversion, embarrassment, silence, inertia, and fossilized narratives that compelled allegiance on pain of betrayal.

The manager of the cemetery had sent me a map showing the location of the grave and, as I approached the ochre-coloured building, above which a Star of David was shining unashamedly in the afternoon sun, I was moved as deeply as the first time I visited my father's grave, which I only did at thirty-five, again after epic procrastination. I was trembling as I followed the immaculately tended gravel paths flanked by gravestones in a riot of different styles, until I saw a large art deco stone bearing the name: FERDINAND MAY. There were no dates, no inscriptions, no names of loved ones, and no Hebrew. Just his name.

Then I noticed that it was a double grave, with single occupancy. Of course: if he died in 1928, my grandmother would have expected to lie next to him when she passed away. Who would have thought, only five years before Hitler took power, that Jews would soon be expelled or murdered?

What also struck me was the speed of assimilation. Thousands of years of tradition over in a single generation. He was the first to leave the Jewish community of Trier; the first to go by a non-Hebrew name; the first of a line of Bible scholars, scribes, circumcisers, and kosher inspectors no longer to be defined by, or even to practise, a religion that had been passed from parents to their children since time immemorial; the first to be buried in a grave with no Hebrew inscription. It seemed amazing to me that he could regard the life of a travelling salesman of ribbons as a step up from being a Bible scholar and a scribe. But he had only taken the first few steps along a path that, in Berlin, might have led all the way to Protestantism, and then Catholicism, and then to a more far-reaching immolation of inherited memory and sensibility, so that one no longer knows who one is or was.

At this moment of arrival, when I encountered his grave and saw the name, I did something I had never done before: I bowed low until I felt I had extended to this man the reverence due to an ancestor whose life was a hinge between two worlds; who continues to lie alone and in dignity in the land of his forebears; and who will hopefully remain there, undisturbed, forever.

48

The Jewish cemetery of Trier

The next day, after a winding train ride from Cologne to Trier, cutting through hills, crossing verdant meadows, overtaking fast-flowing streams, and stopping at hamlets in the beautiful Eifel region, I stood before another ancestral grave: that of Ferdinand's father, my great-grandfather Moshe May. This was an altogether more ancient cemetery, dating back to 1652, and defiled not by the Nazi regime but by Allied bombing, followed by vandals who desecrated it in 1982, and then again in 1983, 1992, and 1995.[34]

My mother had told me about this cemetery. She and my father had come to Trier after that first trip back to Cologne when they had been showered with cakes by the owner of his favourite childhood cafe; and she remembered my father stopping an old man in the street, who was in his nineties, and asking him if he had ever known a Moshe May. Incredibly, the man had. 'Yes, of course,' he said, 'I remember him vividly! The old May! He lived in a house with a turret, and when I passed by he was usually in his living room on the ground floor studying the holy texts. After the death of his beloved wife, he was there more than ever. He was a Bible scholar. A fine man.'

My mother had repeated those words to me so often. The meeting had moved her and my father. They had been taken by the old man to the house with the turret where Moshe had lived and shown the room where he'd studied all day.

'Here lies a kind-hearted descendant of a line of upright people and a family of scribes', begins the inscription in Hebrew on his tombstone, one of the more recent. A few yards away is the grave of Karl Marx's paternal grandfather, Mordechai Halevi ben Schmuel Postelburg, a rabbi who died in 1804. Unlike Moshe's, its headstone is all in Hebrew, with not even the concession of the name and dates of the deceased written in the German form. And there are even older stones, many of them so deeply sunk into the ground that only their tips can be seen, peeking up from the earth.

Then I saw other Mays: Moshe's wife Bella, who died at forty-five. Their little son Eliahu, secular name Eduard, who passed away at fifteen. (Is this why Ferdinand named my uncle Edward, in memory of the little brother he lost?) Their daughter Chava, who lived only to her twenty-first year.

I learned that Trier's Jewish community at the end of the nineteenth century, when Moshe thrived, numbered around 300 – similar to Christburg's, in which Ernst was raised. Occasionally, spouses would be found among the Jews of surrounding villages, but the few families represented in this cemetery mostly intermarried. Three hundred feels claustrophobic; I could understand why Ferdinand, like Ernst, left once assimilation became acceptable – within the community as well as to its non-Jewish neighbours.

Yet, wandering around the tiny plot, which is well-tended and pervaded by timeless quietude, I was besieged by an identity passionately lived – not one fraught with life-sapping riddles, or that flees into a labyrinth of internal exile, as in the lives of the three sisters; not one that takes, as it took me, half a lifetime to excavate in the face of denial, obfuscation, and fury. And again I felt a profound sense of arrival, as I had at Ferdinand's solitary grave the day before; but this time I'd arrived not just at a monument to lost family but also at the portal to an immense heritage, which these stones somehow rendered vivid, real, thinkable, legitimate – and mine. *This* surely was restitution.

I wasn't allowed to visit the cemetery unaccompanied. It is surrounded by a wall and always locked. Access could be gained only by arrangement with the city's synagogue, where I was told to report first and to ask for Peter Szemere. But when I showed up, the receptionist said that he couldn't see me then after all. A party of schoolchildren was visiting and I should return an hour later, when he would be free.

Rather than waiting, I thought, *Why don't I join the schoolchildren's visit?* I slid into the meeting room just as Herr Szemere was starting to tell two dozen teenagers about the basics of Judaism and that it is not an alien religion but rather that of a parent to their offspring: Christianity and Islam.

He did a superb job regaling them with lively biblical stories, but the children were restless and bored. When we moved from the meeting room to the hall of worship, they'd found it amusing and possibly absurd that men had to cover their heads. Tracksuit hoods were reluctantly put on and boys wearing kippas for the first time laughed at each other. It was a disconcerting session, void of any trace of reverence on the part of the children before a tragic history or at the power of faith to keep a people going through unspeakable odds. But I was impressed by what a patient and articulate rabbi Trier had, and afterwards I congratulated him on his entertaining introduction to the story of the Jewish people.

How long, I asked, had he been the rabbi here?

'Rabbi?' He looked puzzled. 'I'm not the rabbi. When we have services, a rabbi drives over from Luxembourg.'

'How long have you been a congregant?' I persisted.

'I'm not a congregant. I'm Christian.'

He saw my surprise and chuckled. 'This is Germany. We don't have enough Jews to fill all the positions in synagogues, so in a small city like Trier a Christian has to contribute.'

'Are you from Trier?' I asked. I imagined that he represented the Jewish community because he was an elder of the town, perhaps with ancestors who had known Jews, like my family, who'd once lived here.

'No, I came from Munich.'

'So why did you look for a position in a synagogue?'

'Because I worked for El Al, the Israeli airline, at Munich airport, and when I had to retire at sixty I needed another job to make ends meet. I spoke some Hebrew from having to deal with Israeli passengers – modern Hebrew, of course, but still better than nothing.

'I'm from a family of Hungarian aristocrats,' he continued. 'We fled the communists in 1956, after the Hungarian uprising against Moscow. We lost all our wealth. In Germany, we had to work hard for a living.'

'And why did you go to work for El Al?'

'Very simple: they paid better than Lufthansa. It's the security risk of working at an El Al counter. You're a terrorist target.'

His journey from Hungarian Christian aristocrat to official of the synagogue at Trier via Munich airport cast me into that clichéd emotion that I try to avoid in Germany: melancholy. Jewish life in this city of my ancestors felt threadbare, empty, artificial – and Moshe's tomb, along with the world to which it so eloquently points, achingly lonely. Unlike in Berlin, where the Jewish ghosts of pre-Hitler Germany still retain a foothold, in this city they were silent. The past is a graveyard.

'For being a terrorist target, the Israelis had better pay you well,' he added with a smile.

The survivor file

My quest to recover my German ancestry had encountered a magnificent gift in Klaus Meltzer. Through him, I found myself closer not just to Theo, but also, and quite unexpectedly, to my father's family, which had always seemed beyond my reach, cocooned in unbreakable silence. Without Klaus I might never have lingered in Cologne and from there gone on to Trier.

And then there was another, equally unexpected, connection to my German roots that offered itself – one that, however, would be decisive in taming my imaginings of a restituted *Heimat* and in disbanding the infantile fantasy of Germany as the magical ur-world that would embrace and root me like a primal parent, forever holding me close. Instead, it would force me to confront how intensely partial, even hollow, any restitution of the past is likely to be.

This was the return, after the fall of the Berlin Wall, of the J. Eichenberg Garment Factory AG, which had started out making shirts and collars, and then diversified into sleepwear and aprons. Until the early 1990s, neither my mother nor her sisters had known that Ernst and Emmy bought 15 per cent of the business in 1924, the rest being owned by a chain of my grandfather's distant cousins, whose descendants were dispersed all over the world, from Colombia to Chile to Britain to the United States.

Eichenberg had been Aryanized on 1 February 1939: forcibly sold to *Deutschblütiger* – people of German blood – at a bargain-basement price that, after successive valuations by the Berlin Chamber of Industry and Commerce, the German Workers' Front, and the Nazi Party itself, had been revised down from an already nominal opening offer. The little money paid to the Jewish owners was then largely confiscated in emigration tax – the *Reichsfluchtsteuer* (or Reich escape tax) – levied on Jews for fleeing a country that had stripped them of citizenship and almost all legal rights, and was soon to exterminate those who were unable or unwilling to leave.

Under Nazi rules, any purchaser of Eichenberg had to meet a non-negotiable condition: the name of the firm was to be Aryanized too. The authorities were adamant that getting rid of Jewish owners and staff wasn't enough. Names conveyed history and meaning, and they had to be racially purified.

This did not please the new proprietors, August Plöger and the brothers Heinrich and Albert Fischer; nor the supervisory board members who had replaced their ousted Jewish predecessors, one an SA-*Oberführer*, the other an SS-*Untersturmführer*. Though they had been given a deadline of five months from the date of expropriation to Aryanize the name, they pleaded and bargained for two long years with Berlin's Police President to keep 'Eichenberg' for its brand value.

Losing the name, they argued, would cause heavy financial losses, as international customers in particular turned to foreign competitors. Moreover, it was *not* intrinsically Jewish: the root '*Eiche*', or 'oak', had 'a primeval German ring' to it;[35] and these Germanic credentials were further boosted by the fact that an SS officer as well as a small town near Kassel bore the same name. Oh, and another firm, called 'Eichenblatt', or 'oak leaf', was continuing to trade under its original name – so surely, they implied perfectly reasonably, an oak's Aryan character was no less robust if it qualified the word 'leaf' ('*Blatt*') than if it qualified the word 'mountain' ('*Berg*'). But, in order to further enhance those primeval resonances, perhaps they could call the company 'Deutsche Eichenberg'?[36]

The Police President's office flatly refused. Moreover, an opinion that they now commissioned from the Chamber of Industry and Commerce revealed that the 'Eichenblatt' company sported a logo depicting an oak leaf. This, the Chamber obscurely concluded, made it a very different case to Eichenberg, which employed no logo at all. Plöger and the Fischer brothers were given a further six months to change the name; 31 December 1939 was the new deadline.

But, again, the trio weren't taking no for an answer. New arguments followed, most bizarrely that the company had, in fact, neither been founded by a Jew nor had a Jewish owner in the previous forty years. After these, too, had been rejected, they switched to a more practical tack, claiming in October 1940 that a renaming was impossible because two supervisory board members were now fighting in the war, which had broken out in the meantime. They were therefore unavailable to endorse a decision that had to be taken by consensus. How about delaying the whole matter until the end of the war?

After checking with the Chamber of Industry and Commerce whether corporate name changes really required consensus and being advised that this was nonsense, and, in addition, sending agents over to the factory to verify that the old name plates were still in place, the remarkably patient Police President's office upped their game. If Eichenberg's new owners didn't obey at once, they would be severely punished and a new name imposed by force.

This worked. Sort of. On 10 May 1941, the day on which Rudolf Hess, Hitler's loyal deputy, flew on his strange peace mission to Britain, they replied that they were 'determined' to give the company a new name, which would be 'United Garment Factory' – Vereinte Wäschefabrikation AG, or VEWAG for short. Herewith, they declared, 'all Jewish elements in the company will finally be removed. Heil Hitler! J. Eichenberg AG'.[37]

It must have taken chutzpah to stonewall the Police President in a totalitarian state for this long, but they continued to drag their feet for yet another year before officially registering VEWAG on 24 April 1942, over three years after the expropriation.

The change turned out not to harm the company after all. It thrived during the war, supplying the regime with jackets and shirts for the Wehrmacht. After Germany's defeat, it was confiscated by the communist regime in East Berlin, where it continued to trade as a state enterprise until the collapse of East Germany in 1990.

Remarkably, the complete file documenting Eichenberg's Aryanization turned up in the attic of a Berlin district court in November 1991, hidden within the company's registration deeds. It almost certainly survived the bombing of the city only because it had been left in the wrong office: records of a business's Aryanization were not generally stored together with its deeds. In the tidy world of German officialdom, where each procedure was like a minor god, that sort of error was exceedingly rare.

Then the Berlin Wall had to fall, East Germany had to collapse, and Germany had to be reunited before the heirs of the original owners could contemplate restitution. Before Mikhail Gorbachev obligingly triggered these world-historical developments, the business and the handsome building that it owned were out of reach, in communist East Berlin.

50

We have Saddam Hussein to thank

We also had the Iraqi president, Saddam Hussein, to thank for our recovery of Eichenberg. When the ferociously anti-Semitic dictator invaded Kuwait on 2 August 1990, Inge-Margot Müller, a descendant of one of its other expropriated owners, happened to be living in Saudi Arabia, where she was married to a German oil executive. As stories of murder and destruction emerged from Kuwait, Inge-Margot was getting nightmarish flashbacks to 1943, when the SS had snatched her mother in Nice and she herself had narrowly escaped arrest.

Now, in Dhahran in autumn 1990, she was taking no chances. If Saddam moved on to the bigger prize of the Saudi oil fields, Jewish civil rights in Saudi Arabia would hardly be high in his priorities. As the Americans were massing their forces in the Gulf for an attack on the occupying Iraqis, she flew to Florida to take refuge with her cousin, Renata de Jara.

Inge-Margot and Renata had been raised in Germany and were granddaughters of Gustav and Henriette Wertheim, the single biggest shareholders in Eichenberg.

The flood of news at the time about Kuwaiti assets stolen by Saddam Hussein and the violence done to their owners by his

henchmen dredged up long-forgotten stories about a factory somewhere in Berlin and its expropriation by the Nazis. Inge-Margot
recalled her mother showing her a building that was divided between
staff apartments at the front and a factory at the rear. And then the
name Eichenberg stole up on her! While the other world drama of
1990, the reunification of Germany, unfolded, the cousins tried to
reconstruct the history of Eichenberg's creation, growth, and confiscation; and they resolved to get it back.

Inge-Margot at once wrote to her elder sister Marion, who had
been thirteen when she last saw the Berlin building and might have
more vivid memories. Marion's reply was discouraging: 'The factory
did *not* belong to our family but was rented!' she mistakenly insisted.
Fortunately, her letter was delayed in the post. Before it arrived,
Renata had left for Berlin, on the hunt for Eichenberg.

Renata was feisty, businesslike, and tenacious, with a face like a
bird of prey and a voice that rasped in mid-Atlantic German-
American tones. She flew to Berlin armed only with the name of
the firm – and the details of a legal secretary there, who had once
done a little work for a neighbour in Florida. The legal secretary
said that she could recommend the perfect lawyer to help: Elke
Stahlke.

It was an inspired tip. Stahlke was forensic, as sharp as her stiletto
heels, deeply committed to restituting expropriated Jewish properties – and patient.

51

The file goes astray

Stahlke needed her patience. It quickly came to light that we had a determined competitor for Eichenberg's restitution: the son of one of the Aryanizers who had 'bought' it from my grandmother, Emmy, and her co-investors.

Hans-Joachim Fischer, son of Albert, maintained that his family had also been a victim of expropriation – when the communists in East Berlin seized the property from them in 1949. As for the Jewish families, they had already been taken care of four decades earlier, in 1954, when a German court had ordered his father and August Plöger to pay 40,000 Deutsche marks in compensation to Herbert Liepmann, Eichenberg's ousted managing director, and a few of the other original investors. He had therefore lodged an official claim to Eichenberg, which he was demanding back in its entirety.

Stahlke's advice was succinct: do nothing. Our priorities, she said, were very different. Most importantly, we had to track down the rightful heirs to Eichenberg, the descendants of all those who had been expropriated in 1939. There might be dozens all over the world. Many of the original owners of properties like ours had been murdered in the camps, or had died natural deaths without informing their living descendants, or were now ill and demented.

At the same time, it would be necessary to navigate the network of official German agencies – diffuse, mutable, but critical – each of which had some sort of responsibility for Eichenberg and to that extent would be involved in its restitution. There was the Treuhand, which had been established in June 1990 to take formal possession of the businesses and properties that had been in the hands of the soon-to-be-defunct East German state, to prepare these assets for sale, and, where they had been stolen from Jews, to return them to their rightful owners. There was the District Court in Berlin and its associated land registry. Above all, there was LAROV – the *Landesamt zur Regelung offener Vermögensfragen* (the 'State Office for Settling Open Questions about Assets') – which verified the identity of heirs and adjudicated rival claims for properties. LAROV was the crucial player: it would be responsible for issuing the final verdict on the restitution.

It wasn't, though, always easy to figure out who had responsibility for what. At that early stage after the fall of the Wall, when the parallel worlds of East and West were colliding and everything was being improvised, no single authority in Berlin had control over former Jewish properties. Eichenberg's building in East Berlin was managed by two organizations with different interests, one of which, the Treuhand, was keen for the building to be sold, while the other, a relic of East German rule that administered its apartments, was resolutely opposed to a sale – understandably, because they had long-term tenants who for the time being had nowhere else to go.

Meanwhile, the Treuhand's character was changing as we were speaking to them. A turgid government bureaucracy was morphing into a commercially savvy real-estate agency. The staff in charge of the Eichenberg file were visibly transforming themselves from uppity officials, whose only interest was to police the rules and do as little work as possible, to a pair of aggressive salespersons intent on convincing us that we had no choice but to have them dispose of Eichenberg's property whenever we found all its rightful heirs. Even their dress changed from the plain outfits of desk-bound East German bureaucrats to the designer clothes of deal-hungry executives. But no sooner had they switched their identity than another German government edict abolished the Treuhand altogether.

Bizarrely, amid the chaos of those times, our Aryanization file went missing. Only one day after Stahlke discovered it squeezed into the company's registration documents, it had disappeared. She was flummoxed: how could a file survive the Third Reich, the Allied bombing, the defeated Nazis' destruction of their archives, armies of occupation, and the division of Berlin, only to vanish just when the past to which it bore such detailed witness could be restituted?

Luckily, she had immediately realized that this was an extraordinary historical document – it turned out to be the only complete Aryanization file that she ever encountered in the dozens of restitution cases she handled after the fall of the Wall – and had photocopied almost the whole thing then and there. As she had stumbled on the file at midday, and the closely supervised room where lawyers were allowed to consult official papers would shut at 2 p.m., she'd quickly copied as many pages as she could using her own portable copier before slipping the file back into the registration documents at exactly the place where she had discovered it, and leaving for a late lunch.

It was just as well she had had the presence of mind to copy the file. Without it, the past might have been a lot more resistant to our claims on it.

Finding the heirs

Now, the hardest part had to begin: tracking down the heirs.

Stahlke decided that there was an obvious place to start: with the only investor who had listed themselves as Aryan when the business was confiscated. This was my grandmother, Emmy Liedtke, into whose sole ownership my grandparents' shares had passed after Ernst's death. An Aryan's descendants would probably still be living in Germany. They would be the easiest heirs to find.

Provided, of course, they were male. Women would have lost their family names on marrying – and Emmy Liedtke had had three daughters.

But thanks to the Nazis' prohibition of mixed marriages, Ernst's disapproval, Ilse's Catholicism, or whatever had stopped her marrying Harald Böhmelt, she had passed the Liedtke name to her son; and so it had been preserved.

On a freezing day in December 1991, he received a phone call from Stahlke. She had started her search simply – with the Berlin telephone directory. Armed only with the address at which Emmy's shares had been registered by the Nazi authorities when Eichenberg was Aryanized, she managed to trace him, and so our whole family.

Finding the other heirs, however, required more than a local telephone directory. They would surely be anywhere but Berlin. Advertisements were placed in newspapers from Sydney to Santiago, with remarkable results. Overnight, feuding relatives couldn't wait to be reconciled. Long forgotten cousins were hungry for contact. Decades of silence were broken by flurries of visits and telephone calls – before communications would cease again, this time probably forever.

Most of the Americans, British, Colombians, and Germans sent in the required proofs of descendance in no time at all. Some others, including the Chileans, were agonizingly slow. The executor of one heir who had recently died refused to cooperate after he discovered that she had left him nothing in her will. It took over four years to track down and complete the paperwork for twenty-one of them, who together represented a tantalizing 76 per cent of Eichenberg's ownership. Only three couldn't be found: Eric Sonnenberg; Frank Lehmann; and whoever the heir was to someone called Adelheid Gerschlowitz.

It was vital to find this elusive trio who made up the remaining 24 per cent of Eichenberg's shareholders. Meanwhile, the post-reunification property boom in Berlin had gone into reverse. The euphoria following the fall of the Wall and the hope that a world capital would quickly spring from the ecstatic fusion of two halves of a city that had been separated by a death zone for nearly three decades were – amazingly, in hindsight – evaporating.

A couple of intrepid investors were keen to buy out the heirs to Eichenberg's property who'd already been traced. They offered half its market value to compensate for the risk that the missing heirs might never be found. But this was no time to give up. The hunt for them had to go on.

53

Pip

The first of the three, Eric Sonnenberg, was the nephew of Herbert Liepmann, the manager of Eichenberg when it had been Aryanized. Renata had searched for all the Sonnenbergs in the UK. Then she switched her search to the US, in case he had re-emigrated. But none of the Sonnenbergs she contacted was an Eric or knew of one.

A year later, she happened to mention the problem on the phone to another of Liepmann's heirs, a London-based lawyer called Rico Jonas. 'You're looking for Eric?' Jonas chuckled. 'He was here for lunch yesterday, on his way from the US to South Africa! He drops in on me twice a year, to and from his annual visit to Cape Town to visit his son. I'll give you his wife's phone number in Philadelphia.'

'But why couldn't I find him anywhere?' Renata asked.

The voice at the other end of the phone growled with laughter. 'He hasn't been called Eric since he was a schoolboy in England fifty years ago. He's Pip now!'

'Pip?'

'He used to go to a friend's house after junior school and, the first time he appeared, the friend's snooty mother demanded of her son: "Who's this little pipsqueak you've brought home? Sit him down and I'll give you both a cup of tea. No, first go and give yourself a good scrub, Pip! You look disgusting!" And from then on the name

Pip stuck to him. He worked, and filed his taxes, and married as Pip Sonnenberg. He only wants to be called Pip!'

Frank Lehmann, the second missing heir, was a nephew of Rico Jonas, who had located Pip. Jonas was eighty-nine when the survivor file had surfaced in Berlin. At ninety-two, just eleven months before Eichenberg was finally restituted, he told Renata: 'It will be a miracle if you get Eichenberg back. It will be even better if I live to see it happen. But if I don't, my will is with my lawyer.'

Jonas died eight weeks before Eichenberg was restituted and left his money to two former girlfriends, one of them a woman who lived in Fiji, the other a professional ice skater based in London – and to Frank Lehmann in New York. The first two were easy to locate, but Frank was harder. Jonas's lawyer had been trying for some time, but his letters had gone unanswered.

Renata decided to fly to New York to track Frank down herself. She would go to the address for him that Jonas's lawyer had given her and, if he was out, leave a message with a neighbour. But when she got there she realized this wasn't going to work: in place of the apartment block was a burned-out ruin. A charred smudge on the face of the building framed a large black hole, where the fire must have started.

So what now? The New York telephone directory still had Frank listed at the black hole and neither the local post office nor utility companies would give out a forwarding address. But then she asked at a nearby store, and learned that Frank was now at a senior citizens' home. The manager gave her its name and even its telephone number.

'Would it be possible to speak to Mr Lehmann?' Renata enquired gingerly, imagining a decrepit figure with tremoring limbs, slumped in a large chair and possibly unable to talk or to remember anything.

'Sure,' the operator said briskly, 'I'll connect you to the director's office.'

'I really don't want to bother the director. Can you please just connect me to Mr Lehmann's room?' Renata said. 'Is he able to take calls?'

'Mr Lehmann *is* the director,' the voice said, becoming impatient.

An assistant took the call. No, Mr Lehmann wasn't in; he was out dancing salsa. He did that every evening, so it wasn't a good idea to call at this time. He rode to the salsa class and back by bike. He also cooked for the old people when the cook was ill or too lazy to turn up.

When he finally returned Renata's call, Lehmann was suspicious, thinking someone was playing a trick on him. He had just lost a long battle with the German authorities over two other Aryanized properties, one of them a seven-room mansion, and had started to put all that behind him when this unknown woman called to offer him a share in just such a property. Odder still, she was desperate for his cooperation.

Nor did the name Eichenberg ring bells. It must be a misunderstanding, he thought. He hadn't known that his uncle, Rico Jonas, had been a childhood friend of Herbert Liepmann; that Liepmann had left Jonas a small share in the business; and that this share had trickled down to him.

For Frank Lehmann, this was a triumph of historical justice. Where he sought, he hadn't found; where he failed to seek, he had come into riches. When he got his inheritance, he didn't give up being the director of the senior citizens' home. He was dedicated to helping old people in their dotage; but now, thanks to the Eichenberg money, he could look forward to a comfortable retirement himself.

54

The missing 1 per cent

With Pip and Frank, we had 92 per cent of the heirs on side. The Chileans, who accounted for a further 7 per cent, were still at war with their national bureaucracy over certifying the paperwork, but at least we knew where they were. There was one missing piece: the heir to Adelheid Gerschlowitz.

So what had happened to Adelheid? The hunt started, as it often did, with an enquiry to Yad Vashem, the Holocaust Memorial. Did they have her on their lists? No, they replied; the only murdered Gerschlowitzs from Berlin were a Jenny, a Flora, and a Nathan, and none of these names rang bells with Renata.

A couple of weeks after Renata received the reply from Yad Vashem, she happened to be in Berlin, and decided to visit the grave of her grandfather, Gustav Wertheim, who was buried in the Jewish cemetery at Weissensee. As she was about to leave, she thought she'd ask an official at the front desk if he knew how you could discover where your German-Jewish ancestors were buried, if all you had was a name and place of birth. Was there such a database?

'Adelheid Gerschlowitz?' He tapped into a computer. 'She's buried right here!'

Renata was stunned. 'So how can we find out more about her?'

'Speak to that young fellow in the next room,' the official replied. 'He's researching the fate of Berlin Jews in the thirties.'

The young man thought this must be a set-up. 'But I've researched the Gerschlowitz family!' he said. 'It was a few months ago now, but I'll get you all the information I have.'

Adelheid, he reported, had been deported to Theresienstadt, survived the camp, and died in Berlin in 1956.

Died in Berlin? That would make the search for an heir so much easier. There must be a whole post-war paper trail on her in this city of files. For a start, if she had been imprisoned in a Nazi camp and then lived in Berlin after the war, she would surely have received some sort of pension from the German government. The bureaucracy that dealt with pensions for Nazi victims was the Entschädigungsbehörde, the Restitution Authority, the obvious next port of call.

Renata thanked the young man and was about to head for the Restitution Authority when he called after her: 'Wait a minute! Adelheid had a daughter called Flora, who was born on 26 June 1893 and was also deported to Theresienstadt. You have an heir!'

He read on; then paused. 'I'm sorry – she was murdered. Her mother survived, but Flora died within a few months.'

This matched the information on a Flora that Renata had received from Yad Vashem; that Flora must have been Adelheid's daughter.

After the usual weeks assembling the necessary papers, Renata tracked down a three-inch file into which the Restitution Authority had compressed Adelheid's life, where she discovered that there was a sole heir: Dr Werner Asch, Adelheid's nephew.

Further enquiries revealed that he had married a woman called Dagmar, who had given birth to a daughter, Judith, born in Berlin in 1961.

So Judith Asch was the heir to Adelheid's 1 per cent and she might be in Berlin, right under Renata's nose. The hunt for Eichenberg's heirs would end, as it had begun, in the improbable setting of the city from which the original owners had long ago been expelled. Finding her would just be a matter of searching the telephone directory.

But it wasn't as simple as that. There was no Judith Asch with

that date of birth registered in Berlin. Renata then tried the maternity wards of hospitals in Berlin: had any of them delivered a baby
with that name on that day? No luck. What about baptismal registries,
both Catholic and Protestant? Dagmar wasn't Jewish and might have
raised Judith as a Christian, but there too Renata drew a blank.

A breakthrough came with a search that Renata placed at Berlin's
Interior Ministry for all birth certificates marked 'Judith Asch'. Four
months later, Judith's birth certificate was located. But Renata could
have no access to it, they said, as she wasn't a direct family member.
Not that a birth certificate would have shed any light on where she
was living over three decades later.

Renata pleaded with the official at the local registry of births and
deaths. Judith Asch, she told him, probably had no near relatives
and this concerned an inheritance from which she would benefit.
He shrugged understandingly, but the rules were the rules. As she
was about to leave, exhausted at this dismal end to years of searching
for heirs, he said, 'By the way, Frau de Jara, why don't you try
enquiring at this other office?' And he slipped her a piece of paper
directing her to the registry of Berlin residents.

Renata had left Germany too young to know that when you move
into a new lodging there the first thing you must do is register at
an office like this. If only she had asked Stahlke, she would have
gone here immediately. And it duly took this office just ten minutes
to resolve the mystery: Judith Asch had a new name. She was now
Judith Bieling.

Renata ran to a public telephone across the road – she didn't yet
have a mobile phone – and grabbed the Berlin directory. There it
was: 'Bieling, Judith'! She left a message saying that if she was the
former Judith Asch, daughter of Dr Werner Asch, and great-niece
of Adelheid Gerschlowitz, then she should call this stranger from
Florida for some good news.

That evening, Judith was amazed to learn that, if she successfully
laid siege to a chain of bureaucracies, she would become an heiress.

But why Bieling?

The answer was easy, Judith told me over coffee in Berlin in 2008:
Bieling was the maiden name of Judith's mother, Dagmar. When
Judith was about to begin junior school, Dagmar wanted her

daughter to think of herself as a Bieling and not as an Asch. The reason for this, she later told Judith, was compassionate: Judith's classmates might insert an 'r' after the 'A' in Asch, and so make her an '*Arsch*' — an arse, a backside — and Dagmar wanted to spare her the taunting and the humiliation.

For Judith, Eichenberg wasn't just about the discovery of some money. It had given her a global family of which she was now part. By 2008, she had already spent Thanksgiving with Renata in Florida and New Year's with Renata's children in California. She and I had met and felt a bond through a common inheritance that was a surprise to us both. The community of heirs was her real windfall.

55

The Aryanizers demand compensation from us

With Judith located, Eichenberg was swiftly restituted, in mid-1995, by an 'incontestable' ruling of the Berlin authorities. A thrilling piece of historical justice had been completed.

But ghosts don't take easily to retirement. Within months of the restitution, a lawyer for Hans-Joachim, son of Albert Fischer, one of the original Aryanizers, appeared on the scene yet again. Now he was demanding back the 40,000 Deutsche marks compensation that his father had been ordered to pay Herbert Liepmann back in 1954. He wrote to Stahlke in October 1995, in July 1996, and again in August 1998. Stahlke did what she did masterfully under these circumstances: nothing.

Part of me sympathized with Hans-Joachim. Wasn't there a case for him to get *some* money back? The Aryanizers hadn't been responsible for Hitler's anti-Semitic obsession, even if they had profited from it. They had invested in a business that would have gone bankrupt if its Jewish owners and managers had been expelled without being replaced. And then in 1949 they, too, had seen the assets of the business confiscated – this time by the communists in East Berlin.

In any event, as the twenty-first century got into its stride, I realized that I wasn't done with Eichenberg either. A passionate desire to meet these Germans who had picked its shares from my grandmother and her co-investors crept up on me, partly because there is something delicious about feeling safe in the presence of a former enemy, especially when they happen to belong to a nation that you still love; and partly because I wanted to discover why this long-defunct business meant so much to them.

August Plöger had died back in 1978 and was unmarried. Albert and Heinrich Fischer had also both died. And sadly, just a year before I cold-called their family home in 2006, so too had Albert's son Hans-Joachim, who had fought so hard to prove that he was the true heir to Eichenberg. But when we spoke on the telephone, which we did twice, for what must have been a total of two or three hours, Hans-Joachim's widow, Annette, seemed neither suspicious – 'why are you calling us after all these years?'; nor condescending – 'of course we personally had nothing against Jews'; nor strenuously apologetic – 'we shouldn't have profited from the Nazi racket'; nor artificially philo-Semitic. I liked the fact that she was none of these things.

Her immediate candour and matter-of-fact tone astonished me. As did the freshness of her memory: there was no pause to recollect long-distant events. She said I was welcome to come and see her family's papers on Eichenberg, which were stored in a trunk in her cellar, and to take copies of any that I wished to have. As a memento, she would give me an original share certificate in VEWAG – the new name that the Aryanizers reluctantly gave the company after the Police President's office won its two-year battle to dispense with the supposedly Jewish-sounding 'Eichenberg'.

Within minutes of making contact, we were deep into history.

At first, she told me that her father-in-law hadn't been a Nazi; he had merely belonged to the National Socialist Motorists Corps. Later in our call, she said that he had, after all, succumbed to full Party membership soon after taking over Eichenberg. Nor had he made a point of seeking out confiscated Jewish firms – he was just looking for good investment opportunities, and there were lots of firms available to be taken over in the late 1930s, not only Jewish ones but thousands that had been brought down by Germany's terrible economic situation that Hitler was trying to sort out. It was, in many ways, an exciting time: 'Nineteen thirty-six to nineteen thirty-nine were lovely years for German people – not for Jewish people, of course, but for Germans, yes.'

Her father-in-law, she said, had really wanted to invest in a hotel in Hamburg. He didn't particularly like Berlin; and he felt more comfortable with the hospitality sector than with textiles. But August Plöger had heard through the Nazi Party grapevine about Eichenberg being for sale and had persuaded him that it could be a money-spinner. Plöger's problem was that he didn't have enough cash to invest in Eichenberg; nor did he have the necessary management expertise. One or two others had turned down the opportunity to co-invest with him before he approached Albert Fischer.

Initially, Albert was worried that he had no experience at all of textiles, or of running a firm of Eichenberg's size, with nearly 300 staff. This would be a huge step up from the car dealership that he and his brother Heinrich owned, which employed about 60 people, and which anyway was doing wonderfully selling the new VW beetle, the pride of Hitler's Germany.

What convinced him, according to Annette, were Plöger's Nazi Party credentials. If Plöger could use his connections to get ministries to place contracts with Eichenberg for soldiers' clothing, then the firm might be a treasure trove. Unfortunately, she said, Plöger was also something of an anti-Semite – unlike her father-in-law, who had taken pity on the ousted Jewish manager, Herbert Liepmann.

On Liepmann's last evening in Germany, after he had sold the business as well as his family's apartment in Berlin, Albert invited him to dinner. It was a convivial occasion, according to Annette: 'My father-in-law didn't give Liepmann money or valuables like jewellery; but he gave him hospitality.' He got a good dinner, with lots of wine, and then he was put up for the night. Liepmann caught a train to the Belgian coast before dawn the next morning, delighted, she maintained, that his business was to be left in such capable hands.

56

How to have a good war

After the Aryanization, Annette said, August Plöger contacted the business's clients at once to tell them that it was no longer Jewish and needn't be boycotted. More importantly, he worked his magic with the ministries – and trench coats as well as jackets and shirts for the army began rolling off Eichenberg's production line. Soon the business was going so well that her father-in-law, Albert Fischer, was able to take 30,000 Reichsmarks out of it and give 10,000 to his son, Hans-Joachim.

But this switch in Eichenberg's production wasn't only good for business, she added. It also got Plöger something else that he wanted from his ministry contacts: exemption from military service. His work at Eichenberg was deemed important to the war effort, which was what you needed to avoid being called up. Meanwhile, Albert switched his car dealership and repair business to servicing vehicles for the Wehrmacht, and this too was regarded as important to the war effort.

Albert's cultured and luxury-loving brother Heinrich was now on Eichenberg's supervisory board, together with its recently acquired SS and SA members. But supervising a garment business was hardly his idea of fun. He got himself assigned to the German Embassy in Paris – no longer a war zone, since France was now occupied – where he was in his element. Paris offered excellent concerts, fine wines, charming women, and lovely country resorts to which he would repair at weekends.

The three Aryanizers were certainly having a good war.

Eichenberg prospered too – until its building in Prenzlauer Berg took a direct hit from a bomb in early 1945 and partly burned down. But by then the owners had already suspended most of its production and hauled its equipment off to a safer part of Germany. Albert Fischer gathered all the money from the business that he could lay his hands on, as well as some of the portable assets, and distributed it among friends and colleagues whom he trusted to hide it for him until the fighting was over. He then fled westwards, to his home town, on one of the last trains out of Berlin, which was by now besieged on all sides by the Red Army.

Albert Fischer's trust was misplaced, Annette said: the cash all vanished. But Eichenberg never left his mind. He had invested so much in it, after all. Not just to buy it; more costly were upgrades to the machinery, new staff to replace the Jews, a 'social fund' that the *Deutsche Arbeitsfront*, the Nazi-controlled union, had demanded, improvements to the work and leisure areas ordered by the *Amt Schönheit der Arbeit*, the Office of the Beauty of Labour, and, immediately after the war, extensive repairs to the bomb-damaged building.

On top of investing all this in the business only to see it confiscated in 1949, along came Herbert Liepmann a couple of years later demanding compensation for the Aryanization. As far as Albert Fischer was concerned, she continued, the 40,000 Deutsche marks that the compliant court ordered be paid to Liepmann and his relatives in 1954 confirmed his own moral right to Eichenberg. It also redoubled his determination to get it back.

So, in the mid-1950s, he went to East Berlin, which was still easy to do in those days, before the Wall had been built, to see what had happened to Eichenberg's building since the communists turned it into a 'Property of the People'. When he saw it, he was overcome by emotion and yearned to have it restituted to him. He saw himself in that edifice: his work, his history – and his future. He immediately engaged a lawyer to lobby the East German authorities.

But the lawyer's letters went unanswered. Albert then had a fresh idea: he and Herbert Liepmann should mount a *joint* approach to get the building back! The support of a victim of Nazism might induce the communists to be more sympathetic. The Jew and the Aryanizer could be a winning team.

But Liepmann had no trouble resisting the temptation to get into bed with a man who, as he saw it, had connived in stealing his family's business. Not that the East German government would have accepted the idea anyway. Far from welcoming Westerners to run privatized enterprises, it was nationalizing everything in sight. Albert Fischer's proposal was out of the question. He left East Berlin, never to return.

57.

'Progress!'

Before he died, Albert told his son Hans-Joachim to continue battling to get Eichenberg returned to their family.

Taking his father's wishes to heart, Hans-Joachim travelled to East Berlin with Annette not long after Albert's death. They walked for an hour or two around the dilapidated building. The parts that Albert had paid to have repaired in the 1940s were still pristine, but otherwise it looked weary with neglect. Yet the visit only stiffened Hans-Joachim's resolve to take it over and restore the range of products that it had made before the Aryanization. He began looking for an apartment for his wife and their children, but when Annette saw the tiny communist dwellings with their shabby interiors and run-down yards, not to mention the empty shops, she put her foot down. 'You can go there, but without us,' she told him. 'I am not living in a communist country, for any factory in the world. This whole Eichenberg business destroyed your father's marriage' – Albert divorced in the late forties after his years in Berlin had estranged him from his wife of nearly four decades, whom he had left in their home town – 'and if we go back to it, it will destroy ours.'

'He thought that I'd like the boat on the Wannsee!' she added.

'The boat?'

Eichenberg, according to her, owned a boat on the Wannsee for entertaining its clients – along with a boathouse, or a share in one.

Eichenberg's corporate boat was news to me. It certainly hadn't tempted Annette to move to East Berlin. Nor was she prepared to compromise by living in West Berlin while her husband worked from Monday to Friday in the communist part of the city. That would have required him to cross the Wall twice a week, with all the security and the searches – an insane idea, she said.

As she spoke, I wondered if my grandfather's boat on the Wannsee, which he and his family had occasionally sailed on summer weekends, was the same boat. My mother was always greatly amused by Ernst's pride in it. It was one of her father's touchingly naive ideas, she would say. Apart from being a financial millstone, Berlin's long winters under low-hanging grey clouds made it unusable for much of the year; Ilse alone knew how to work it; and they could all think of better things to do with their free time than schlep out to the Wannsee only to expend hours preparing it to sail and then closing it up again at the end of the day.

Not to be deterred – or believing that his wife would change her mind once the factory was his again and she had laid eyes on the boat nestled in its wooden hut – Hans-Joachim engaged a lawyer to explore how he could get the business back. But he received the same advice as his father had a decade earlier. Even if he and his family became East German citizens, he was told, restitution in any form was unthinkable because the factory had been taken over under Nazi Aryanization laws. It wasn't that the communist government cared about its expropriation from Jewish ownership, Annette emphasized; rather they weren't going to help anyone who had benefited from Nazi policy.

After their meeting with the lawyer, they retraced their steps back to Eichenberg's building. Hans-Joachim took out his camera and looked about him furtively. A passing pedestrian glanced at this Westerner and said sternly: 'Over here, you are not allowed to photograph.' He quickly took a few pictures with his camera concealed under an open coat, noticing the new name of the company: *Fortschritt!* – Progress!

Back home, he put the photos in that trunk in his cellar, which

Annette had mentioned in our first telephone call. He would regularly go down there to dust them off and to imagine a new life in the communist east, reunited with his rightful inheritance and investing his future in *Fortschritt!*

58

The elusive share certificate

In late 1989, Annette said, days after the fall of the Wall, Hans-Joachim was struck by exactly the same idea as Renata and her cousin Inge-Margot would have during their conversation in Florida a year later – except he didn't need Saddam Hussein to jog his memory. That property in Prenzlauer Berg! Now the moment had *really* come to get it back! At first, he thought that the best plan would be to do a deal with the heirs of the former Jewish owners, much as his father had tried to do with Herbert Liepmann. They would surely want to talk: after all, it wasn't easy for people scattered around the world to repossess an old business and get it started again.

But then he thought better of it. Why go into coalition with the Jewish heirs? His case was surely stronger than theirs. As his father had rightly argued, it wasn't their family's fault that the original owners had been thrown out; but once they were, the place would have gone bankrupt if someone hadn't come along and rescued it. And if they had stayed, would they have been able to persuade Göring's Ministry to buy jackets and shirts off them? Could they have afforded repairs to the bomb damage, immediately after the war? Of course not. But beyond all that, his family had suffered a greater injustice than the Jewish heirs had; for at least Herbert Liepmann had received compensation back in 1954, whereas the communists had grabbed Eichenberg without paying his father a penny. Hence he was entitled to its restitution. He engaged a law firm to press this case.

Though not entirely without logic, Hans-Joachim's arguments were hardly going to cut ice in 1990s Germany, and his claim for restitution was officially rejected in 1992. Like his father before him, he never got over the loss of Eichenberg. He would say: 'My goodness! How can all this that my family built up, with so much love and effort and money, now be gone?' And then, Annette added, he would try to console himself: 'We were like the German aristocrats who lost their ancestral estates behind the Iron Curtain.' After the communist takeover of East Germany, she said, they also suffered the confiscation of what they loved and was rightfully theirs. He recognized there was nothing he could do, but he couldn't accept it.

Again, like his father before him, he told his son always to remember Eichenberg and how much their family had done for the firm. Shortly before he died in 2005, Annette said, he gave his son a share certificate of the company. 'Keep that in memory of our beloved Eichenberg,' he had said. 'Let its memory live. It was ours.'

Annette had been telling me all this in our phone calls; her openness amazes me now, as it did then. Her story flowed whole and vivid, as if it had occupied her for years. Though I had no further pressing questions to ask, I wanted to see that trunk in her cellar, stuffed with Eichenberg papers. Above all, I coveted the share certificate bearing the firm's Aryanized name, VEWAG, that she'd offered to give me. Perhaps it was just the thrill of holding a document that non-Aryan hands couldn't have held in 1942, when the new name was registered; and of touching history in however token a way.

I decided to visit her on my next trip to Germany, a few weeks later.

But our evening was uneventful. Annette and I had already exhausted the subject in our calls. And being face to face was oddly inhibiting, as if trying to establish a personal connection made it harder to discuss this intensely personal matter; whereas, talking as strangers down a phone line, we'd been unguarded and relaxed.

When the time came to leave her house, it felt an abrupt change of gear to remind her of the trunk and the share certificate.

'Of course!' she exclaimed. 'Come down to the cellar, but I'm not sure there is as much there as I had thought.'

There was nothing – not a single paper about the firm. There was a lot about other family businesses back to the 1930s; and there were documents from the 1940s and '50s that seemed to concern the car dealership.

'No Eichenberg papers at all?' I persisted.

'Oh, I did find a photocopy of the 1954 court judgement about the 40,000 Deutsche marks that we paid Herbert Liepmann and the other Jewish people from England,' she said, as we were leafing through yet another file on the car business. 'I put it upstairs on the coffee table. You can have that, if you wish.'

'I know that document; it's in my own Eichenberg file,' I told her.

'Well, they got the 40,000 and then the building back. I think they should at least have refunded my husband what his father spent repairing the damage inflicted by British and American bombs. We should have got that money back!'

She spoke in a strident tone that had earlier been completely absent. But now was hardly the time to reopen all that history. Besides, her husband's lawyer had already demanded, several times, that we refund the 40,000 – though, as far as I knew, he hadn't also claimed the money that Albert had spent repairing the bombed roof.

'And the share certificate with the Aryanized – the new – name?' I asked again as we climbed back up from the cellar.

But she had changed her mind. I wasn't going to get the trophy I wanted.

Her voice became colder still, as if the tangibility of the Aryanized share certificate brought home her family's loss of Eichenberg with a vividness that banished the charm of reconciliation with us, the descendants of the original owners. The only document she was prepared to give me, she repeated, was a photocopy of the 1954 court judgement that had gone against her father-in-law and that, in her mind, justified financial compensation from the Jewish families to hers.

But I already had that – in duplicate.

'Why can't you give me one of the certificates in the name of VEWAG?' I asked yet again. 'It would mean a lot to me – and you said that you had several of them.'

I was about to point out that a share certificate in an abolished company, denominated in an abolished currency, and issued by an abolished state was surely of no practical use to either of us, when she said:

'You never know, one day my son or *his* descendants might need it.'

59

Restitution? No, thanks

Only one member of our family wanted to hear nothing from me about the Eichenberg saga: my aunt, Ursel. Every time I tried to speak to her about it, she cut me off.

Ursel was so appalled at being confronted by this spectre of the Nazi past and of those fatal Jewish origins that she repeatedly told me she intended to repudiate her share of Eichenberg, insisting that it should go directly to her children. To be required, half a century after securing her non-Jewish status, to furnish German officials with proof of her parentage or of legal succession, was adding insult to injury, even if this time the motive was justice and the aim restitution. Whenever I raised the subject, her face froze in fury at history's impertinence in thrusting on her, yet again, the status of a victim and a Jew. The rest of the Eichenberg lot could take the bait mockingly proffered by the wheel of fortune, but not her.

Something about the immensity of her repudiation awed as well as dismayed me. It wasn't that a handsome payout couldn't tempt her to suspend the rule that her Jewish origins must never be recognized. Rather I couldn't help respecting her capacity to feel the pain of having once been marked out for social death – pain surprisingly easy to repress. Since her youth, she had, as I saw it, been oppressed by the emotional isolation of even the most assimilated German Jews from their host society; by their Sisyphean striving to be exceptional just in order to be accepted as ordinary; by the family mantra of 'only the very best'. She despised the cliché that the German and Jewish traditions had been triumphantly symbiotic; for her, they were like two people who, however erotically attracted they might be to one another, are lethally incompatible. She refused the conviction, fervently held by my mother and later by me, that there was an unsurpassable harmony between the heights of German *Kultur* and of Jewish spirituality. For Ursel, this was nonsense on stilts, which had exacted a terrible psychic cost from Jews and had inevitably ended in catastrophe (a view that placed her, with supreme irony, in the company of some of the most distinguished German-Jewish intellectuals, such as Gershom Scholem, the great scholar of Kabbalah). And although I still cling to that conviction, I grudgingly admired her independence of mind.

And, it seemed to me, her distaste for Eichenberg and for the consolations of restitution was motivated by something else too: the reality that there is no recovery from being a victim of the Third Reich. There is no justice or apology that can make good such degradation. Not even truth can. Truth can offer victims dignity of sorts, but the damage is irreparable.

I used to visit Ursel as often as I could in her cozy apartment in Munich, where she ran me baths overflowing with foamy pine essence, treated me to her incomparable comic imitations, and bought me my favourite food, which as a teenager was shrimp with pink cocktail sauce, a luxury that would have been unthinkable in my mother's austere home, where gastronomic indulgence was that reconstituted crème caramel.

At lunchtime, we might amble into Käfer, an elegant restaurant, and the maître d' would greet her with a bow and escort us past a phalanx of servers to her table, where she would order a *Pfeffersteak*, a side salad, and a glass of champagne, eat a couple of pieces of steak and discreetly drop the rest into the waiting mouth of her dachshund, Romeo, who was nestling at her feet. When Romeo sometimes bit a neat incision into the couture of a woman at the next table or left a permanent dental imprint in a husband's trousers,

Ursel apologized with such sovereign charm that recriminations died on our neighbours' lips. She softened the stiffest countenances with her uncanny portrayals of people's tics and obsessions. You could see her conjure mind and body, both still remarkably plastic in her eighties, into a role, and how the cabaret performer, the character dancer, and the classical stage actor would all get into their strides.

One day, on a brief visit to Munich, she presented me with a sealed envelope, which was waiting for me on a table by her front door. 'That's for you,' she said curtly, as soon as I arrived. 'I place all my interests in the Berlin *thing* in your hands.'

I was amazed. A short note gave me power of attorney over her interests in Eichenberg, 'though', it added puzzlingly, '*not* the interests of other investors', as if these were somehow hers to dispose of.

'What am I supposed to do with this?' I asked.

'Do whatever you like. I don't want to hear anything more about this business. It disgusts me.'

'But this is about justice,' I protested. 'Your parents invested in this.' I deliberately said 'parents': any mention of her father's name drew her into a vortex of panic and rejection, as if some black hole imperceptible to the rest of us were sucking her into its annihilating core.

'And what about your children? They'll understandably be furious if I have power of attorney over their inheritance. I'm not doing this, Ursel.'

'You deal with it,' she snapped, as though exiling the whole matter from Germany to a safe distance in faraway England.

But I was certain that I was going to do nothing with that letter, whatever her motive for writing it. I decided to file it away and speak about this poisoned chalice to nobody.

60

Romeo in Bayreuth

Romeo was the other reason I relished my trips to Munich. He was a remarkable dog, and not only because of his taste for fillet steak, or the uncanny way in which his moods would mirror Ursel's. Musically, too, he seemed to have very clear preferences. He loved opera but found piano sonatas and chamber music boring. He listened quietly to Mozart for hours, curled up on his cushion, occasionally half opening his eyes to check in with his boss; but he appeared to find Wagner intolerable. If I persuaded her to play a recording of *Parsifal*, his luxuriant little body would freeze, he would look uneasily around him, shoot us a disapproving glance, uncurl himself, and lumber sufferingly out of the room.

Here, as in many things, he was perfectly attuned to Ursel, who also loathed Wagner. She was repelled, it seemed to me, by what she saw as the solemnity and mystery, the sacred dignity, with which his music invests melancholy, vengefulness, and insatiable eros; and by the bogus, indeed dangerous, way in which, she thought, it fetishizes ancient Teutonic myths.

For many years, my mother, brother, and I were the beneficiaries of her Wagner aversion, for she gratefully offloaded onto us the tickets she received for the festival at Bayreuth from two kind-hearted doctors, Jochen and Eva Kabelitz, who invited us to stay with them for the week-long pilgrimages we ended up making each summer.

The tickets, rare as gold dust in those days – the waiting list was said to be eight years from the time you first applied – cascaded down to us along a line of Wagner refuseniks, who seemed to treat them as temptations to histrionic degradation, to be handled with gloves and pinched noses. The Kabelitzs, who were offered the tickets by neighbours, passed them on to Ursel, and from her they found their way to us, but not before being rejected by her close friend, a doctor called Charlotte Pommer.

Charlotte had first met Ursel through Lexi Alvensleben – and was the original source of her connection to the Kabelitzs. Enormously courageous, ethical, and sensitive, she had been one of the few doctors in Nazi Germany to refuse to work on the bodies of executed victims of the regime. As a young graduate in Berlin in 1941, assigned to the laboratory of Hermann Stieve, a distinguished anatomist who regularly received the corpses of freshly hanged prisoners from the nearby Plötzensee Prison, she one day saw the bodies of three dissidents whom she personally knew lying on the dissection table. She resigned at once, only to be moved to the surgical department at the state hospital of the police in Berlin, where she did all she could to support and protect those in the resistance movement who crossed her path. In March 1945, she was arrested, interrogated, and sentenced to prison, which she escaped a few weeks later amid the chaos of the collapsing Nazi state.[38]

It was thanks to Charlotte Pommer's rejected tickets for Bayreuth that I fell in love with Wagner's music. Not that my devotion to the cult was immediate. When my mother first took me and my brother to worship at the temple, I was seventeen, and found the *Ring*, with its four operas over sixteen hours, unbearable not only in length but also in what I then took to be their baroque, self-indulgent kitsch, the tedious grandiloquence of their motifs and heroes, and the way the music could endow the pettiest emotion with heaven-smashing grandeur. After the first act of *Siegfried*, my brother and I went on strike. We told our mother that we wouldn't be going back after the interval, and instead curled up in front of our hosts' television and watched thrillers and action movies. Until, returning in raptures to the Kabelitzs' house in the second interval of the final opera, *Götterdämmerung*, and finding us playing with Romeo in the garden, our mother demanded that we attend the last, climactic act. 'Children,' she announced, 'you *cannot* miss this. You will not know why until you hear it!'

Her summons had a quality I knew well: it opened my eyes and ears to a liberating realm of sensibility – a realm ignored, so she seemed to say, at the risk of becoming a stunted person. I was smitten from the first moment of that act, unable to understand why I had been so bored. Despite the troubling appeal of Wagner's music to the baser instincts as well as to the noblest, its conjuring of purity out of corruption or decay, and its capacity to disorient, even degrade, ethical sense, since that evening I have never ceased to feel emancipated by its bewitching evocation of intimacy – lost, craved, attained, unattainable.

Ursel usually drove over from Munich to join us on those magical days, and would sit on the terrace of the Kabelitzs' house smoking cigarettes and picking the meat and smoked salmon out of the sandwiches that Eva had prepared for the hour-long intervals. Romeo was at her feet, warming himself in the sun that seemed to shine with particular gentleness over Bayreuth and the hills around it, snapping into alertness only to receive morsels of unwanted food that his mistress dropped onto the flagstones.

Not that Romeo always waited for delicacies to be tossed into his mouth. Though he preferred being fed to feeding himself, and was a deft catch even from the far side of a room, he sometimes found the temptation to grab irresistible. One of those moments was at a birthday party I had in the countryside near Munich, where a magnificent Black Forest cake awaited me.

We were chatting under the afternoon sun on that summer's day, and I was about to be marched into the house to inspect the multi-layered construction that had taken many hours to prepare, when Romeo slunk out of the kitchen pointedly averting his head. Something was clearly amiss. We called and whistled to attract his attention, but he continued tracing a wide arc around us, ignoring even Ursel's summons of last resort: a stern tone of voice which he generally knew to obey. Only when she surprised him from behind did he spin anxiously towards us, his eyes sunken and guilty – and his snout snow white.

He was still trying to lick the incriminating evidence from his whiskers as we rushed into the kitchen to find the cake's three layers meticulously separated from one another and the cream cleaned off both sides of each layer, leaving only the liqueur-infused chocolate sponge. Stray cherries soaked in kirsch were lying rejected on the counter, which glistened with Romeo's saliva.

The entire birthday cake had to be abandoned. But what again impressed me was his discernment. He drew the line at alcohol: like Wagner, it just wasn't for him.

61.

Mother's last 'last visit' to Berlin

On a Saturday evening in October 2009, I am on a train, returning from Paris to London, when my phone rings. It is my mother.

'Simy, I have never felt so bad in my life,' she says, sounding frightened and vulnerable. 'I don't know what's happening, but I have never felt like this.'

She has a tight chest and feels like she is dying. I know it must be serious because she is always 'unbelievably well' and 'as strong as a horse'. And it is true: in her then ninety-five years, she has never had any illness except for colds, and even those fizzled out in her eighties, since when I haven't known her unwell at all, aside from one nasty attack of shingles. Until eighty-five, she was still hiking every summer in the Swiss Alps and was able to play the violin without the slightest shaking of her bow arm or impairment of her hearing. And she has never worn glasses, whether to see near or far.

Three tense hours later – I call her every few minutes because I want to comfort her and know that she is still alive – I arrive at her house. She looks fine, and she is in great spirits. 'It was nothing,' she says, 'I feel completely normal.' But I am worried. 'Mother, let's go to a hospital for a quick check,' I urge her. 'You did say you'd never felt so bad in your life.'

She refuses. I sit with her for an hour or two, and become

convinced that she is indeed fine. Perhaps it was one of her occasional panic attacks, for which she has beta blockers at the ready.

The following evening, she calls me again, at about the same time. 'Simy, this is terrible. Please come over now. Please.'

I rush over and tell her we are going to A & E, whether she agrees or not. 'All right,' she says, 'but no ambulance. If you call an ambulance, I will certainly die.'

We get into my car and drive to the nearest hospital. On the way, she abruptly complains of chest pain. It is Sunday evening, at about 8 p.m. By midnight, the results are in: she's had a major heart attack, maybe two. They are going to keep her in for one night.

At 4 a.m. I'm awoken by the telephone. 'This is reception at Cardiology,' the voice announces. 'Your mother is standing here in her coat, demanding to leave. She says you promised to collect her an hour ago, but we aren't allowed to release her after the diagnosis she's had.'

I jump into my car and arrive at the hospital to find her surrounded by a senior cardiologist, a junior doctor, and a nurse. She is accusing them of being as bad as Nazis, incarcerating her against her will, and interfering in private questions of health, which are none of their business.

'I'm sure you've experienced this before,' I apologize. 'This is the first time she's been in a hospital bed since my brother was born.'

'Actually, no, we haven't experienced this before,' the junior doctor puts in. 'We cannot let your mother go until she is out of immediate danger.'

They are in collective professional lockdown.

I try to persuade her to stay, at least until that afternoon, but she refuses. If I don't drive her home, she will walk out, this minute, and find a taxi in the street. If that isn't possible, she'd prefer to die.

A few minutes later they surrender.

Over the following days, my mother declines dramatically. She is soon bedridden and hardly able to take even fluids. Sometimes she can't recognize me, or else thinks I am her father, then her brother, then another relative she hasn't seen for years.

A week after the heart attack, the doctor takes me aside while visiting her house and warns me, in that pitilessly matter-of-fact voice sometimes assumed by medics when delivering terrible news, that my mother has seventy-two hours to live. Everything is going wrong, he says. Her blood chemistry is all over the place; the ECG is a jagged disaster; blood pressure is yo-yoing; and her body is 'shutting down' – a euphemism for dying. There is nothing to be done: she is far too old for surgery and medication would be useless.

Now it is only a matter of planning the funeral.

Six weeks later, my mother and I are on a flight to Berlin. After recovering enough to get out of bed, to start reading and going out again, and to maintain her house in the immaculate way that she likes it, she wants a break and asks me if I'd accompany her on yet another last visit to her native city. She is determined to go to a concert every day for the week that we're going to be there. She loves Berlin; it's never stopped being her *Heimat*, she says. And she's never, for a moment, felt happy in exile. 'Never, for a moment,' she repeats over and over. In fact, she announces a few days before we leave, she wants to move back, three-quarters of a century after emigrating.

I duly agree to arrange the visit, though I'm doubtful that she will relocate to a Germany that has changed out of all recognition since the 1930s. Nonetheless, I engage someone in Berlin to look for suitable care homes and draw up a shortlist for me to visit on another trip to the city. The plan to move back, impractical though it is, thrills me: the idea that there will, after all, be a return; that Hitler's expulsion will finally be defied. I glimpse the promise that life can be lived for real, rather than in an 'as if' or provisional way.

In my euphoria, one obvious point doesn't occur to me: that she might end up living under one roof with an ex-Nazi or two, or find herself at breakfast next to someone with just the sort of body language that would make her want to flee Germany faster than she escaped that hospital in the middle of the night.

We land in Berlin at around 9.30 one evening. A friend has generously lent us his apartment on Walter-Benjamin-Platz, and after depositing our cases there, we rush to an Italian restaurant as it is about to shut, persuading the maître d' to provide us with pasta, salad, and a bottle of red wine. At 1 a.m. Mother is tucked up in bed, exhilarated as she always is – at first – to be back on her home turf: the one place in Germany, she insists, that never had broad Nazi sympathies, indeed whose natives mocked Hitler and his absurd speeches and marches. The Führer, according to her, was a political squatter who had set up his headquarters in hostile territory. He knew that he would never win over Berliners, with their abrasive independent-mindedness.

Every day of this homecoming involves a visit to a museum in the afternoon and then a concert in the evening. On one of those days, the concert is a matinée, after which we have an early dinner and then go on to the theatre. The play is Kleist's *Der zerbrochne Krug*, but we have really gone for the actor, Klaus Maria Brandauer. It's almost sold out, and we get pretty much the last two seats. Up in the gods.

Things do not go well after dinner. It takes half an hour to walk the hundred yards or so from the restaurant to the theatre, with frequent stops for Mother to catch her breath. Arriving with little time to spare before the performance begins, I discover that Bertolt Brecht's Berliner Ensemble has no elevator, which will mean climbing nearly fifty steps. I try to persuade her that this would be absurd. What's the point? She has just had a heart attack from which she nearly died. Why now risk anything for the sake of a play, which we might hardly be able to see or hear from that height anyway?

She is, as ever, unpersuadable. The heart attack was nothing serious, she declares. It is nonsense that she nearly died. All nonsense. I shouldn't be taken in by 'the hysteria of those doctors, whose professional interest it is to find problems.'

After about fifteen steps she complains of breathlessness and stops to recover. She seems paralyzed, unable to go either up or down, and is losing her balance. Again, I suggest that we abandon the play. Again, this is just the spur she needs to continue. She resumes her climb. Then she gets chest pain. Now she is accusing me of causing her chest pain by trying to call off the evening. I struggle to remain calm by telling myself that, if she passes away now, it would be while doing what she wants to do, in the city where she wants to be. She would die almost exactly where she was born, in the one place that she says she has never stopped loving.

Some minutes later, with the performance bell ringing relentlessly, we find ourselves in the highest part of the theatre, with all the students, only to realize that we have to climb several more steps in order to reach our row, and then to shuffle past a dozen people to our seats near the middle.

There we sit for two and a half hours, with no air conditioning, in sweltering, oxygen-deprived conditions, too far from the stage to see the tiny actors or make out much of what they are saying.

It is only as we are leaving that crisis hits. My mother sees a man in the foyer and freezes.

'I feel so terrible,' she says. 'I need to get out of here immediately.'

'But we *are* going, Mother. What's the matter? I told you it was all too much, the heat, the Kleist, the climb . . .'

'It's nothing to do with any of that,' she snaps, a look of panic on her face. 'It's him,' she says, pointing weakly at the man. 'He's so tall.'

'Tall? So what? You're crazy, Mother!' I try to lighten things by poking fun at the absurdity of her concern.

'Oh God, I have to leave Berlin at once. I have to leave Germany. I never want to come back. He's so tall,' she repeats in the same horrified voice, which is now alarmingly breathless. 'Those ghastly lanky limbs. And that disgusting confidence. I know those types. *They* were the Nazis. Oh, I wish we'd never come here.'

'But lots of people are tall,' I remonstrate. 'Come on, let's go. This is stupid.'

'You don't understand,' she ripostes angrily. 'You know nothing of those people. If you think I'm moving back here, you're sorely mistaken. I wouldn't dream of it.'

There is no arguing with her. She looks frail and pale, and I fear the worst. Perhaps her recovery hasn't been so robust. For sure, the whole trip is a folly. I reprimand myself for packing a concert and the theatre and dinner in a noisy restaurant into a few hours.

As she begins to recover her composure, I walk her slowly through the foyer to the exit. Negotiating the steps down to the street, we run straight into the tall man chatting to his companions.

'That sure felt a long play,' he drawls in an American accent, 'especially with no intermission. I doubt they'd ever put on something as impenetrable as Kleist on Broadway and fill the house. And with so many young people in the audience. Brandauer was worth coming to see, but I don't think I understood more than a smattering – that kind of German is way too hard for me.'

'Anyway,' he adds as he and his friends walk off, 'Brandauer's a lot more entertaining as the baddie in that James Bond movie.'

62

Mother's death – My 'return' to Germany begins

My mother's near-death experience prompted me to ask her a question that had been an unspoken taboo for decades. What were her funeral instructions when the time came?

I thought I'd start from an incontestable premise. 'Mother, we are all going to die someday. It might not be soon, but it will happen. When it does happen, do you want to be buried as a Catholic, in a Jewish cemetery, or in a secular graveyard?'

This brought everything back to what I thought was the insoluble problem of identity.

'Throw my body into the nearest ditch!' she commanded. 'It's over anyway, then. The person no longer exists, so what does it matter?'

I told her that I would need more precise instructions than that.

'In the Jewish cemetery where your father is, where they *all* are,' she said, as if nothing could be more self-evident.

'Are you sure?' I asked, astonished. 'But you've been a Catholic all your adult life. Are you sure you don't want a Catholic burial? And what about last rites?'

'I want to be in *that* Jewish cemetery,' she said.

I asked her the same question many times over the following years and always got the same answer. Her reply never had a redemptive quality: it never conveyed the sense that a repudiated heritage had finally been embraced; or that a source of banishment from the world was now a harbinger of solace. Just as with her sisters at the end of their own lives, there was no 'closure', such as that attributed to Rahel Varnhagen, the writer and Berlin salon host, who, according to her husband, proclaimed on her deathbed in 1833: 'The thing which all my life seemed to me the greatest shame, which was the misery and misfortune of my life – having been born a Jewess – this I should on no account now wish to have missed.'[39] My mother never uttered such explicit words of reconciliation. She just changed her mind – and announced her decision as if the previous decades of tortured denial hadn't happened.

But *I* did feel a profound sense of redemptive closure when, after her death, five months short of her hundredth birthday, we buried her where she had wanted to be: in *that* Jewish cemetery, 'where they all are.'

Walking down the gravel paths between the graves, I could see why this was where she had chosen. I recognized names I hadn't seen or heard since my youth. Esther Salamon, who had been a devoted friend of Luise Borchardt. The Freyhans, music lovers from Berlin. These were her people. Like her closest childhood friends, Marianne Nussbaum and Marianne Imberg, Mother's circle, whether intimate or professional, had always been almost exclusively Jewish, not *because* they were Jewish but because, for all her insistence that she wasn't of it, that was where she felt most at ease. That was her world.

She rests in the Liberal Jewish Cemetery in London's Pound Lane, a stone's throw from my father, from Eddy, and from so many of the colleagues, friends, enemies, and rivals who filled her life.

The move back to Berlin was not to be. *This* was her return.

And then there is my own uncompleted 'return'. In January 2017, three years after my mother's death, I finally begin the process of claiming German citizenship, and at the same time of finding an apartment to buy in Berlin, looking to the future as well as to the past. I decide to go back to Germany, initially for half of each year, in order to try to be there in an everyday way, threaded, I hope, neither with nostalgia nor with an excessive yearning for future safety, but instead with patient, waiting attentiveness, so that my German inheritance might be in calm, realistic relationship to the country as it now is.

On 2 January 2017, I turn up for my appointment at the German Embassy in London – the place, fuller with significance for me than any other building in London, where my father died over half a century earlier, falling back with that terrible thud; the place where my mother encountered the barking Nazi government official in 1937 and, slapping down her expired German passport, became stateless; the place where she regained her own German citizenship, sixty-one years later, in 1998; and now the place from where my journey back to Germany will begin.

It feels like a no man's land as I pace the anonymous waiting area, penned off from the embassy proper by a separate entrance and a security barrier. I'm glad I have to await my turn for an hour or more. The slow grind of officialdom intensifies the giddy feeling that I am about to find a way back into hundreds of years of belonging. Somehow the banality of the everyday makes the journey of home-coming more vivid, not less. I have a sense of the density of reality similar to what I felt in the park when Sally told me and my brother about our father's death. Loss of father. Gain of father's homeland. The two have been locked in dialogue all my life.

This incredible sense of an end to a life suspended in exile isn't dented by the anticlimax to my wait. When I get called, an official behind a glass pane that looks as if it could be bulletproof tells me that I've used the wrong application form. Descendants of refugees from Nazism, unlike other applicants for German nationality, must apply for naturalization under article 116, paragraph 2 of the German Constitution, which states that:

> Former German citizens who between January 30, 1933 and May 8, 1945 were deprived of their citizenship on political, racial, or religious grounds, and their descendants, shall on application have their citizenship restored. They shall be deemed never to have been deprived of their citizenship if

they have established their domicile in Germany after May
8, 1945 and have not expressed a contrary intention.

And then, four months later, after spending a few days in Auschwitz-
Birkenau with Anita Lasker-Wallfisch – a survivor and old friend of
my family, who had invited me to join her for this life-changing visit
– I fly to Berlin to look for an apartment.

By chance, the marketing suite for the new development that I
visit at the insistence of the real-estate agent who's helping me find
a home, is on almost exactly the opposite side of the Tiergarten to
where my mother and Ursel and Ilse and Ernst and Emmy lived.

But it isn't just Blumeshof that's not on today's map of Berlin –
the address I'm trying to get to isn't either. My grandparents' home
has been wiped off it; my potential new home isn't yet on it. I get
lost wandering down brand-new streets so bereft of place and patina
that they seem like a practical joke played on this city of unrelenting
history. One of them, which matches the name given to me by the
agent, snakes around a vast crater presided over by a skyscraper
crane, at the foot of which diggers and bulldozers zigzag like crazed
aliens. Eventually I spot the building number I'm looking for, but
the doorman at the deserted glass tower says this isn't it.

I return to the S-Bahn train station where I'd arrived a few minutes
ago and see a stall selling currywurst, Berlin's contribution to fast
food, and behind it glimpse a woman with flaming orange hair, who
might know the whereabouts of an address that must be one of the
few places on the planet out of Google's sights.

Seeing me approach her stall, her eyes fix me with that defensively
aggressive, sardonically humorous look which is a trademark of
Berlin. While I'm still a couple of yards away and haven't yet said
a word, she blurts, in local dialect: '*Junger Mann, hier wird jejessen
und nicht jefragt!*' – 'Young man, here one eats and doesn't ask!'

She perceives, from my uncertain gait or from the questioning
expression already forming on my face, that I'm going to ask her for
help of some kind – and that she won't make a penny out of me.

There's everything of this city's magnificent spirit not only in what she says but in how she says it: biting, ironic, tough, critical, cozy, and mocking. Rude and yet strangely warm. I begin to mutter something about being in a hurry now and coming back another time to buy a sausage, but the withering scepticism in her eyes makes the almost empty promise die on my lips. It's only after I cease to present myself as a supplicant and concede that she has better things to do than explain the local topography that, interspersed with a rant decrying the developers who are ruining her city, she tells me precisely how to find the marketing suite, which it seems I've already passed a couple of times.

It feels odd to walk into that glossy atmosphere, surrounded by brochures and coffee machines and immaculately dressed sales people and a model of the huge development that will spring up nearby. I'm so close to the primal source, Blumeshof, which could exist in only one place on earth; yet I'm inspecting the kind of home that could be anywhere in the world.

Far from buying off-plan, or looking in this part of town, which feels far too urban, I told the agent that I wanted to find a small apartment near the woods and lakes in the far west of Berlin, and not in a new-build but in one of the houses with high ceilings and art-deco entrances from the turn of the twentieth century. But she encourages me to give this a go as it's near the river and a stone's throw from an expanse of green – so it almost meets my criteria. Besides, if I change my mind, I can always sell my 'option' to another buyer – perhaps for a premium. I'd better hurry, she warns. A French woman has already reserved an entire floor. An Indian man has put down a deposit on another floor. People from Hamburg and Norway and America are all racing to sign contracts as she and I speak.

But aren't I supposed to be returning to my roots? Is this not-yet-existing building a home or an asset? Will anyone live here or will it be a pied-à-terre for investors? The whole point is that I don't want to consider myself a foreigner in this city. This is to be my new home in Germany and not a perch in a foreign land.

After lingering at the crater, and trying to imagine myself living above it, I retrace my tracks back to the woman with the orange hair, who is turning over a row of sausages on her grill; and then, walking on, I reach the six-lane Strasse des 17. Juni, which commemorates the workers' uprising in East Berlin in 1953 that was bloodily quashed by the communist authorities and the Red Army. On the other side of the road is the Tiergarten – a part of it that I've never been to. I decide to go for a stroll before returning to commit myself reluctantly to one of the apartments.

No sooner am I inside its hallowed precincts than I am amazed to find myself in front of the Rousseau Island of family legend – the island around which my mother had ice-skated as a child and that she thought was spelled 'Russo' – one of those names marking a beloved world that lives defiantly within me. So this is where it is! So it really exists! I am euphoric, but also pervaded by gentle dread – not the dread of loss, but the dread of discovery. Will the loved one be forever elusive? Am I being vapidly sentimental?

Naively, greedily, I want to possess and imbibe this sacred space so deeply that its reality will be 100 per cent present to me; so that it can never slip away again. And, on the other side of the park, the bombed Elysium of Blumeshof comes into focus, drawing me close, and I feel my grandparents standing next to me, living at full throttle and yet pervaded by despair, warning me and welcoming me. I can see its network of rooms, Ernst's study, Emmy's reading room, the piano at which she accompanies herself singing *Lieder*, the girls' rooms, the Christmas table, the steaming goose, the cloths embroidered with a big woven 'L' for Liedtke. I can hear Ernst ringing the bell. And I can hear Walter Benjamin asking of my grandparents' apartment, as he did of his own grandmother's upstairs: What words can describe 'the almost immemorial feeling of bourgeois security that emanated from these rooms'? The 'solidity' and the fragility – it is all there, in black and white.

But I'd better go back to the marketing suite. If I don't take an option on one of those apartments, the woman from France or the man from India might buy it up too.

63

A devastating discovery

Is return really possible? Even if you gain citizenship, as I did in May 2017, almost exactly eighty years after my parents were stripped of theirs; even if you find that the philosophy, the literature, the music to which you have the most powerful and natural affinity is that of your forebears – can the foundations that they lost ever be reclaimed? Without artifice or force?

The discovery of Klaus Meltzer and Eichenberg had opened up avenues to a lost homeland, but they couldn't restitute it. In particular, I was amazed how little the return of Eichenberg, with its tangible asset, the handsome building in Prenzlauer Berg, meant to me. The possibility of historical justice – the fact that there were laws and bureaucracies dedicated to it – was exhilarating. But Eichenberg as a living entity was, of course, irretrievably gone. None of my direct family had ever lived there, so there were no ghosts to whom I felt close; the employees, managers, customers, and machinery had vanished; and the money was useful to my mother, but didn't bring our Germany closer. A house can be restituted, but not a home.

And then, on 8 May 2017, just one day before I go to the German Embassy in London to collect my newly arrived certificate of German citizenship, a bombshell: Klaus Meltzer turns out not to be a lifeline to my murdered great-uncle, Ernst's brother Theo.

* * *

In Auschwitz with Anita Lasker-Wallfisch a few weeks earlier, we
are shown a book of names tracing a vast circle and listing the six
million exterminated Jews.

I hasten to the 'L's, searching for my mother's family name,
Liedtke. There, I see who I am looking for: Theodor Liedtke. But
not one; three. Two of these turn out to be the same Theodor, my
great-uncle, both entries showing the victim as born in Christburg
on 10 June 1885. One says that he died in Sachsenhausen in 1942,
as my mother and Ilse had always told me, and as the package of
his last possessions seemed to confirm. The other stuns me: it says
that he was deported to Auschwitz on 1 March 1943.

So he didn't die lugging stones at Sachsenhausen, or from a shot
to the back of the head? So Ilse and Hedwig were both wrong?
Beating back my imagination's attempts to visualize this infinitely
gentle soul being packed into a cattle truck, I notice that another
Theodor Liedtke was also deported to Auschwitz, also from Berlin,
and also in 1943. He arrived just a few weeks later. Unlike our
Theo, he was born in 1887 in Berlin, rather than in 1885 in
Christburg.

I hurry back with Anita to our hotel opposite the camp's main
gate; and, while she smokes a cigarette in a chair that the reception
staff have placed for this sole purpose just outside the entrance, I
get to work on Google. In minutes, I have discovered an entry on
the other Theodor Liedtke, the one born in 1887 in Berlin, in a
book on the confiscation of businesses and property from Jews in
Germany, extracts of which can be read online.[40] I learn that, in
September 1942, Himmler decreed that all Jews still within
Germany, even if they were already incarcerated in concentration
camps like Sachsenhausen, or working as slave labourers, were to
be transported to Auschwitz.[41]

Back in London, I email the author to ask for his sources. By
return, he sends me an Attorney General's report to a Berlin regional
court, dated 7 November 1941, concerning the other Theodor
Liedtke, and regrets that he can find nothing further on ours, except
confirmation from the German Federal Archives that he was indeed
deported to Auschwitz, and so did not die in Sachsenhausen, information that remains too painful to contemplate.

The other Theodor Liedtke, the Attorney General charges, owns an apron store and has a daughter called Ellen, into whose name he attempted to transfer his property in Berlin in 1940. This was exactly what Klaus Meltzer had told me, except that Klaus had said the transfer had happened in 1938 or 1939. In addition, and as Klaus said too, this Theodor was arrested for breaking the law, convicted by a civil court, and thrown into prison.

The report appears to solve the mystery of Ellen's mother, who, it says, wasn't Jewish and died in 1938. Moreover, I discover the real reason for his arrest, which wasn't theft, as Klaus had said. The real reason was that Theodor Liedtke had falsely claimed he was a Hybrid of the First Degree rather than a full Jew – in other words, that he had only two Jewish grandparents rather than four. Indeed, in 1938 he had submitted petitions to have this racial status officially recognized, presumably in part so that his business and property should not be Aryanized, which would prevent him passing them to Ellen.

Though all these petitions had been rejected, in August 1940 he nonetheless went ahead with his plan to transfer his property into Ellen's name. It occurs to me that this might be what Klaus meant by 'theft': if a full Jew's property had to be Aryanized, in gifting it to his daughter he was, in effect, stealing his own property from the Aryan hands into which the law obliged it to be sold.

The gift was Theodor's undoing: the lawyer whom he'd engaged to notarize it reported him to the authorities for failing to disclose that he was a full Jew. As a result, he was charged with the high crime, under the Nuremberg Laws, of concealing his ethnic identity. He was sentenced to eighteen months in jail, at the conclusion of which he was deported to Auschwitz and murdered.[42]

My mind flits to Ursel's success in achieving Aryan status, and I marvel even more at how she pulled it off. At how a Nazi official as high-ranking as Hans Hinkel could be persuaded to intervene on her behalf; to order his underlings to tell the Reichstheaterkammer that all concerns about her racial origins should be dropped; to engage in direct correspondence by letter with this unknown young actor; to welcome her to his office. I'm horrified and relieved at the influence of Carl-Ludwig Duisberg, scion of IG Farben, one of the greatest industrial conglomerates of Germany, complicit in the Nazi project of enslavement and extermination; but then wonder at the risk that he and his wife, Ursel's friend Jola, took on her behalf.

And I see with a clarity that I'd never allowed myself the fork in the road before which Ursel stood in late 1941: in the one direction, the stage, safety, and an ancient aristocratic title; in the other, the mounting perils of being a Hybrid of the First Degree as she became a racial reject, one of the living dead. I can hardly bear to recall the heart-rending moment in her letter to Hinkel where she thanks him for giving her back the life she had lost. How can I or anyone possibly criticize her repudiation of what was, to her, a lethal heritage?

But these thoughts are quickly overtaken by the new reality: Klaus Meltzer isn't my cousin after all. He isn't a link to our Theo and so to Ernst. He hasn't opened a door to their lives. Clearly, he is the grandson of Theodor Liedtke the apron-store owner. His insistence that Theodor had been arrested and indicted as a criminal, which my mother rejected as nonsense, was not true of our Theodor. His certainty that Theodor had a wife – Klaus's grandmother – was true of his Theodor, not ours. There was, it turned out, no evidence that ours led a double life. Perhaps my great-uncle's housekeeper Hedwig had been so devoted to him that she really had been filled with joy every time he returned, even after going out for a few minutes. Perhaps the package that Ilse received, complete with his *Judenpass*, followed not his death but rather his transfer to a greater hell even than Sachsenhausen.

I feel a double loss of what I thought had been restored. Of Klaus, of course, and through him of a fuller sense of Theo's existence than my mother's descriptions of her and Ursel's Saturday afternoon visits had given me: his life as a father, as a lover, as an owner of property, and as an entrepreneur. His life as a man of secrets, who wasn't the open book that everybody imagined they saw. But, more poignantly still, of the 'consolation' that Theo died close to home, from a quick method of killing, which Ilse insisted was the way at Sachsenhausen, and not in an extermination camp, with its unspeakable rituals of nakedness and the panic of asphyxiation as the Zyklon B pellets start to work. Instead, I struggle to adjust to the vision of him having to endure that journey in the cattle truck and, if he survived it, the reception process at Auschwitz, which Anita had recounted to me in such detail during our visit to the camp: the shaving, the showering, the shouting, and then, at his age – fifty-eight, too old to be useful as slave labour – the gas chamber.

It seems stupid, this sense of loss, because my connection to him had been so tenuous anyway. But only now do I realize how much the discovery of Klaus, and what I thought was his umbilical link to the life of Theo, and through Theo back to Ernst and Emmy and Blumeshof, meant to me. Thanks to Klaus, Theo had come right up close: a life that had previously appeared to me in only three faint images – Theo at the Saturday teas with Mother and Ursel, Theo the salesman at Tietz's department store, and Theo the prisoner at Sachsenhausen, in all of which he was present but barely visible – had filled out into a man with street-smarts and a villa and a wife and a daughter, with her Hitler-adulating prospective parents-in-law and his place in their living room under the portrait of the Führer. And all this recovered life was embodied in Klaus, the man in the attic with Gregor the mad parrot and the menorah and the certificates signed by Göring. Now, though, our Theo seemed further away, flatter than ever, as if his whole benevolent, blameless life had been lived with one foot already in the grave.

64

The woman and the dandy

Quite apart from the impossibility of restituting a lost or stolen past, I am surely yearning for an idealized homeland that never existed. I might even be indulging in the sorts of fantasies that cost Ernst his life – except that my fantasies, unlike his, are *wholly* unrealistic. I am convinced that, in his day, the famous German-Jewish cultural symbiosis, from which each party had so immeasurably profited, even if only one had done the loving, really had existed. Whereas, after Hitler, the Holocaust, and the evisceration of so much German culture in the Third Reich, the intense creativity of that relationship was destroyed, at least for the time being.

Even German philosophy, to which I have devoted most of my adult life, has recently been making strenuous efforts to abandon its traditional ways of thinking, instead craving to become more anglicized, precisely as I moved in the opposite direction, discovering my own philosophical habitat in the German mind, from Hegel to Heidegger, via Schopenhauer and Nietzsche – thinkers who rivet me and speak to me, even when I don't understand them.

Nor do I have any answers to my big questions: Could love for a lost Germany forge a path to intimacy with the new? Could that German-Jewish world of *Bildung*, with its breadth and humanity, whose wounded but defiant spirit lived on in our London home, have a vibrant, if utterly different, future?

One reality has helped me, like, I am sure, many other children of refugees from Nazism, find a path back to Germany: the country's amazing determination to apologize and do justice to the Jews – amazing because, as a rule, human beings do everything they can to avoid responsibility for the horrors that they perpetrate against each other. Yet here were the Germans, or at least vast numbers of them, doggedly taking responsibility and atoning, not – or not only – because the world was demanding it of them, but because they *needed to* in order to go forward as a nation. Their self-respect, and so their identity as Germans, depended on it. This is a breakthrough in how peoples behave to one another; a profound contribution to civilization.

Which other people has ever done this systematically, let alone made repentance and reparations to its historical victims. central to its own identity – and so a source not just of shame but also of strength and national renewal? The British for the Kenyan Mau Mau? The Americans for the My Lai massacre in Vietnam? The French for the horrors of the Algerian War? Any of those three nations for the incalculable suffering inflicted on black people by slavery and the slave trade?

Distressingly, I also come across flashes of anti-Semitism in today's Germany – and by no means just on the uncouth, *unsalonfähig*, far right, to which many people would like to think it is confined, but also in more furtive and more polite forms among the otherwise tolerant majority. There are undoubtedly deep pockets of resentment about all the restitutions and reparations, along with the endless pressure to remember and to repent, as if the Jew were an omni-present moral sadist, holding a whip over the German conscience and never allowing it peace or self-respect. Who knows how much bitterness towards Jews already lies latent in Germans after so many decades of drilling themselves into shame, of being told that the words 'Germany', 'crime', 'guilt', and 'apology' are synonymous?

And there are also occasions when the action of a Jew provokes scary outrage: the sort of outrage that blames a people and not an individual; that says, 'He did it because he is a Jew.' This has to be acknowledged too, though it doesn't diminish my love for Germany one iota — and I would prefer to pretend that it isn't happening, or at least that it is harmless.

When it does happen, people seem to be getting a lot off their chests, quietly and in private. The conversation I overheard in a cafe in Berlin's Charlottenburg district in April 2007 still hurts, all these years later.

A man and a woman are sitting at the next table, the woman snappily dressed in a two-piece suit, the man more dandyish, with fashionably unkempt hair and a silk cravat stuffed into his open shirt. The woman seems to have lots of cultured friends, speaks of private views at trendy art galleries and premieres at the opera that she has recently attended, and works two days a week for a prestigious charity together with other well-connected people. Her companion has been to many of the same openings and premieres, made films in his youth, then worked in the gallery world in another German city, and now spends most of his time writing. After about a quarter of an hour, their conversation takes an abrupt turn:

'He has that *typically* Jewish arrogance,' the woman says. Her voice sounds relaxed, but her face is etched with hate.

'Did he survive the war here with his family, or how come we have a Jewish entrepreneur here, of his age?' the man replies. 'Or is he one of those Russian immigrants?'

'No, he's not Russian. His parents returned after the war, I think. They were in England or America. I despise the way he talks and struts.'

'If he were a German, wouldn't you just say he was an arrogant *person*?' an embarrassed voice says behind the woman. I hadn't noticed him until then. He is with them, though the table is too small for them all to fit round it and he looks stuck onto her side like a squirrel on a tree trunk. 'You wouldn't say he was an arrogant *German*.'

'Of course, I blame Germans too when they do bad things,' the woman replies.

'But you blame Hans or Peter, you don't blame them *as* Germans,' the third person continues. 'Anyway, he's a friend of yours, that entrepreneur. I've seen him at your parties several times.'

'Yes, but nowadays I just meet him at X's, the novelist. Another Jew. Though I avoid going there. I can't stand the way he tries to ingratiate himself into Berlin society. He invites Germans over for his Passover evenings every year, as if he craves our recognition. It's excruciating, though his rituals are quite amusing. Harmless, really.'

'What are his books like?'

'Well, you know, he has his pretensions. I doubt they are particularly good. I have no idea if they sell. He wants to create a sort of salon – to be *in*. Pushy. That type.'

'What I find really disgraceful,' the dandy says, 'a scandal, is the Kirchner.' He is referring to the controversial restitution in 2006 of a painting by the expressionist painter Ernst Ludwig Kirchner to the heirs of a Jewish art collector who had once owned it. 'That painting belongs to us; the Jew sold it in the thirties for a proper price; and now they are using their typically Jewish techniques to get it back. And, of course, our cowardly Berlin Senate, a bunch of innocents, falls for their blackmail and gives it back. *Those* people in London and New York have had enough from us!'

'Those people are in any case immoral,' the woman corrects him sternly. She pauses as outrage bloats her countenance. 'I find the thing sickening,' she continues, and her face twists itself into a mask of revulsion.

Now the atmosphere is getting really unpleasant. An avalanche of hate is gathering pace. The third person looks on helplessly. He seems trapped in a dilemma: to defend the Jews would merely arouse the woman to further incrimination; but to say nothing might look as if he is acquiescing in her charges, or, worse, sees them as unanswerable.

'Yes, that's actually what one always said about them,' the dandy replies caustically, and his expression becomes animated. 'People will again say: "The Jews" . . .' – he says the word awkwardly, so he begins again – 'People will say: "Jewish people cannot be trusted; they are only out for themselves!" Jewish people had better watch out for that. The Kirchner is ours.'

He keeps glancing uneasily at the woman, as if frightened of her vehemence but also not wanting to be outdone by it, fearful perhaps of appearing feeble or unpatriotic or too compromising in the face of foreign evil. 'They've had enough justice from us Germans; this is now *exploitation*,' he adds pointedly, spoon-feeding her a morsel of her favourite food.

Although he is the less venomous of the two, I find him the more sinister. He seems indifferent to the Kirchner, yet he is getting swept along by the murky joys of indignation. He is dark, but in a weak way.

'Anyway, this has nothing to do with justice,' the woman goes on. 'And the worst are those Jewish lawyers with their success fees. Taking a commission on the plunder – disgusting! The auction houses, the banks, the law firms, they are all controlled by Jews in America, and they are just taking us trusting Germans for a ride.' She fumes and hates, and the dandy tries to fume and hate along with her. A powerful aroma of poison drifts over from their table.

'What about your own restitution?' the third person asks the woman, with seemingly feigned nonchalance. 'You didn't object to that.'

This is clearly his way of taking a little revenge on her. He looks hurt.

The dandy is surprised. 'You got restitution?'

'Oh, I took no interest in that. My brother did it all. He interests himself in all that sort of stuff.'

'How come you got restitution?' the dandy presses.

'Well, my grandmother had an interest in a building in the Czech Republic that her family lost after the communist takeover. After the Wall fell, we were offered some money.'

'You took a lawyer and fought hard to get that money,' the third person interjects. At last he is summoning some confidence.

The dandy doesn't seem bothered one way or the other. The woman shrugs, as if the whole thing has nothing to do with her, though she doesn't deny she accepted the money. She shrugs to perfection. If the third person thinks that she is rattled by her own hypocrisy, he is mistaken.

Later that evening, unable to free myself of the conversation in the cafe, I realize that what mystifies me most about it isn't that the woman was blaming a people rather than a person: that, as she saw it, there would always be Jews eager to exploit the Germans' honest decency and burden of guilt for their own revolting ends. What really mystifies me is the spiritual feel of her hate. Spiritual because her hate seemed to see the Jew as personifying greed raised to the level of desecration; and because it seemed to inspire her with the kind of moral zeal to resist and vanquish the desecrator that is typically afforded by religious faith. Who knows how much theft and exploitation, or indeed rape and murder, committed by locals against locals, had gone on in Germany while the Kirchner affair was raging? I imagine that the woman would have been appalled at such crimes, but when she thought of the Jew who got the Kirchner back, she didn't only see criminal behaviour; she saw sacrilege. We were in the realm not of the miscreant but of the blasphemer – in short, the realm of the sacred.

65

A London club

Back in London, I am recounting the exchange in the Berlin cafe to someone whom my mother would have called 'typically English'. He is a vivacious seventy-year-old economist, the epitome of old-school graceful manners, though I'd need a semiotic auto-translator to figure out what he really means.

I begin to tell him the story as we're having a pre-lunch drink at his club, where only fleeting eye contact seems permitted and the air is filled with a uniquely English complacency, neither strident nor gushingly self-congratulatory, but confident that nothing in life can be too bad to prevent England from continuing in more or less the way it always has done, with crises maybe, but not catastrophes, and in which the de rigeur demeanour is flippant unflappability.

I'm deep into the Kirchner when he notices the time and interrupts to suggest that we proceed to lunch, which is awaiting us in the ornate dining room, with its chandeliers, red plush carpet, silver cutlery, and decanted Bordeaux at the ready. As we walk in, he a pace in front of me, I see that his right arm, held stiffly downwards, is twisting restlessly and his shoulder is jerking very slightly, as if he is agitated by the burden of some great responsibility, but is too discreet to reveal it. Perhaps, I muse to myself, this is how members of the ruling classes signal their status to one another; for the dining room is surely full of them.

Winding our way between tables, my host becomes more remote. We sit down at the far end of the room, order, and then, perhaps having forgotten the interrupted Berlin tale or simply finding direct talk of Jews and racism too uncomfortable, he launches into a tirade against the policies of the European Central Bank and the US Fed. For a minute or two I hold on to the argument, but then the propositions, premises, inferences, statistics, ratios, and quotations from Keynes and economists unknown to me start slipping out of my control, and I am unable to decide what exactly follows from or entails what. I panic: we aren't even on our first course yet.

A few minutes into this disquisition, his eye fixed on the middle distance as if addressing Keynes's ghost, there is a lull, presumably meant as an opening for me to comment. Since I have no idea what to say, or any firm purchase on what is at stake or why we are discussing international finance, and my silence as well as his relentlessness are making me nervous, I try to change the subject.

'Does your club now admit women?' I enquire.

'Only in the evenings,' comes the staccato reply.

'Well,' I continue, 'if you want to preserve male-only lunches, you could use one room for them and another of these palatial rooms for women-only lunches.'

My host remains impassive. At the next table, a well-heeled man is lunching with another well-heeled man. A signet ring glistens contentedly on his amply fed finger.

I repeat the point, fearful that perhaps he hasn't heard me. Fear is a dreadful thing: it can be parent to whole classes of stupidity.

His stern demeanour swivels in my direction; it seems to say: 'I did hear you the first time.'

Instead of stopping, I persist. 'Well, of course, Aristotle, the most influential philosopher of friendship in Western history, is adamant that the truest friendships can exist only between those who are ethically good as well as alike in their virtues. His conclusion that only men are capable of such friendship is repugnant, but do you think his ethical point could be extended to any same-gender intimacy?'

'Yes,' he says, 'I understood your earlier point, but I disagree. I would find it rather more convenient if they would admit women for lunch in this room.' And then: 'But if you like my club so much I'd be happy to propose you as a member.'

'Oh no,' I say, panicked at the prospect of allegiance to such an utterly alien world, 'I've always resisted joining any club. They're not for me.'

He then returns to the world economy and I to my silence. I don't manage to finish my story. But I feel so out of place here and, by contrast, the promise of belonging that shines in distant Berlin beckons so potently that the poison seems to have drained from the woman and the dandy. Or, rather, the poison isn't prevalent enough in today's Germany to warrant any great alarm. Or, if it is prevalent, it still wouldn't find its way to someone like me, who, with his abstruse interests in philosophy and music and German culture, and with his evident love of Germany, is too harmless, too respectable, and too inconspicuous to be its target.

Or perhaps, like Ernst, that is just what I want to believe.

CODA

Dinner at the German Embassy

The only day of the year on which I rigorously avoid going out is 22 February, the anniversary of my father's death. Not out of sadness, but out of piety. That was the day he collapsed at the German Embassy in London, a day on which he usually hovers duskily about me, emerging into that painfully unreachable presence that the dead achieve when we dare to grasp their absence.

But I didn't have a moment of doubt about accepting an invitation to dinner for 22 February 2018.

At the German Embassy in London.

I couldn't believe the coincidence. Was some puppeteer of destiny playing a morbid joke on me? It felt like I'd been belatedly asked to a seance.

The dinner was in honour of Anita Lasker-Wallfisch, with whom I had visited Auschwitz ten months previously. It was to mark a speech that she had recently delivered, on Holocaust Remembrance Day, to a packed session of the German parliament. It was a speech of such unyielding magnanimity and composure, so unburdened by torment or anger, that it became hard to imagine – though I have known Anita all my life and first saw the number 69388 tattooed onto her forearm as a small boy, when our families used to go to a local swimming pool together at weekends – that she had endured the unimaginable hell of that 'death factory', as she calls it, for even a day, never mind for over a year.

Anita knew both my parents before I was born. My uncle, Edward May, was one of the first people she met when she arrived in England after her liberation. Her husband, Peter Wallfisch, and my mother had a piano and violin duo for over fifteen years. She gave birth to her daughter, Maya, and my mother to my brother, Marius, within twenty-four hours of each other; and, as a child, Maya used to spend many Saturdays with us when her parents were away working. Among Anita's numerous kindnesses to me, I particularly remember our trips to London's Heathrow airport after my father died, when I'd make myself a cozy 'bed' in the back of her Mini Estate and she'd generously wait at the top of Terminal 2's car park while I watched aeroplanes taking off and landing, often daydreaming about leaving England and becoming a refugee myself.

And then the most obvious thought occurs to me last of all: Anita is the only family friend still alive who knew my father. She knew him far better than I ever did, and when she speaks of him it is as vivid as if she had seen him yesterday. That she should be here, in the German Embassy, on the anniversary of his death, fills me with gratitude.

I am late – the last guest to arrive – and as I ascend the steps to the door of the ambassador's residence on Belgrave Square, I am suffused by the nauseous thrill that, all these decades later, fate has decided that I am ready to stand, on this day of all days, on that sacred, terrible ground – ground that witnessed a series of events still opaque to me.

I scan the cavernous entrance hall and the doors leading onto it. Might any of these conceal the meeting room where he and Ursel and Franziskus and the lawyer met?

The doors are all shut. Only a small corridor-like space that now functions as a cloakroom is open. I leave my coat, scrutinize the space as fast as I can – it looks far too small to accommodate a meeting – and hasten up the sweeping staircase towards voices upstairs.

A childlike thought thrills and embarrasses me: this is not just the German island in London on which my father died; it is also now my home – I am naturalized and this is the embassy of my nation. And there – I see her from the top of the staircase – radiating her usual vitality, is Anita, sitting on a sofa, sipping champagne, holding court.

I was expecting a large dinner, but it is like a family gathering, with only eight or nine guests, hosted by the chargé d'affaires, Tania Freiin von Uslar-Gleichen. As we sit down at the impeccably laid table, a split-screen film starts playing in my mind, against which I struggle in vain. On one half of the screen I see shouting guards, ferocious dogs tearing at the flesh of living humans, dying children, plumes of smoke, a lake on fire; the ground is vibrating as I remember it doing in Japan when seismic tremors strike. There is screaming everywhere – but nobody is being heard. And, on the other screen, courteous government officials are receiving visitors and an atmosphere of 'solidity' and peace reigns: the solidity of Blumeshof and the peace you might find in a cloister on a sunny day, or in the Swiss Alps with falling streams, still ferns, and majestic glaciers.

I hear the words 'And the vegan option is for madam?' as a meal that looks identical to mine, minus the salmon and with fluffy potatoes made with nut oil rather than butter, is placed respectfully in front of the guest opposite me, Anita's daughter Maya. And I marvel that such care is possible.

Then I again hear the sound of my father collapsing backwards with an awful thud. And a long-forgotten memory comes to my aid: how, after he died, it was Ursel alone who brought some levity into our home. Not for her the solemnity of a wake, which can make bereavement all the harder to bear. The next day, she was boogying alone to 'Chattanooga Choo-Choo' in the corridor outside my bedroom, still in her nightdress, a blaring radio in her hand. She had set up a camp bed next to my parents' bed – I remember her and my mother talking all night, a confiding and consoling babble of German in the next room. The simple cart that had carried the coffin to its grave and the way it bumped along the gravel path had seemed bizarre to her, she told me many years later; but she had never been to a Jewish funeral until then. Her humour deflected us, magically, from the defiant presence of the freshly dead, and I loved her for it.

I turn to the kindly embassy official sitting next to me and ask whether the building we are in was always reserved for the ambassador's residence.

'No,' she says, 'there was a time when we just had this building.'

'So it housed all the offices too? The whole embassy was squeezed in here?'

'Yes – it must have been a squeeze!'

'When was the newer building – the one with the offices and large white external staircase – constructed?'

'In the late 1970s, I think.'

'So, before that, in the 1960s, the offices were definitely here, where we are now?'

'Yes,' she confirms.

At that moment, Anita says with a broad smile to the chargé d'affaires across the table, 'This man has just become a German citizen. He's a German now. Or again.'

'Oh, so you're one of my flock,' the chargé d'affaires shoots back.

'Delighted to be!' I answer, relieved to be distracted.

'Wasn't that a very hard decision?' the official sitting next to me enquires gravely.

'Not at all,' I hear myself say. 'Nothing could be more natural. After all, I *am* a German. It's the right thing to do.' I feel tears rushing at my eyes, threatening to unmask the emotion I am really feeling. Tears of relief at some sort of resolved identity – not just my identity: my father's too. He was a German. As well as a Jew. In my father's house there were *two* homes, and he left a place for my life in both. I remember my scorn for Ursel's denial of his Germanness at dinner in the Swiss chalet, when I was eleven. Now, to keep those tears at bay, I force myself to think as vividly as I can of his grave – as, oddly perhaps, I often do when trying to distract myself from present pain, such as when the dentist is delivering an anaesthetic to the back of my mouth and they almost touch a nerve.

The official looks surprised by my answer.

But distraction is impossible, least of all by thinking of his grave. I'm closer to his last moments than I've ever been; and I hear my mother recounting for the hundredth time, on a loop of bewilderment, that telephone call from this very place – from some room just yards from where I am now sitting eating salmon with fluffy potatoes topped with melting butter. I hear her say it yet again. Like her own father's death, she never got over it: never freed her mind of the scene. I wish she could have. I used to beg her to try. She referred to these two men as '*die beiden Väter*' — the two fathers. In her later years, she had photos of them next to each other on a shelf in her bedroom, and would look at them again and again for reassurance.

'Is that Mrs May?' the voice at the other end of the phone enquires. 'This is the German . . .'

From the tone of grave finality, my mother knows at once that something catastrophic has happened — so she tells me when she thinks I'm old enough to hear about it.

'I am so sorry to have to inform you . . .'

'Where is he now?' she asks, trying to forestall the cold politeness of a death announcement.

'I am awfully sorry to have to tell you that your husband collapsed during . . .'

'Is there a doctor at the embassy?'

'No, but we are very near St George's Hospital, and we've called for an emergency . . .'

She arrives at the German Embassy, a coat draped over her night-dress, just as a man and a woman in green overalls leap out of the back of an ambulance and vanish into the mansion, while a paramedic sits in the back preparing for an imminent arrival.

My mother peers inside.

'Yes, madam?'

'Is this for Walter May?' my mother enquires meekly.

'And who are you?' the voice says.

At that moment, a stretcher appears at the door of the embassy, and in the group behind it are Ursel and Franziskus.

The corpse, wrapped in a blanket, is rushed into the ambulance, its complexion, my mother tells me, a grey-blue, its eyes impassively ignoring her confused attempts to make contact with them and to understand what he has been through.

Riding with my father to the nearby hospital — located in a hand-some building that, in the 1990s, became a luxury hotel and celebrity haunt – she holds his cold, shockingly limp hand, unsure if he is dying or already dead, staring at his ashen face, which seems frozen in an expression of pain and confusion, neither evincing life nor resolved into the gruesomely unburdened calmness of the freshly dead.

'Would you like to see him once more?' the pathologist asks Mother after they reach the hospital and he has been taken away.

She declines.

As we make our way from the dining room back to the grand staircase after dinner, I see more closed doors on that upper floor. I slip into a bathroom – perhaps one he used? It certainly looks unmodernized. I don't know if it is intended for visitors, but its door is open. As I'm washing my hands, I catch sight of my face in the mirror and wonder if my father ever imagined his six-year-old son as a middle-aged man in a suit and necktie – with, like him, a passion for fine food and wine. And my reflection, staring back knowingly, seems to say: 'You were right, long ago in the park when Sally told you he'd died, that your father would never again witness your life. But you were also right about the freedom that you were certain he'd bequeathed you at that moment – when your world became flooded not only by emptiness and doom, but also by reality and light. You've been harbouring his two homes all this time – and the freedom to build a future with that inheritance.'

I step out of the bathroom, back onto the upper floor, where we'd had dinner. It is now abandoned, and I relish lingering for another minute in its vastness, cocking my ear for any voices that might speak to me from its silence.

Downstairs is also deserted, except for a young member of staff and the attendant peering patiently out of the cloakroom. The front door is wide open and through it the dark of the night and a hubbub of voices nudge their way in. The trust, perhaps the naivety, of that unguarded door makes me feel exhilaratingly free and safe. The attendant asks for my ticket, though there is only one coat left, and as she takes it off its hanger my eye gets dragged beyond the coat rail to a large room beyond that I hadn't noticed earlier. Was that where he met his end? It seems to be the right location for a meeting room, near the entrance and away from the diplomats' offices.

I'm embarrassed to linger – the cloakroom attendant must be eager to go home, and the others are waiting outside – but I can't help probing. 'Is that spacious room for meetings?' I ask her. 'For visitors? It must be perfect for people who you don't want crawling all over your embassy; it's right by the front door!'

'No, it's for staff,' she replies, unfazed by my gawping at the room, where I'm imagining my father listening attentively to the other three, or perhaps in the middle of interjecting something – then the instant he falls back gasping for breath, his mouth jacked open. I want to ask her if she knows what the room was used for back in the 1960s, to play for time so that I can go on imbibing its atmosphere.

But there are no answers. And everyone is waiting outside.

I make for the front door just as Anita and a clutch of guests are disappearing into a taxi.

Watching her speed off, I realize how intensely comforting her presence has been: as a witness whose memory blesses his life with reality – so that, this evening, he could fill me with so much more than his fearful absence dotted with a few vignettes of kindness. With Anita, in this house, on this day of the year, I feel closer to my lost father and my lost country than ever before. Though I am still far from their shores, I know that I will not cease searching for them both. Earning the past – discovering it, harvesting it, and transforming it into a future – is indeed a life's work.

Maybe, I think, he too, his inextinguishable trace in the embassy, which has lived alone there for so long, felt protected by her.

'We must keep in touch,' the chargé d'affaires says as the taxi disappears and we are alone on a corner of the great empty square. 'You are one of ours now.' And she tells me about an exhibition on German-Jewish artists-in-exile, sponsored by the embassy, that is opening the following week, promising to send me an invitation. I climb into my car, which is directly in front of the building, marvelling that, in an age of hyper-security, when no risk can be taken and nobody can be entirely beyond suspicion, it is permitted to park outside the embassy of a country that has been targeted by terrorists.

It is all so embracing, so un-barking, so unassuming. Like the question that, as I drive home, keeps replaying itself in my mind, and that seems to speak for my new Germany, for the refusal to answer drama with drama, or tragedy with redemption, as the daughter of a Holocaust survivor who had arrived at Auschwitz sure that she would be selected to die is asked, with such taken-for-granted respect, by her German host:

'And the vegan option is for madam?'

ACKNOWLEDGEMENTS

I owe an immense debt to the late novelist Aharon Appelfeld and to the philosopher A. C. Grayling for repeatedly urging me to persist with this project. Without their encouragement, my many years of discussion with, in particular, my mother and my two aunts – all three of whom I had bombarded, since my childhood, with questions about their lives and those of their parents, uncles, and grandparents – might never have made their way from my memories and scattered notes into print.

I am hugely grateful to friends and colleagues who kindly read the manuscript, in whole or part, at various stages of its writing, in particular Lydia Goehr, A. C. Grayling, Tim Judah, Anthony McCarten, Tom McCarthy, Hella Pick, Martin Ruehl, and Rosie Whitehouse.

I extend very special thanks to Daniel Wildmann, Director of the Leo Baeck Institute in London, who devoted innumerable hours and his formidable expertise to vetting my treatment of German-Jewish history, and from whom I have learned so much; and to Bill Swainson, who advised me extensively as a freelance editor, and under whose guidance the text went through several iterations.

Invaluable research assistance and expert advice was provided, at different times, by Boris Behnen, Ulrike Ehret, Julia Hörath, John Owen, Hester Vaizey, and Kim Wünschmann, and I want to record my gratitude to each of them. Kim and Julia discovered files in German archives of which I might otherwise have remained ignorant. In addition to his superb research, Boris kindly obtained the necessary permissions to reproduce and publish documents from those archives. Thank you to all their staff, especially at the Bundesarchiv, the German federal archive.

Renata de Jara and Elke Stahlke, the client–lawyer dream team, who spearheaded the restitution of a building and business in Berlin that had been Aryanized in 1939, and in which my grandparents had had a stake, kindly checked and approved the relevant chapters.

I thank Anita Lasker-Wallfisch for inviting me to join her on a four-day visit to Auschwitz in 2017, as well as for many discussions and reminiscences in her kitchen over takeout Thai dinners and her delicious home-made soups. Of the close-knit German-speaking Jewish circle in London in which I was raised, she is the last surviving member, and in particular the last to have known both my parents since before I was born. She is someone to whom I feel a deep bond of gratitude.

Finally, huge thanks are due to my wonderful agent, Caroline Michel, for championing this project, as well as to Tim Binding and Laurie Robertson and the whole team at Peters, Fraser and Dunlop. I extend equally huge thanks to my magnificent – and patient – commissioning editor, Georgina Morley, at Picador, with whom it has been a tremendous pleasure and privilege to work. I am indebted to Marissa Constantinou for her painstaking work and all her support; to Chloe May (no relation) for skilfully and meticulously guiding the text through to publication; and to Nick Humphrey, who brilliantly, and with necessary brutality, excised surplus verbiage, further proof that slimming and toning can be good for the health of an organism.

Most finally, I should like to thank Lord Byron's Manfred for his encouragement –

> Sorrow is knowledge: they who know the most
> Must mourn the deepest o'er the fatal truth

– but even more so W. B. Yeats:

> We must laugh and we must sing,
> We are blest by everything,
> Everything we look upon is blest.

NOTES

1 Franz Kafka, *Letters to Milena*, translated by Philip Boehm (New York: Schocken Books, 1990), pp. 217–8.

2 Toni Morrison, *Song of Solomon* (London: Random House (Vintage), 1998), p. 333.

3 'Walking the Way of the Survivor; A Talk With Aharon Appelfeld', Philip Roth, *New York Times*, 28 February 1988.

4 Walter Benjamin, 'A Berlin Chronicle', in *Reflections*, translated by Edmund Jephcott (New York: Schocken Books, 1986). All my quotations from this work are taken from pp. 41–3.

5 Letter to Alma Mahler in August 1914. Cited in Alex Ross, *The Rest Is Noise: Listening to the Twentieth Century* (New York: Farrar, Straus, and Giroux, 2007), p. 72.

6 Source: J. Eichenberg AG expropriation file. List of shareholders and their racial origins submitted to Berlin's Police President. Location: 'Akte zur Enteignung der J. Eichenberg AG', Handelsregisterakte, HRB 22680 später HRB 51960, Landesamt zur Regelung offener Vermögensfragen, Berlin.

7 Joachim Günther (Hrsg.), *Neue Deutsche Hefte*, Band 24, Heft 1 (Berlin: Neue Deutsche Hefte Verlag, 1977), p. 173.

8 As quoted in Henriette von Gizycki, *Kaplan Fahsel in seinem Werdegang unter Zuhilfenahme seiner Briefe und Aufzeichnungen* (Berlin: Germania Verlag, 1930), p. 120. All translations of Gizycki are mine.

9 Gizycki, p. 103.

10 Gizycki, p. 120.

11 *Falschheit und Arroganz.*

12 Gizycki, p. 15.

13 Gizycki, p. 18.

14 Gizycki, p. 20.

15 Gizycki, p. 52.

16 Gizycki, p. 57.

17 'weckte den jugendlichen Sinn für einen neuen Rhythmus und Humor, für eine neue Selbständigkeit und demokratische Freiheit' – Helmut Fahsel, diary entry, cited in Gizycki, p. 17.

18 Verein für Kraft und Schönheit.

19 Gizycki, pp. 18–20.

20 'Ich strebe nach Vollkommenheit des Körpers'. Gizycki, p. 12.

21 Was ein junger Mann wissen muss.

22 Annali von Alvensleben, Abgehoben (Hamburg: Christians Verlag, 1998), p. 18.

23 The Reichssippenamt was charged with Erb- und rassenkundliche Untersuchungen.

24 A Mischling ersten Grades, which I have translated as 'Hybrid of the First Degree', was defined as a person with two Jewish grandparents and was forbidden to marry an Aryan German. They were, though, free to marry each other. Saul Friedländer, Nazi Germany and the Jews: The Years of Persecution 1933–39 (London: HarperCollins, 1997), pp. 145–51. A Mischling zweiten Grades ('Hybrid of the Second Degree') was a quarter-Jew: one with a single Jewish grandparent.

25 Quoted in Christopher R. Browning (with Jürgen Matthäus), The Origins of the Final Solution: The Evolution of Nazi Jewish Policy, September 1939– March 1942 (Lincoln: University of Nebraska Press, 2004), p. 404.

26 In August 1935, the Genossenschaft der deutschen Bühnenangehörigen, which actors had to join in order to become members of the Reichstheaterkammer, demanded proof of Aryan background from all its members (not just from newcomers). It was a long-drawn-out process – the last demand for proof was sent out in February 1938. Florian Odenwald, Der nazistische Kampf gegen das 'Undeutsche' in Theater und Film 1920–1945 (München: Herbert Utz Verlag, 2006), pp. 193–6.

27 Bundesarchiv Berlin, BArch, R9361V/16995.

28 BArch, R9361V/56771. My translation.

29 BArch, R9361V/56771. My translation.

30 Werner Finck, Witz als Schicksal – Schicksal als Witz (Hamburg: Marion von Schröder Verlag, 1966), p. 60.

31 Christabel Bielenberg, When I Was a German, 1934–1945: An Englishwoman in Nazi Germany (Lincoln: University of Nebraska Press, 1998), pp. 111–2.

32 Eisernes Kreuz 2. Klasse, Einsernes Kreuz 1. Klasse, Ehrenpokal der Luftwaffe, Deutsches Kreuz in Gold.

33 Ritterkreuz des Eisernen Kreuzes.

34 Annette Haller, Der Jüdische Friedhof an der Weidegasse in Trier (Trier: Paulinus Verlag, 2003), pp. xvi–xvii.

35 'Der Name Eiche sowie Eichenberg haben einen urdeutschen Klang.' My translation.

36 Source: J. Eichenberg AG expropriation file, letters to the Berlin Police President's office of August Plöger, 1 July 1939, and of his lawyer Walter Patschan, 26 August 1940. Location: 'Akte zur Enteignung der

J. Eichenberg AG', Handelsregisterakte, HRB 22680 später HRB 51960, Landesamt zur Regelung offener Vermögensfragen Berlin.

37 Source: J. Eichenberg AG expropriation file. Location: 'Akte zur Enteignung der J. Eichenberg AG', Handelsregisterakte, HRB 22680 später HRB 51960, Landesamt zur Regelung offener Vermögensfragen Berlin.

38 This paragraph on Charlotte Pommer is indebted to Sabine Hildebrandt, *The Anatomy of Murder: Ethical Transgressions and Anatomical Science during the Third Reich* (New York: Berghahn Books, 2016), pp. 165–6.

39 Hannah Arendt, *Rahel Varnhagen: The Life of a Jewess*, translated by Richard and Clara Winston (Baltimore: The Johns Hopkins University Press, 1997), p. 85.

40 Christoph Kreutzmüller, *Final Sale in Berlin: The Destruction of Jewish Commercial Activity, 1930–1945*, translated by Jane Paulick and Jefferson Chase (New York: Berghahn Books, 2015), p. 277.

41 Kreutzmüller, p. 328.

42 Kreutzmüller, p. 277.

SOURCES

Everything recounted in this book is based on one or more of my notes, my memory, my impressions, my views, and my interpretation of events. In addition, wherever I could expand and verify stories by consulting official archives, notably in the case of my aunt Ursel's achievement of Aryan status in 1941 and of the restitution of J. Eichenberg AG in the 1990s, I have done so.

I am grateful to the following archives, from whose files I have quoted and/or reproduced images: Bundesarchiv Berlin; Bundesarchiv–Abteilung Militärarchiv, Freiburg im Breisgau; Landesamt zur Regelung offener Vermögensfragen Berlin; Staatsarchiv Bremen. Detailed references are given at the appropriate points in the text and can be found in the notes. Credits for images are recorded in the list of illustrations.

My narrative of events and times before my birth, or that I otherwise did not witness first hand, is, overwhelmingly, the result of years of discussion with – verging on interrogation of – my mother and her two sisters. From a young age I was compulsively interested in their lives and choices, in part as a way of finding my own grounding in a family and a history that seemed as elusive as they were endowed with cultural riches – so that many of the footholds that I thought I had secured turned out to be provisional, or illusory, or forbidden, or all three.

In particular, I interviewed my mother extensively about her life – and the lives of her sisters, parents, uncles, and grandparents, as well as of my father and his brother – over a period of eighteen years, from 1988 to 2006.

I also had long discussions with the late Klaus Meltzer about his life, as well as those of his parents and grandparents, and it is with his enthusiastic blessing and approval that I recount aspects of his own family story and of our encounters. He also kindly gifted me photos from his albums, two of which are reproduced here.

Though I had closely followed the restitution of J. Eichenberg AG in the 1990s and had access to the confiscation and restitution files through my mother, who was one of its direct heirs, many additional facets of the story that I tell here come from conversations with the two people closest to it over the longest period: Renata de Jara, who represented the largest portion of heirs and was the court-appointed *Nachtragsabwicklerin*, entrusted with managing Eichenberg's liquidation; and Elke Stahlke, the lawyer engaged by Renata and the person who first discovered the Aryanization file from the Nazi period. I cleared the entire text in chapters 49–54 with both of them. In addition, Judith Bieling checked and approved the chapter relating to her. Some names in those and related chapters have been changed to protect the identity of the people concerned.

In addition, the names of the priest in chapters 29 and 31, the pastor in chapter 32, and the friar and priest in chapter 33 have been changed.

I quote extensively from the biography of my great-uncle Helmut Fahsel by Henriette von Gizycki: *Kaplan Fahsel in seinem Werdegang unter Zuhilfenahme seiner Briefe und Aufzeichnungen* (Berlin: Germania Verlag, 1930). The English translations here are my own.

Where I use quotation and direct speech to relay conversations, I cannot and do not vouch that every word is faithful to the original; but I am as certain as I can be that I have conveyed their meaning and essence truthfully and accurately. Scenes or dialogues that my interlocutor did not directly witness, such as between the Rosenthals and their Jewish lodger in chapter 18, but which were related to them first hand, are unverifiable; but the content is as I recall it being transmitted to me, in this case by Ilse.